LAW AT THE VANISHING POINT

For Renée

Law at the Vanishing Point

A Philosophical Analysis of International Law

AARON FICHTELBERG
University of Delaware, USA

Routledge
Taylor & Francis Group
LONDON AND NEW YORK

First published 2008 by Ashgate Publishing

Published 2016 by Routledge
2 Park Square, Milton Park, Abingdon, Oxon OX14 4RN
711 Third Avenue, New York, NY 10017, USA

Routledge is an imprint of the Taylor & Francis Group, an informa business

British Library Cataloguing in Publication Data
Fichtelberg, Aaron
Law at the vanishing point : a philosophical analysis of international law. - (Applied legal philosophy)
1. International law - Philosophy
I. Title
341'.01

Library of Congress Cataloging-in-Publication Data
Fichtelberg, Aaron
Law at the vanishing point : a philosophical analysis of international law / by Aaron Fichtelberg.
p. cm.
Includes bibliographical references and index.
ISBN 978-0-7546-7251-7
1. International law--Moral and ethical aspects. 2. Law--Philosophy. 3. Critical legal studies. I. Title.

KZ1256.F53 2008
340'.1--dc22

2007035645

ISBN 9780754672517 (hbk)

Contents

Series Editor's Preface

The objective of the Applied Legal Philosophy series is to publish work which adopts a theoretical approach to the study of particular areas or aspects of law or deals with general theories of law in a way which focused on issues of practical moral and political concern in specific legal contexts.

In recent years there has been an encouraging tendency for legal philosophers to utilize detailed knowledge of the substance and practicalities of law and a noteworthy development in the theoretical sophistication of much legal research. The series seeks to encourage these trends and to make available studies in law which are both genuinely philosophical in approach and at the same time based on appropriate legal knowledge and directed towards issues in the criticism and reform of actual laws and legal systems.

The series will include studies of all the main areas of law, presented in a manner which relates to the concerns of specialist legal academics and practitioners. Each book makes an original contribution to an area of legal study while being comprehensible to those engaged in a wide variety of disciplines. Their legal content is principally Anglo-American, but a wide-ranging comparative approach is encouraged and authors are drawn from a variety of jurisdictions.

Tom Campbell
Centre for Applied Philosophy and Public Ethics,
Charles Sturt University, Australia

Introduction

The Future and Legal Theory

World politics are changing in dramatic ways. The old forms of relations, old modes of association, the old rules of international relations that have dominated the political imagination for centuries are dying, sometimes quietly, sometimes shrieking hideously. Talk of human rights, trials for war criminals, and the rule of law in the international sphere, notions that were considered merely rhetorical, naively idealistic or outright dangerous until recently have begun to take on a life of their own. Conversely, terms such as "sovereignty", "self determination", and the very term "international" itself, terms considered sacrosanct for centuries in discussions of global politics, have been cast into doubt in theory and substantially weakened in practice. Further and more concretely, modern technology, new forms of mass communication, new forms of economic relations, and new modes of transportation have exerted increasing pressure on existing political relations, stretching them close to the breaking point. Whether these changes bode ill or well for humankind is an open question; the question of whether these changes force us to rethink the nature of global affairs, global politics, and global law is not quite so open.

Despite these rapid and dramatic geopolitical changes, political philosophers, political scientists, and legal theorists have largely stuck to their traditional theoretical models. Seeing conventional categories of domestic political philosophy and legal theory (which almost without exception view the state as the primary unit of social and political life) as adequate for the job, most political theorists have approached international issues, be they moral, legal, or political from the standpoint of discrete, sovereign political entities. "Orthodox accounts of reception and diffusion of law, at least in modern times, have been unduly influenced by formalist, state-oriented conceptions of law, which tend to downplay or overlook the other, often more elusive, elements that go to make up a legal culture" (Twinning 2000, 53). To use a notable example, John Rawls' work *The Law of Peoples* (1999) laudably articulates a moral view of international relations in a "realistic utopia" ruled by principles of justice and law, but remains unjustifiably attached to a sovereignty-based model of international affairs. While he does go to some length to distinguish between "peoples" and "states", Rawls remains bound to the conception of world affairs as comprised of independent bodies who enter into relations with each other. At the other extreme, Peter Singer (2002) and Martha Nussbaum (1996) have rejected the conception of international politics as rooted in the sovereign state, only to replace it with a cosmopolitan ethic that effectively ignores the diverse forms of political, economic, and social relations that have developed across the globe. While political philosophy has acknowledged the phenomenon of globalization, it has yet to take it seriously enough to incorporate its changes into the foundations of its various philosophical systems.

The reliance upon the sovereign state as the foundation of political philosophy has had a number of detrimental effects on theoretical attempts to understand international law. The belief that all political and juridical legitimacy stems from the state has led to a stark cynicism towards international law and the role of norms in international relations in general. In its theoretical form, this skeptical view has run from Thucydides to Hobbes to Hans Morgenthau as the school of international relations realism. All of these thinkers have rejected the legitimacy or efficacy of international treaties on the grounds that states will ultimately do what they will. Thus, there is a direct link between the conceptual reliance on the sovereign state on the one hand and skepticism towards international law on the other. An immediate rejection of the legitimacy of corporate bodies such as states or intergovernmental organizations has handicapped serious attempts to understand the functioning of the international polity. The onset of globalization has exposed the weaknesses of both views as empirical claims about the nature of political relations. Such views have ultimately obscured the possibilities, promises, and dangers to be found in contemporary international society, a context where neither sovereign states nor individuals stand as the essence of the political (Henkin 1999).

Among the goals of this work is to get beyond the conceptualization of global political and legal relations as being completely "inter-national" and view it in a more sophisticated fashion, and examine the results of such a project for the philosophy of international law. Once we abandon the modern nation-state as the foundation for a theory of international law (as well as international relations), we will see that the nature of legal theory changes substantially. In this study, I will not work from the "ground up" by starting with smaller forms of political association such as communities, cities, or states, and then proceed upwards in order to justify international legal norms. Instead, my analysis will be (for lack of a better term) holistic, that is to say, I will begin by examining international law independently of the traditional nation-state (usually considered to be the very life-blood of international law) and then go backwards to see what role the state (and the individual that comprises the state) plays within international law, rather than what role international law plays in relation to the state (to this extent then, this work is "constructivist" in orientation (Checkel 1998)). This, I believe will lead us to understand international law in a different, and substantially more positive light. Thus, by consciously or otherwise relying upon the conceptions of the state inherited from traditional political and legal theory, philosophers have made things both too easy and too hard for themselves. By trying a different approach I hope to make it more useful, if not easier.

The purpose of this work is to use the tools of contemporary philosophy to seek to come to a better understanding of the nature of international law as it is presently developing and to attain a better grasp of its "reality". I will seek to offer a philosophical account of international law that achieves several goals: First, it articulates a methodologically defensible delineation of what international law is when considered as a phenomenon of study (this is the formal, or methodological dimension of my analysis). Second, its method is used to explicate significant matters of substance within international law itself, specifically issues of legal personality and the law of humanitarian intervention. Finally, from the standpoint of this account of international law, we will be able to address traditional criticisms of international law as a legitimate body of study. Here I will argue that international law does have a genuine role to play in the understanding of international relations, and I will attempt to articulate how this role may best be understood. The achievement of these three goals, then, will be the central aim of this work.

This work, by its very nature, is interdisciplinary and, because of this, it may inadvertently produce some confusions and misconceptions in readers who have deep roots in some more traditional approaches. Rather than allowing this confusion to linger through the reading of this work, thereby leading to the raising of faulty objections to its ideas (as opposed to the good objections, which I encourage), I should say a few words about the difference between philosophical and (international) legal discourses and how this work seeks to bridge the gap between these two worlds.

Some of the arguments offered here may seem overly technical, even pedantic to those used to the more casual arguments made in legal theory and international relations theory. Dwelling on logical and semantic distinctions may seem to amount to unproductive hair-splitting to those engaged in the analysis of law in a more pragmatic vein. Similarly, the introduction of philosophical terminology may seem like an attempt at obfuscation through jargon. However, I believe that the liberal use of technical language and the abstract forms of reasoning found in philosophy in this work is not only helpful, but ultimately necessary for an adequate and defensible analysis of international law. Criticisms that have been taken as devastating in the relevant literature have rested upon analyses that (whether explicit or otherwise) have been philosophical in nature, mandating a response that employs all of the tools necessary for the task. Finally, this is a work of philosophy, and I would be remiss if I did not use all of the philosophical tools at my disposal to complete the task to the best of my ability. A building is only as strong as the materials used in its construction, which in turn lies heavily upon the quality of the tools available. If my discussion of concepts such as wide reflective equilibrium is unclear, I bear full responsibility for this, but regardless of the clarity of my language, the concepts I deploy, I believe, are necessary for the task at hand, however pedantic they may seem.

On the other side of the coin, philosophers may find some of the legalistic jargon and some of the aspects of legal reasoning, not to mention the political and historical events that are dealt with here, to be somewhat unfamiliar. I have tried my best to translate legal terminology into the philosophical idiom, but no translation is perfect and I expect that a certain amount of confusion is unavoidable. Interdisciplinary work, if it is to be truly interdisciplinary, must avoid completely subordinating one discipline's assumptions and terms to those of another, and I have resisted turning this work into simply another philosophical treatise which doesn't engage with international law on its own terms. A genuine synthesis of disparate disciplines is a difficult feat and the prospect of leaving both sides dissatisfied in the effort is ever-present. I sincerely hope that this is not the case with this work and that philosophers, legal theorists, and practicing lawyers will find something interesting and useful within these pages.

A Note on the Term "Theory"

Not all theories are the same in character, not all philosophical projects deploy identical methods, nor do they aim for identical goals. For this reason, it is worthwhile, before proceeding, to spend a moment explaining what it means to give a theoretical analysis of an institution such as international law. The central aim of this work will be to develop what I will call an "account" of international law. That is, I will attempt to develop a theoretical picture that coheres with what is conventionally considered to be international law by practicing experts and scholars (the reasons for preferring this approach will be spelled out in Chapters 2 and 3). From the development of such a picture, I hope to show a number of important things about the law and the nature of international relations more generally. This is not the preferred method for arbitrary reasons; rather this approach will do some theoretical work in the remaining chapters. One of the significant consequences of this approach will be to suggest that many of those who are skeptical of international law have misapprehended it and that their criticisms ought to be abandoned.

This work, then, will have an empirical flavor to it, seeking to understand international law as it is embedded in human social and political life. In general I will eschew large, metaphysical claims about *the* foundation of international law and *the* function of law in the international environment. Similarly, I will avoid many overtly prescriptive claims about the desirability (or normative status) of international law. Rather, I will accept a more or less common-sense assumption that law is a complex phenomenon that can serve a variety of functions and be desirable for a variety of reasons. This means that the ensuing chapters will borrow as much from the philosophy of social science as from legal and politacal theory and ethics. I recognize that for some, used to a more conventional justification for the law, this may seem unsatisfying. However, there are defensible reasons for taking this approach and its advantages will be spelled out through the remainder of this work.

While there have been numerous scholarly efforts to combine the study of international relations with international law, this work is not, directly at least, a part of that tradition.[1] In many ways, the approach I will set out here does not accord a strong role for IR theory for understanding international law. Rather than seeing international law as primarily part of a general theory of international politics or of legal compliance, I will seek to show that international law penetrates deeply into global politics, more than simply at the level of inter-state relations or the interactions of other collective agents. Rather, this work is pluralist in nature, arguing that international law is a phenomenon best understood through numerous disciplines, eschewing the role of general theories of any kind. This means that historians, sociologists, anthropologists, and even psychologists may contribute something meaningful to the understanding of international law and its role in human affairs. There is no single correct way to understand the effects of law on international politics and too strong a reliance on general laws of political relations causes one to overlook the complex intersections between law and social life.

---

1 The "IR-IL" literature has grown immensely over the last 20 years. For some of the most prominent contributions, see Slaughter (1999, 2004), Arend (1998), and Abbott (1989).

Further, most, though not all, international relations theories still rely on the sovereign state as the analytical centerpiece of their theories. While there are some exceptions to this rule, much international relations theory either postulates the existence of sovereign states and from there seeks to grasp the role that law plays in the global order. Even those theories that are conducive to law, that is, those IR theories which believe that law matters in international politics, see the fundamental problem of international law as one of constraining the actions of sovereign states. This, however, is one level of analysis, and there are many other interesting and important questions that should be asked at the sub-national level as well as at the level of individual human beings. Of course, the sovereign state is an essential part of international politics, but how law impacts on state behavior is not the only question to ask about the role of international law in global political life.

If there is an overarching "point" to this work, it is that international law does not need other disciplines in order to operate effectively in international society. For most functioning legal systems, theory is a sideshow, separate from the practical activity of actual lawyers. More conventional fields of law may rest on foundations that are no more secure than international law's, but this does not mean that these systems are on the verge of collapse. Rather, they function because they are accepted and generally useful for everybody involved (nobody asks "what is the basis of obligation for Constitutional law?" with the belief that much hinges on the answer). As part of their education, international lawyers are taught to accept the *prima facie* legitimacy of their field and deal with theoretical questions only when absolutely necessary.

International law is an exception to this rule. Often scholars of international law feel a need to be closely aligned with theories of international politics or law to be legitimatized. Perhaps this stems from an insecurity about the status of international law, a legal system that lacks a direct means of enforcement, and the scorn that international law receives in the public and from some in academia. Regardless, I hope that one contribution of this work will be to show that there is a limited need for "theoretical foundations" for international law. Rather, international law can stand on its own as a field of law and as a field of political analysis.

Acknowledgements

Innumerable people have looked at parts of this manuscript, offering encouragement, advice, and criticism. In particular, I would like to thank Nicholas Fotion, David Bederman, Abdullahi An-Na'im, Michael Sullivan, Amit Pandey, Henry Dyson, Timothy Terrell, Roger S. Clark, Mark Janis, Rosslyn Higgins, Wouter Werner, Terry Gill, Anne Bowler, Ronet Bachman, Reed Coats and Joel Best, along with many who anonymously looked at various parts of the manuscript at different points in its development.

Chapter 1

Skepticism Towards International Law

Skepticism towards international law has a long history, having been professed by some of the most esteemed legal theorists and philosophers, not to mention politicians and diplomats. However, as with all forms of skepticism, skeptics towards international law are involved in numerous different projects with different ideological, theoretical, and political agendas behind their efforts, some of which stand in direct conflict with each other. In addition to the different purposes to which their skepticisms are put are the conflicting natures of their respective skepticisms, that is, what the skeptics believe international law to be and on what grounds they reject it (and what they mean by the notion of "rejection" itself). Thus, before we can begin to evaluate properly these objections to developing a theory of international law, we must first seek to understand the different views and some of the assumptions (philosophical and otherwise) upon which they rest. Once we have grasped the central criticisms of international law, we will be in a better position to develop a resilient, positive theory.

The central goal of this chapter then will be to sketch out some of the major forms of skepticism that have been asserted regarding international law and their different ramifications for this legal regime. While I will link each set of objections with a particular name or set of names, there may be other theorists and philosophers who fit into each category (and some that combine these categories more-or-less consciously).[1] Thus this list is neither complete nor comprehensive, it is merely an effort to make some sense of the main forms of skepticism towards international law. The first type of skepticism I will designate the "definitional semantic" rejection of international law (linked with the positivist jurisprudence of John Austin), the second is the "descriptive realist" approach (belonging to some of the classical and more recent adherents to the realist school of international relations theory), then the "prescriptive realists", associated with the international relations theory realists as well as diplomats like Dean Acheson and Henry Kissinger, and finally the objections from the Critical Legal Studies (CLS) movement (affiliated with the "New Stream" school of international law and the postmodern legal thought of Martti Koskenniemi). Once I have outlined and evaluated these different skeptical views and commented upon some general themes running through them, I will then be in a position to develop a theory that will respond to what remains compelling in these objections. This positive goal will be the project of the ensuing chapters of this work.

I should offer one further comment about the kinds of criticisms that I will discuss in this chapter. I will only be concerned with criticisms of international law

1 For a particularly interesting blend of these different criticisms in relation to the international law of human rights see Watson (1979).

that object to it *in principle*, and not necessarily in practice. This is to say, I will not concern myself with those who argue that at this or that time international law was or is ineffective but *could be* effective sometime in the future. Nor will I concern myself with criticisms that merely point to weaknesses in the contemporary international legal order (for example, the belief that international law is useless given the current structure of the Security Council of the United Nations). Rather, I will analyze views that hold that by its very nature and by the very nature of the entities that it tries to constrain (in most cases sovereign states), international law is either non-existent, irrelevant, or morally unacceptable. It will be a part of my response to some of these criticisms that they have conflated the theoretical component of international law (its status in principle) with its current international efficacy (its status in practice) and thereby overstated their case. As we will see later, I will agree that international law at times is ineffective and at times has been irrelevant to understanding a series of events, but that these are not grounds for rejecting international law as an important force in international relations either at present or in the future. Thus I will claim that in current practice international law may seem at times to be non-existent, although I think that those who hold such a view frequently overstate the case, but this does not mean that it isn't found elsewhere, and this is therefore not a good reason to reject international law as such.

Definitional-Semantics (Austinian Positivism)

One popular form of skepticism, frequently associated with John Austin's brand of legal positivism, seeks to show that international law is "not really law" and therefore it is a mistake to apply the term to rules that guide international relations. According to this view, the term "international law" is an inappropriate use of the word "law" based upon some pre-existing standard that the legal theorist herself uses. Such a view starts with a more-or-less articulated or defensible standard of "genuine law" and then seeks to show that what is dubbed "international law" does not meet its criteria and thus should be removed from the domain of legal studies. Given this conclusion, such a theorist argues that scholars should change their language regarding the nature of the norms that are at play in international relations and start calling them something else. Everything that we thought was law and speak of as law but does not meet the stipulated requirements must be understood as something other than law and described by some other term.

Of course, Austin's critique of international law is the most often cited version of the definitional-semantic critique (although there are others).[2] For Austin, law is conceptually bound up with commands emanating from a single source. Standing behind this source and providing the rules with their legal quality is a sanction – punishment for disobeying the command. "Laws properly so called are a species of *commands*. But, being a *command*, every law properly so called flows from a *determinate* source." It is only because the commands may be enforced by the

2 For a heavily cited, although brief discussion of this form of critique which includes some important non-Anglo versions see Koskenniemi (2005, 125–6).

powers that be that they are considered law. Lacking such a unitary authority, and lacking a single originating point, it is impossible to describe international law as true law. "And hence it follows that the law obtaining between nations is not positive law: for every positive law is set by a given sovereign to a person or persons in a state of subjection to its author… The duties which it imposes are enforced by moral sanctions: by fear on the part of nations, or by fear on the part of sovereigns of provoking general hostility." While conventional laws are determined by a single authority and are enforced by "evils", international laws are not, and therefore the term "law" cannot be appropriately applied to this legal regime.

Such an argument for rejecting international law must overcome several significant hurdles before it can fulfill its goals. First, it must show that there is only one proper conception of "law" (or "real law"), with a set of necessary and sufficient conditions for the appropriate application of the term. Otherwise, such criticism has accounted for only one kind of law, and not law as such. This is the most strictly philosophical part of the analysis (and is nowhere given by Austin himself). Second, such conditions for genuine law must be laid out in a satisfactory and defensible way, one that serves the purpose of broad legal analysis. Austin has attempted to do this with his determination that "law" is best understood as commands of the sovereign that are backed by sanction (Austin 1995, Lecture I). If this primary definition of law captures the true, ultimate essence of law as such and thereby sets the standards that any act, decision, rule, and so on must meet before it may be justifiably described as law, only then may it be used to dismiss international law as a false form of law.

It has been pointed out by critics that Austin's aim in his *Province of Jurisprudence Determined* is not to capture the variation and nuances of the use of the term "law" in ordinary language, but rather to account for the "true essence of law" apart from the everyday use by the laity. Whether there is any correlation between Austin's definition of the term and our everyday understanding of the word (such as its relation to justice) is effectively irrelevant for his analysis. As Gerard Maher describes Austin's method:

> What we should note for present purposes is that such reality of law is not necessarily expressed in the language of those whose social life it regulates. Indeed, *Austin's* avowed aim in trying to set out the boundaries for legal theory was to cut through the variety of matters commonly called law and deemed legal, and instead to present what for him were the distinctive features of law as it existed in all societies and or as it must exist in any society… [T]he task of jurisprudence is to bring out the reality of law which ordinary (legal) discourse tended to obscure (Maher 1978, 409).

For lack of a better term, we can call Austin's overall approach "Platonist" as he is claiming to uncover the true, unchanging essence of a term regardless of how we may use it in ordinary language. If his use of the term does not match our ordinary language then so much the worse for ordinary language. We will see that many cogent criticisms of Austin take issue with this Platonist method and the relationship between philosophical reflections and social institutions like law.

According to this approach, all other uses of the term "law" must either be understood in terms of this definition or be rejected as mistaken. Thus Austin allows that certain rules that do not seem to be commands of a sovereign are in fact laws because they may be explained or adequately understood through his so-called command theory. For example, laws that create rights (such as freedom of speech) do not initially appear to be commands backed by sanctions. However, Austin argues that these rights-conferring laws are in reality laws imposing duties, and thus are easily reconceived in terms of the command theory. "Every law, really conferring a right is, therefore, imperative: as imperative, as if its only purpose were the creation of a duty, or as if the relative duty, which it inevitably imposes, were merely absolute" (Austin 1995, p. 38, col. 2). The *right* to freedom of speech then is in fact a *duty* of others to allow a person to speak freely that in turn is the product of a *command* that the agent refrain from preventing speech. Thus, along with the primary cases of commands to do or to forbear from doing a particular act (such as laws prohibiting murder), are laws that are ultimately reducible to this primary definition and thus may still be considered valid uses of the term law[3] (we might call them "laws by reduction").

Having developed such a legal theory, such a skeptic must then develop an account of international law, delineating its nature and scope and defending this description against other, competing accounts. Austin's initial description of international law as, "Laws which regard the conduct of independent political societies in their various relations to one another. Or, rather, there are laws which regard the conduct of sovereigns or supreme governments in their various relations to one another" (Austin 1995, Lecture V, p. 41) is disappointingly unsophisticated. Elsewhere he elaborates:

> Society formed by the intercourse of independent political societies, is the province of international law, or of the law obtaining between nations. For (adopting a current expression) international law, or the law obtaining between nations, is conversant about the conduct of independent political societies considered as entire communities: *circa negotia et causas gentium integrarum.* Speaking with greater precision, international law, or the law obtaining between nations, regards the conduct of sovereigns considered as related to one another (Austin 1995, Lecture VI).

Thus Austin has given us a description of international law: It is conceived of as the norms pertaining between sovereigns, agents that in municipal law are the source of the content of law as well as the source of legal sanctions. On Austin's view, it is this model of law that must be contrasted with the definition of genuine law articulated above.

While Austin does not attack other definitions or understandings of international law at length in his *Province*, it is worth noting that his view is quite different from many of the prominent theorists of international law or, more appropriately, "the

---

3 Paradoxically enough, however, Austin does admit certain uses of the term law that are not reducible to his primary definition yet remain legitimate objects for jurisprudential study, cases such as "acts of *authentic* interpretation" and "laws to repeal laws" for example, "are other objects improperly termed laws (not being commands) which yet may properly be included within the province of jurisprudence" (Austin 1995, 37, col.1). Of course, why *these* are legitimate, and others are not remains an unanswered question for Austin.

law of nations" that proceeded him. Grotius, frequently considered the "father of international law," did not look to the existence of autonomous political entities and their interrelations to establish and delineate his law of nations.[4] Other scholars of the natural law tradition similarly reject the assumption that international law is defined as the legal relations holding among sovereigns but would point to larger metaphysical or theological doctrines in order to describe it.[5] Austin's conception of international law wasn't accepted by many of his contemporaries and it is hardly a truism that the nature and sources of law are in fact how he characterizes them.[6]

The final step of the argument must be to show that international law thus defined does not meet the aforementioned criteria and thus is not really law. Because the only means of enforcing the norms of international law is public opinion, and because they lack a single source for determining their obligations, international laws cannot be conceived of as genuinely legal. Equally important, they are not obligatory in the ways that legal norms are obligatory. "The so called law of nations consists of opinions or sentiments current among nations generally. It therefore is not law properly so called." And elsewhere:

> And hence it inevitably follows [from the above definition], that the law obtaining between nations is not positive law: for every positive law is set by a given sovereign to a person or persons in a state of subjection to its author. As I have already intimated, the law obtaining between nations is law (improperly so called) set by general opinion. The duties which it imposes are enforced by moral sanctions: by fear on the part of nations, or by fear on the part of sovereigns, of provoking general hostility, and incurring its probable evils, in case they shall violate maxims generally received and respected (Austin 1995, Lecture VI, 201).

---

4 See for example the introduction to *The Laws of War and Peace* where Grotius cites a vast number of sources for the law of nations without ever appealing to the concept of sovereignty (Grotius 1949, 1962). For more on the connection between Austinian positivism and other movements in international legal theory in the first half of the 19th century see Nussbaum (1954, 224–30).

5 Prior to Austin, Blackstone had defined "the Law of Nations" as "a system of rules, deducible by natural reason, and established by universal consent among the civilized inhabitants of the world; in order to decide all disputes, to regulate all ceremonies and civilities, and to insure the observance of justice and good faith, in that intercourse which must frequently occur between two or more independent states, *and the individuals belonging to each*" (Blackstone 2003, 407). I will discuss the connections between "international law," "the law of nations," and "transnational law" as I understand it in the next chapter.

6 To be fair to Austin, he does in fact confront Grotius and Pufendorf on the issue of the nature of international morality (Austin's term for international law) arguing that "they have confounded positive international morality, or the rules which actually obtain among civilized nations in their mutual intercourse, with their own vague conceptions of international morality as it *ought to be*, with that indeterminate something which they conceived it would be, if it conformed to that indeterminate something which they call the law of nature" (Austin 1995, Lecture V, 287).

Austin's reasoning then is by a simple deductive process: all laws must meet requirements *a* through *x*. International laws, properly understood, do not meet these requirements. *Ergo* international laws are not genuine law.

As a result of this reasoning, international law is not true law, but is rather relegated to a lower status as "positive international morality" in Austin's view. Moral norms, in contrast to legal norms, do not carry any jurisprudential weight, which is to say they are not the objects of study for a genuine science of jurisprudence. They are motivated not by a sanction (that Austin defines as an "evil or inconvenience" of punishment), but by a fear of falling out of good graces with one's peers (Austin 1995, Lecture V, p. 143). What is key, however, to Austin's distinction between the "law" and "morality" is that the latter does not involve any real obligation from its subjects. As Austin puts it:

> Being liable to evil from you if I comply not with a wish which you signify, I am *bound* or *obliged* by your command, or I lie under a *duty* to obey it. If, in spite of that evil in prospect, I comply not with the wish which you signify, I am said to disobey your command, or to violate the duty which it imposes (John 1995, Lecture I, p. 33).

Thus Austin's distinction isn't merely one of mere semantics: one of the central concepts of legal theory, obligation, disappears with those norms that do not cohere with his definition of law as a command.[7] Not only does international law fail a simple semantic test that purports to describe the nature of law, it fails to be normative in a legal sense: It fails to impose any *real* duties.

Within the framework of such an approach, there are three ways to salvage international law: first, one may reject the proposed definition of law, as was done effectively by H.L.A. Hart in *The Concept of Law* (Hart 1994, 82–91). Second, one may reject Austin's characterization of international law, claiming that he has misunderstood its nature and that in fact it really does meet his criteria. Later, I will offer a rejoinder to Austin that combines both types of responses: I will argue not only that Austin has mischaracterized the nature of law in general, but he has also misunderstood the nature of international law in particular.[8]

A final, more radical critique of Austin's approach to law and its related critique of international law is to reject the central premise of his argument: namely, the assumption that words have fixed meanings that we may discover through logical or semantic analysis. While there are many cogent philosophical arguments from a variety of sources that would give reason to reject the approach to the analysis of meanings offered by Austin, we need look no further than to Ludwig Wittgenstein's conception of a "family resemblance" in the determination of meaning. For Wittgenstein, there is no primary sense to words, but rather a complex set of relations such as in the various meanings of the word "language." As he puts it:

---

7 As Hart has shown, Austin's argument that "evil" or "sanction" necessarily entails obligation is perhaps the most specious part of Austin's reasoning. See Hart (1994), esp. pages 82–91.

8 This is not to say that Austin's concern regarding the "unenforceable" nature of international law is not warranted and worth considering. I will address this issue in further chapters.

> Instead of producing something common to all that we call language, I am saying that these phenomena have no one thing in common which makes us use the same word for all, – but that they are *related* to one another in many different ways. And it is because of this relationship, or these relationships, that we call them all "language" (Wittgenstein 1963, §67).

A computer code such as BASIC is a language, ASL is a language, and love is a kind of language. While they are all "languages," there is no central definition that holds them together. Thus, just as the term "language" has no privileged reference or meaning, the term "law" need not denote any particular thing or property, and any attempt to make it so is falsifying our use of language for the sake of a dubious theoretical consistency.

A view similar to Wittgenstein's was brought to bear on Austin's approach to international law by Glanville Williams in his 1947 article "International Law and the Controversy Concerning the Word 'Law'." Here, Williams accurately accuses Austin of illegitimately elevating one arbitrary definition of law, one tailored to describe a narrow set of phenomena (namely domestic criminal law), to the status of the essence of law as such:

> The power that Austin assumed for himself, to define the meaning of the words he used, he should have accorded also to others. Every one is entitled for his own part to use words in any meaning he pleases; there is no such thing as an intrinsically "proper" or "improper" meaning of a word. The nearest approach to the "proper" meaning is the "usual" meaning... But Austin was not seeking the usual meaning of the term 'law'. If he had been he could hardly have denied that the phrases "law of nations" and "law of gravity" were usual ones, and moreover phrases that were usual among the best writers (Williams 1945, 148).

Thus for Williams, it is not that Austin's understanding of the essence of law is inadequate (although certainly he believes this to be the case), nor is his account of international law itself flawed (undoubtedly true), but rather Austin's project rests upon a dubious assumption. If there is no essence to the meanings of words, no proper meaning as Austin intended, then there is no good reason to believe that perfectly normal usages of the term "law of nations" in books by Grotius, Pufendorf, and others are not equally proper uses of the term. This said, there is no real reason to reject international law on some seemingly arbitrary definition of what law ultimately is.[9] While I will later reject some of the more radical consequences of this approach (especially the conclusions that the New Stream draws from it), its charge of a false essentialism seems to me to be correct, at least in relation to Austin.

While these replies to Austin's critiques of international law have cogency, they may not be enough to completely respond to Austin's views. Clearly, Austin is not pulling his definition of law out of thin air. Rather, he is rooting his analysis in a deeper intuition shared by most people who think about the subject: law is fundamentally

9 While the philosophical foundations of Austin's critique of international law may be dubious, we will still have use of Austin's approach throughout this work as pointing to some interesting and useful features of law and disregarding the larger philosophical issue of whether we can come to an "essence" of law.

about making certain behaviors obligatory, or at least non-optional. Domestic law is obligatory because it is enforced by a government or a sovereign with police officers and a military to back it (or him) up. International law is not obligatory for states or other international actors precisely because it is not enforced. This definition is not arbitrary, but rather reflects a deeper understanding of the techniques of social control that are shared by others – techniques that are clearly lacking in the international field. Thus, Austin is not merely using an arbitrary definition of law to pillory international law, but rather he is seeking to clarify our pre-existing intuition about the connections between a set of norms and the use of sanctions as a means of social control. The endurance of Austin's critique stems not from the somewhat weak definition that he gives regarding the foundations of law, but rather emanates from a deeper understanding of the nature of law as such.

Of course, anybody who works in international law is familiar with Austin's critique and its enduring legacy. Clearly, Austin is pointing to an important part of the legal ideology of many people both inside and outside of the academy.[10] However, it is unclear how far one should uncritically accept such popular intuitions about the term "law" regardless of how entrenched and widespread they may be. The belief that laws require enforcement to be "real laws" is one that obscures as much about law and our beliefs about law as it reveals and it deserves a certain amount of skepticism. While many people both inside and outside of academia share such views about the nature and structure of law, many do not. Robust legal traditions, whether Islamic law (Shariah) or Canon law, remain potent forces in societies without possessing a bureaucratic means of enforcement, and many parts of domestic legal systems don't meet such criteria. Sociology of law, particularly the legal consciousness movement, has shown that public attitudes towards law are as much shaped by perspectives of right and wrong as with enforceability, that is, compliance is as much a function of attitude towards the law as administrative enforcement (Tyler 1990, 3–7). The assumption that law requires enforcement and that enforcement is what makes certain behavior mandatory is an ideology that should be critically assessed by looking at law in a broader social context. It is not simply playing games with language to assert that the term "law" can mean different things to different people in different contexts. Part of the remaining analysis will be subjecting such intuitions to rigorous analysis as well as a good deal of skepticism.

Realism: Descriptive and Prescriptive

A second genre of criticism of international law stems from what is usually called the "realist" or "realpolitik" school of international relations.[11] This movement is not as

10 Of course, Austin is not the first person (by far) to express such intuitions about the nature of laws. The Roman general Pompeius Magnus is reported to have said, "Stop quoting the law to us. We carry swords" (Tacitus).

11 In order to prevent confusion between the "realist" school of international relations and the jurisprudential school of "legal realism," I will always refer to the latter by its full name. Thus, when I use the terms "realism" or "realists" alone throughout this work, I will be referring to the school of international relations discussed in this section.

much concerned with Austin's jurisprudential and semantic project of defining law (and thereby defining away international law), as with de-legitimizing law's claims of having any effective role in world politics. Like any other major intellectual movement, the "realist" moniker is applied to a vast number of different theoretical positions (along with the views of a number of politicians and diplomats such as Acheson and Kissinger) and thus we should be careful about speaking too broadly about their views.[12] However, if we were to point to a common thread running through these various thinkers, it is a belief in what we might call the irreducibly political character of international relations and the ensuing need for flexibility, prudence, and at times raw power to negotiate the anarchy of global politics. Rather than the inflexibility and uniformity of international legal rules, the realists see diplomacy and brute force as the real motor of world affairs and claim (usually) that this is how things ought to be.

Following Charles Beitz, we can break this school down into two different (though related) types of claims, a *descriptive* claim and a *prescriptive* claim (Beitz 1999, 20). The first is the roughly social-scientific view that the empirical study of international relations seems to show little or no need for international law, and thus we should not take these laws seriously when studying existing international relations. To use a term from contemporary philosophy of mind, we can say that international law is *epiphenomenal* in the causal nexus of world political affairs for the descriptive realists. The second claim on the other hand is the moral-practical thesis that either there is no normative reason to follow international law or that these rules ought to be rejected when they conflict with other imperatives (such as national interest).[13] On such a view, diplomats have a moral obligation as representatives of state to disregard international law when necessary. *Raison d'état* trumps any putatively legal obligations that leaders may have to other international actors. In its stronger variant, prescriptive realists maintain that there is no normative justification for international law and thus it is not worth regarding in any important political decision. Rather than a social scientific basis of criticism, the prescriptive realist is arguing, interestingly enough, from a moral standpoint.

The two forms of realism represent the perspectives of two different types of individuals. The first sees international law from the standpoint of the hard-nosed social scientist seeking causal explanations for (as well as predictions of) political change in international society. On the other hand, the prescriptive realists view these laws from the standpoint of the practicing politician whose sole aim in world affairs is assuring the security of her state against all challenges and, if possible, expanding its power, wealth, and influence. For the realists, then, the diplomat and the scientist (and not the international lawyer or the judge) provide the ultimate perspective from

12 Some of the central texts of International Relations realism are Morgenthau (1967) and Waltz (1959).

13 As Fernando Tesón has argued, one of these views does not necessarily entail the other. That is to say that the *fact* that international relations are not governed by law (as per the descriptive realists' claim) does not entail that they *ought* not be so governed. This said, I will be dealing with these two theories separately with two distinct criticisms of international law (Tesón 1997, 48).

which the status of international law ought to be gauged and its usefulness evaluated – and from these perspectives it is seriously wanting. We will now discuss each of these perspectives in turn.

Descriptive realism

Descriptive realists rest their views on a number of complicated and interlocking philosophical (and purportedly scientific) claims that argue for the irrelevance of international legal norms. Put more succinctly, international legal norms are epiphenomenal. Here international law is rejected for its uselessness in understanding international affairs. As Beitz describes this view in relation to moral norms:

> If we seek something like scientific knowledge of politics – say, a body of lawlike generalizations with at least limited predictive power – we are unlikely to make much of progress by deriving our hypotheses from moral rules appropriate to individual behavior (Beitz 1999, 20).

This argument asserts, then, that legal norms play no effective role in international politics and in the deliberations of world leaders, and thus should be removed from any serious study of international relations. Thus, when we say that international legal norms are epiphenomenal, we are saying that there is a one-way relation between laws and political behavior, that political circumstances may give rise to the precepts of international law, but that these laws do not in turn influence the agents that are subject to them (Reus-Smit 2004, 16).[14] Thus, these norms may exist on paper and may be cited by governments as a justification for particular acts, but they do not play any real causal role in any of the events in which they are cited.

To put a finer and more empirical point on this claim as a social scientific theory of international relations, one could say that a complete and satisfying account of these relations may be formulated without *ever* claiming that international law plays a significant role. In fact, international law could be removed from the narrative of international politics and nothing significant would be lost. A theory is designed to explain the behavior of a set of agents (presumably, in this context, states), and the most compelling account of this behavior does not require mention of international law any more than it requires reference to divine providence as explicated in the book of Revelation from *The New Testament*. Attempts to appeal to international law as serving any function in empirical events would require either falsifying the phenomena or interpreting law-governed behavior so loosely that it could *never* be falsified. Thus, like any other discredited purportedly explanatory view regarding international relations (such as divine providence), international law plays no satisfactory explanatory role in political behavior and should be left to the realm of naïve idealists. On this account, we should reject both providence and international law as valid accounts of world politics and rely upon more adequate explanatory tools such as national interest and power to explain current and past events and predict future ones.

---

14 See also, Bederman (2000) and Arend (1999).

Many contemporary realist theories that make some version of the epiphenomenality charge base their views on rational choice/game theoretic models, rather than bare theories of psychological motivation. By modeling international relations as a set of rationally self-interested actors, and situating them in numerous "games" or scenarios that are meant to emulate real-world situations, the realist can deduce likely outcomes. Of course, given the lack of a clear international enforcement power, there is no reason why international law should fit into the calculations of international actors. For rational choice theory, international law is removed from the scope of analysis at the outset.

The most significant recent contributors to the field of international law from a rational choice perspective are Jack Goldsmith and Eric Posner. In their book, *The Limits of International Law*, they argue that without an effective enforcement mechanism, international law (particularly customary international law) cannot play any significant role in determining the behavior of international actors. "International law emerges from states' pursuit of self-interested policies on the international stage. International law is, in this sense, *endogenous* to state interests. It is not a check on state self-interest; it is a product of state interest" (Posner and Goldsmith 2005, 13). While Posner and Goldsmith do not believe that international law is "irrelevant" or "unreal", their view entails exactly this conclusion.[15] "Under our theory, international law does not pull states toward compliance contrary to their interests, and the possibilities for what international law can achieve are limited by the configurations of state interests and the distribution of state power" (Posner and Goldsmith 2005, 13). Thus international law works when the relevant agents want it to work. When they do not want it to work, they may conveniently ignore it with few consequences. Thus for Posner and Goldsmith, international law has no independent influence on international affairs beyond its role coordinating state interests.

Their method depends on a number of assumptions about international politics, some of which are explicit and some of which remain implicit. While Green and Shapiro have correctly pointed out that it is a mistake to oversimplify the rational choice movement or assume that it is monolithic in its outlook, they point out that there are a number of general points upon which all rational choice scholars agree. Specifically, they argue that there are five assumptions under all rational choice theory (Green and Shapiro 1996, 14–17):

1. That rational behavior is identified with the "maximation of some sort" of utility. That is, it assumes that agents are concerned with realizing their own desires to the greatest degree possible.
2. There must be a certain consistency or rational pattern to rational behavior.
3. Agents maximize expected (not actual) utility. That is, they use their best judgment to determine which choice is likely to maximize their payoff.
4. Individual agents (usually, though not always persons) are the unit of analysis.
5. Rational choice models apply generally to all agents.

15 As they assert, "International law, especially treaties, can play an important role in helping states achieve mutually beneficial outcomes by clarifying what counts as cooperation or coordination in interstate interactions" (Posner and Goldsmith 2005, 13). As we will see in later chapters, what it means for law to be "real" can differ widely from theory to theory.

These five assumptions, accepting that there are nuances between different theorists, comprise the basic building blocks of modern rational choice theory.

When taken out of economics and general political theory and placed in the context of international relations and international law, a second collection of assumptions appears. Specifically, assumption 4 above is transposed into a discussion of states. Thus states are assumed to be rational agents with definable interests that govern their behavior, and that they wish to maximize these interests. As Posner and Goldsmith put it: "Put briefly, our theory is that international law emerges from states acting rationally to maximize their interests, given their perceptions of the interests of other states and the distribution of state power" (Posner and Goldsmith 2005, 4). Moreover, "Both ordinary language and history suggest that states have agency and thus can be said to make decisions and act on the basis of identifiable goals"(Posner and Goldsmith 2005, 5). Thus, for Posner and others in the rational choice tradition, international relations mirrors the relations of *homo economicus* – the scientifically discoverable, rational, and individualized pursuit of self interest. The game of human conduct remains the same, only the types of actors have changed.

Rather then recategorizing international law as an "international morality" as Austin wished to do, descriptive realism seeks effectively to eliminate law from any scientific analysis of world politics, or at a minimum to marginalize it as an explanatory tool for understanding it. It's not that international law is "not really law," but rather it is useless for understanding actual international relations and thus is best abandoned. It becomes, in the words of one critic "the most active training ground for the imagination," a set of spinning gears having no real connection to the turning motor of world affairs. Whether international law is really law isn't a question that even gets off the ground for the realists (who are equally critical of the "positive international morality" that Austin advocated). Insofar as these rules are useless for understanding anything about world politics, their nature is irrelevant. Thus, rather than redefining (or, to be more technical, reducing) the norms of international law to ethics as Austin had done, the realists advocate eliminating international law from a serious science of international relations entirely.[16]

However, as mere theory, rational choice or other schools of international relations theory cannot undermine international law. Rather, to make any *strong* claims about the irrelevance or limited utility of international law, they must make further empirical claims about it. This is to say, they must some how "hook into" the real world and explain events. This would make these theories stronger than mere theory and would move them into the realm of empirical explanations of actual events – explanations where international law is shown to be without value. Upon such grounds, anybody wanting to understand the real world is justified in turning her back on international legal norms and looking elsewhere to justify a claim (otherwise a defender of international law could simply respond by developing her own theory). There are two possible routes by which one could argue that international relations does not

16 The analogy between the role (or lack thereof) of legal norms in international relations and the role of intentional "folk psychology" in materialist models of the mind will be an issue that I will take up later. However, there is an obvious analogy between the eliminativist project of materialists and the project of International Relations realists.

require an appeal to norms: the theoretical argument from *moral psychology* on the one hand, and the empirical argument from *explanatory adequacy* on the other.

The philosophical assumption of descriptive realism as a moral psychology is a claim about the sources of human motivation in general and political motivation in particular. Frequently, these theorists claim that legal norms do not independently influence the behavior of agents but must be buttressed with incentives such as a desire for particular goods or a desire to avoid particular evils. Namely, such a view (sometimes called "externalism" in ethical theory)[17] supposes that psychological motivations that could motivate an individual to follow the law in a pure fashion (such as a sense of duty), are useless for influencing the behavior of states in the international sphere.[18] While a single person can (perhaps) follow a rule out of a pure sense of duty or obligation, the unique character of states is such that the various internal and external pressures affecting foreign policy exclude such noble motives.[19] Thus, given the unique nature of the state and the structure in which the state is situated, there is no possibility that legal norms could influence the behavior of the state and constrain its pure self-interest. Thus we can safely remove international law from our analysis before even beginning to study international political relations.[20]

However, the research agenda of descriptive realism does not base its case solely upon this tenuous (or at least arguable) psychological ground. Scientific claims can never dwell solely at the theoretical level but must produce empirically satisfactory results in order to carry water. So we might sharpen the point of descriptive realists thus: if we look at international politics in a sober fashion, divorced from naïve moralisms, we will find that the real motor of all political events is the desire for states to protect themselves from harm and to further their own interests whenever possible. Whether or not one accepts the externalist account of motivation discussed above, one cannot but be impressed, or so the argument goes, by the vast amount of confirmation such a view receives in the realm of world history. History cannot but reveal that norms and laws fall upon deaf ears when they conflict with national interest and serve merely as elegant garb for whatever current power relations and current national interests dictate. This is the reality that their moniker aims to capture. The key to the descriptive realist argument then is empirical, not merely psychological, and thus descriptive realism stands or falls as an account of actual, not theoretical, international relations.

How can we gauge the appropriateness of international relations realism as a scientific program? The best way to examine realism is to confront it on its own grounds, as a scientific theory with significant competitors: we examine the issue as one of explanatory adequacy asking whether realism meets any scientifically

17 See Darwall (1996)..

18 Charles Beitz has noted that *moral* skepticism regarding the behavior of states entails a similar skepticism regarding the behavior of individuals (Beitz 1999, 5–27).

19 It is interesting to note that H.L.A. Hart argues that states are capable of feeling an obligation before law (Hart 1994, 230–31).

20 While I will not dwell on the issue here, frequently psychological arguments of the realists regarding the rationality of states and the epiphenomenalism of international law rest upon conceptions of rationality developed from rational choice theory.

satisfactory standards of explanation. Modern theories of international relations must be compared to the data at hand (as well as to alternative accounts of international relations) to determine whether there is an "international law." This is to say, we are best able to evaluate this claim of the epiphenomenal character of international law by laying it against other, competing accounts of a given phenomenon and from there determining its success or failure in relation to these other accounts (such as those appealing to the efficacy of international law). If realism is to live up to its title, it must actually *be* the best possible explanation of the realities of political events, and this requires that we look at the facts at hand.

Take a relatively recent case of world political importance, one that we will discuss in detail in a later chapter: the arrest and attempted extradition of former Chilean dictator Augusto Pinochet by England in 1999 (at the request of the Spanish judge). In such a case the realist would assert that the events surrounding the case were dictated solely by non-legal factors such as the respective national interests of England and Spain. The existence of the treaty against torture that the Spanish judge and British Law Lords both claim motivated their actions and decisions in this case was mere pretense and nothing more for the descriptive realist. The only function that law served was as rhetorical cover for the selfishness of the respective European powers. Precisely what the interests of Europe would be in this case is unclear, but this does not mean that they do not exist, asserts the realist; they are only well hidden by the powers that be.[21] The realist thus claims that with such an account one need not appeal to dubious and high-minded legal norms to explain why Spain and England have done as they have, but need only turn to "concrete" factors such as self-interest and power.

Prescriptive realism

The prescriptive form of the realist critique does not argue that international law plays no role in existing international politics, but more dramatically, that it *shouldn't* play any role there. For the prescriptive realist, it is not an issue of whether these laws are in fact "law" (as with Austin), or the issue of the role of these laws in shaping empirical political behavior (as with descriptive realism). Rather, the issue for this genre of realism is whether humanity in general, or this or that state in particular, is better off if they consider legal norms in the formulation and conduct of foreign policy or whether these laws can ultimately be justified from a normative standpoint.

The prescriptive realist could, in some cases, concede that international law meets some positivist criteria of legality but would argue that the stakes of international politics are so high that these laws ought to be ignored when they conflict with sound foreign policy and the well-being of the state. Similarly, he could agree that legal norms play a real role in world politics (unlike the descriptive realist), but would argue that they shouldn't play such a role and should be abandoned when

21 It has been suggested, for example, that the arrest of Pinochet has served the ideological agenda of a united Europe in separating itself from its frequent and overbearing ally, the United States.

necessary. The issue for the prescriptive realist then is not about the legality or efficacy of international law in world politics, but rather its morality. In other words, the prescriptive realist is not questioning the efficacy of international law, but rather its legitimacy or its wisdom.

There are numerous justifications that could be marshaled for such a claim, and as with descriptive realism there are a number of different views in this camp. However, we will only deal with three of the strongest types. First, I will discuss the perspective of the *prudential diplomat*, second, that of the *moral relativist*, and finally the *republican.* Each view asserts that there are no moral grounds for following international law but argue this point from different standpoints and, in turn, offer different accounts of the ethical foundations of normal political and cultural life.

The prudential diplomat asserts that following rules prescribed by international law forces an unnecessary rigidity upon delicate and complex diplomatic affairs. Legal rules, the prudential diplomat asserts, are frequently created in abstraction, away from real-world politics and cannot adequately cope with tricky, novel situations. Even those rules that are in fact created by diplomats and foreign leaders, and negotiated through treaties are questionable as these people cannot possibly foresee the complex political events that will take place after these laws have been put into effect. In light of these political realities, hypocrisy, duplicity, contradiction, and flexibility (along with a highly selective memory) are the virtues of the diplomat, and despite a certain repugnance, these are the virtues that allow for the common good. Unfortunately, these skills, however laudable in the political sphere, must frequently run counter to behavior recognized as lawful by those outside the world of diplomatic affairs. Were diplomats hamstrung by a set of abstract, inflexible rules, they could not effectively respond to the difficult problems that it is their task to resolve. Thus, despite the noble intentions of international lawyers, when they fashion treaties and compose essays on international law they often wind up causing more harm than good.

In his short essay, "Diplomacy in the Modern World,"[22] George Kennan eloquently represents the view of the prudential diplomat. According to Kennan, bluntly put, the idealism embodied in international law is ultimately destructive to human life when it seeks to impose its dictates upon the Byzantine and morally precarious wheeling and dealing of world diplomacy. "The legalistic approach to world affairs, rooted as it unquestionably is in a desire to do away with war and violence, makes violence more enduring, more terrible, and more destructive to political stability than did the older motives of national interest" (Kennan 1996, 105). The legal attitude and the variety of expectations that come from this attitude undermine efforts to quickly and peacefully solve international political problems through diplomatic channels. Kennan cites as examples of this attitude the belief that all states are willing to subordinate their interests to the rule of law, the assumption of the absolute stability and sovereignty of states. Such a view of global politics, "ignores the tremendous variations in the firmness and soundness of national divisions" (Kennan 1996, 103), it overlooks "those means of international offense… which by-pass institutional

22 Originally published in Kennan (1985, 91–103). Reprinted in Beck et al. (1996, 99–106). All page references will be from Beck et al. (1996).

forms entirely or even exploit them against themselves," and finally "it forgets the limitations on the effectiveness of military coalition" (Kennan 1996, 104). Rather than the rigid structures of international law binding the acts of states and the construction of foreign policy, diplomats would be better able to advance the common good as well as their own interests if they could be left to their own devices. Rather than deploying a crude and inflexible set of rules, the prudential diplomat sees the wisest form of international political decision-making as one of political compromise and moral flexibility.

Again briefly returning to the *Pinochet* case discussed above, we can see how the prudential diplomat would deal with the former dictator and why she would find his arrest and prosecution unwise, regardless of any legal obligations to the contrary. Given the dictator's relative political impotence (when arrested he was 83 years old, in poor health, and possessed little political clout in his native country), there seems to be no real benefit in his prosecution for anybody. Rather, prosecuting the general would undermine political stability in his homeland, possibly reviving his bedraggled image in the Chilean right, and thereby reinvigorating the ideology that cost so many lives during Pinochet's regime. In the worst case, his arrest could so incense the Chilean military that they could (conceivably) initiate a coup in Chile out of anger for the government's inability to return their former patriarch.[23] Finally, it could negatively influence all future attempts to persuade dictators to relinquish their power to more benign political authorities as they fear future prosecution.[24] Thus, while he is unquestionably guilty of the crimes of torture and murder, the benefits of prosecuting the man (presumably deterring future dictators and perhaps giving his surviving victims and the families of the deceased a certain degree of peace of mind) are dramatically outweighed by the potential costs for the Chilean people as well as those under the heel of other dictatorships. An adherence to the relevant criminal treaties, while certainly well intentioned, serves the interests of very few at the cost of peace and Chilean stability, whereas other approaches to the problem would (or at least could) have been less destructive.[25]

I have characterized the second form of prescriptive realism as a form of relativism. On this view, the various cultures of the world are so different from one another that there could not possibly be a set of valid legal norms that would cover all of them. Each society is unique, possessing different notions of justice, different conceptions of the rule of law, and different traditions regarding the nature and purpose of political and moral life. Such diversity makes the conception of a form

---

23 I should note that in retrospect none of this happened. The prudential diplomat's arguments frequently rest upon worst case scenarios.

24 For one example of this sort of reasoning, Rachel Bronson in a *New York Times* column entitled "Think It Over: Indicting Today's Dictators Is Not a Good Idea" argued: "The problem with war crimes tribunals, which have become fashionable for human rights activists and the US Congress, is that they sacrifice the lives of the living in order to provide justice for the dead. By limiting a regime's incentives for giving up power, war crimes tribunals have the potential to perpetuate the very regimes they target" (Bronson 1999).

25 It is worth noting that behind the prudential diplomat's reasoning must be a sort of consequentialism or act utilitarianism. That is to say that the sort of diplomacy that is least likely to have destructive consequences determines its moral desirability.

of law that could legitimately cover and bind all these forms of society a highly dubious one. Either these laws would be the false universalization of one particular group's values or the "law" would simply be a meaningless set of pseudonorms with no binding force. In either case, these trans-cultural rules are not laws in any recognizable sense. The relativist is completely justified if they reject international norms that conflict with their own, particular ways of life.

These relativists are frequently suspicious of claims of universality found in documents such as the Universal Declaration of Human Rights and often view them as mere covers for the hegemony of Western values. In addition, they frequently cite the historical origins of modern international law in the political history of Western Europe (and its imperialist aggression elsewhere) as grounds for asserting that these laws are an exclusively European creation that is unfairly and unjustly imposed upon other, non-Western societies. For some, these laws have stacked the deck, so to speak, against smaller, newer states *vis-à-vis* their older, more established counterparts, undermining the interests of the weaker states in the international arena. For others, the values that international law promotes are at odds with traditional, culturally specific value systems, effectively destroying their ways of life. Because they do not really represent the interests and/or values of all states and communities, they cannot be treated as legitimate international laws.

Thus, the argument goes something like this: either the form of international law (that is, its nature) or the content of this law (that is, the specific rules of conduct embodied in modern international law) are borne from the experiences and interests of a small group of cultures and not those of humanity in general. As a result, these rules remain foreign to other value systems and other political entities that were not fortunate enough to partake in the development of international law or whose traditional values are incompatible with it. As a result, these laws are a foreign imposition upon newcomers to the world stage. The rules of international relations, as embodied in international law, are not their rules and they should not consider themselves bound to these rules. The great variety of nations with their radically different cultures cannot, in principle, be bound to one particular set of legal codes and no laws could possibly be satisfying to all cultures. Therefore, international law as a set of rules that somehow transcend cultural boundaries is destructive to the (presumably laudable) uniqueness of particular cultures, is not binding upon them, and therefore ought to be ignored by those who choose to do so.[26]

A final sort of prescriptive realist, who I have dubbed the republican, takes her inspiration not from the unique characteristics of international politics, but rather from the normative basis of domestic political leadership. According to this line of thought, political leaders are chosen (optimistically) to represent the interests of the

26 Such views are frequently expressed around issues of human rights and democratic legitimacy in Asia and the Middle East. Here it is claimed (by people such as Malaysia's former Prime Minister Mahathir) that human rights laws are in fact a "western liberal idea" forcibly imposed upon "Asian values."

citizens of their state.[27] Political leaders should not see themselves as beholden to anything but the will (and thereby the interests) of those who have placed them in their positions of power. If the interests of these people conflict with international legal rules, then these leaders have a moral obligation to violate these laws for the sake of their domestic constituencies. Thus the republican maintains that the political leader does have an obligation to follow the law, but this obligation stops short at her nation's borders. Beyond this point, she is duty-bound to follow what she believes to be the best interests of the people who have granted her power and not the demands of an international law that may work against her own people. Similar to Austin then, the republican maintains that international law fails to produce any real obligation on the part of domestic leaders. However, for these skeptics it is not because law analytically requires force (and thus, the sovereign) to be effective, but rather because the sovereign's legitimacy is wholly an issue of domestic politics – international law fits nowhere in the analysis.[28]

This taxonomy of realism is at once both elaborate and a drastic oversimplification. There are a number of different positions in the field of international relations and international legal theory that, for the sake of both brevity and simplicity, have been forcibly "married" in this analysis. However, what I have described as the central theme of realism, the primacy of politics (consisting of power, interests, and diplomacy) over the rules of law in the international sphere has been shown to run throughout each of these different positions. Whether they are scientists, political philosophers, or diplomats, realists consistently maintain that there is "something else," be it raw power, the common good, or cultural difference, that prevents international law from truly functioning autonomously, or that must trump the claims of law in the international sphere. Thus the realists can together be seen as rejecting the value of law in understanding and evaluating international politics and this claim unites them. Whether their evaluations are correct will of course be an issue that will be discussed later in this work.

27 As Tesón outlines this argument: "Under liberal democratic theory, the government is the agent of the people. It is employed by the citizens of the state to serve *their* interests. A consequence of this agency relationship is that significant deviations from this purpose, such as when the government advances only its own interests, are grounds for criticism or, in the extreme, for declaring the illegitimacy of that government... Under this view, the duty of a government to serve the interests of its subjects is the paramount rule in international relations. A government does not owe any duty to foreigners because they do not stand in any contractual relationship with it" (Tesón 1997, 48).

28 One response to this view has been suggested by Haskell Fain: "It would be nice if there were sound reasons for holding that some of the rules of the international political community… are legally superior to *any* rule of domestic law... But no argument in that direction will work until one has thoroughly undermined the contractual idea of the state and all the legal notions that attend that idea" (Fain 1987, 56).

other. Kennedy does not seem to offer any independent justification for structuralism (not an uncontroversial anthropological theory), nor does he attempt to explain how abandoning the prevalent discourse regarding international law somehow makes things better (beyond the tautology that we are better off because we are no longer in the dominant discourse). In addition, Kennedy's steadfast refusal to offer a positive theory of international law in the place of the traditional ones gives the thoughtful reader good motivation to refrain from accepting his argument (taken in isolation) as the final word on the matter.

Thus, in order for Kennedy's approach to have any theoretical bite, for the New Stream to function as an effective critique of international law, it cannot simply change the subject but must develop an additional criticism of the traditional practices and assumptions of international legal theory. Were such a critique effective, Kennedy's anthropological program would make sense, or at a minimum such a critique would suggest that we ought to abandon the traditional assumptions and methods of international legal theory. This sort of critique is offered by one of Kennedy's fellow swimmers in the new stream, James Boyle, in his frequently cited article: "Ideals and Things: International Legal Scholarship and the Prison-house of Language" (Boyle 1990). For Boyle, the point is not simply changing the subject in international legal theory, but rather to offer compelling reasons *why* the subject should be so changed, what the fundamental mistake lying behind traditional theoretical accounts of international law in fact is. Thus, in order to understand the New Stream as a genuine critique of international law, we ought to examine the merits of the analysis offered by Boyle.

For Boyle, the problem with conventional legal theory is its pernicious tendency to "turn concepts into things" by a process that he refers to as *reification.* To explicate this notion, Boyle outlines some of the various projects of conventional international legal theory ("trying to give a convincing account of the normative source," "describing a normative meta-system," "the creation of models, etc.") (Boyle 1990, 328) at the outset of his article and then concludes:

> All of these activities have been described as "definitions" of international law, or as attempts to answer the question "Is international law, law?" It is still true, despite Wittgenstein, that when people feel unsure as to what they should be doing, they try to define the *essential elements* of their activity and thus, like medieval philosophers, to find refuge from the world in a prolonged contemplation of the word. My thesis in this article is that this fascination with definitions is not simply a "mistake". Indeed I will argue that it is the manifestation of something rather more important: a pervasive reification that operates on the level of everyday politics as well as in the conceptual netherworld of international legal scholarship (Boyle 1990, 328).

Boyle's point here is that there is a common and completely faulty human tendency to understand concepts and words, uniquely human, social creations without an essence in themselves, as though they were wholly independent things available to an objective analysis. Malleable and wholly contingent entities are given the properties of physical objects, immutable and analyzable.

This human tendency towards reification is both ubiquitous and generally innocuous. However, it can have its destructive side when it is used to conceal serious and contentious political doctrines by claiming to be simply giving a neutral description of a concept or possibilities are foreclosed because they cannot be justified by such a description. This is the problem with the traditional theories of international law, where ideologies are allegedly hidden behind purportedly objective doctrinal and conceptual analyses. Such acts "rely on the *power* that can be exercised by incorporating a contentious political choice into the act of 'representation'." By claiming to be merely a reporter (or a neutral theorist), ideologically loaded choices can be passed off as mere "definitions" or representations of their objects. Deploying such a method, one can slip a political and moral agenda under the radar of political struggle in a particular debate. Reification, then, is the attempt to pass off contentious views as simple facts, such as when one claims that marriage is (by definition) a relation between a man and a woman, or that by their very nature the African-Americans are unfit for complete citizenship. For Boyle, then, the key weakness of traditional theory is its attempts to cloak the theorist's deeply felt political values within a purportedly neutral theory or description of international law.

Boyle uses this notion of reification to attack both the natural lawyers and the positivists, arguing that insofar as both claim to be giving definitions of law, they fall into an intractable set of problems (Boyle 1990, 328). "Through the use of hypothetical examples and ingenious scholastic conceits, both have attempted to show that *they* rather than the other group have actually discovered the 'essence' of law in general and international law in particular" (Boyle 1990, 330). Because the two presuppose that there is a timeless essence to law, but paradoxically enough find this essence in competing sources (for the positivists, the consent of states, for the natural lawyers, the dictates of right reason), their arguments must inevitably prove inconclusive.

> Theorists founded their discussion of sources on a definitional question. They claimed that the authoritativeness of their arguments depended on the "universal quality" of their definitions of law. Yet they could only be convincing when they covertly appealed to some "purpose," be it the operational perspective of practitioners, or the teleological perspective of internationalists. In order to maintain their arguments, they had to believe (or at least, seem to believe) that their purpose was woven into the essence of law (Boyle 1990, 339).

The point here is that any purported definition of a social construct such as international law *must be circular*, presupposing some position or "purpose" (here the interests of either the internationalist or of the practitioner) that is wholly arbitrary from a theoretical standpoint and lacks independent justification. This choice of purpose then determines in a more-or-less logical fashion the choice of essences attributed to law as well as to its key features. But this initial choice *must* remain unjustified, and thus the definition of law offered by the international legal theorist must ultimately remain arbitrary.

Thus, conventional international legal theory according to Boyle suffers from a set of misguided "medieval" metaphysical principles. This critique comes from neither a political nor a social-scientific perspective, but rather rejects the methodological prejudices of international legal scholarship and its underlying philosophical assumptions.

> [O]ne would have to embrace a complicated and unlikely set of ideas in order to believe that there was some point to a search for the "essence" of law.... For a start, one would have to ignore the central insight that "social constructs," such as law, do not have some pre-existing shape prior to human intervention. The idea of finding the essence or the real source of law distracts us from the reality that, in a very important sense, it is being created by our categories and definitions rather than being described by them (Boyle 1990, 332).

Thus the central methodological assumption of conventional legal theory, that one can give a neutral account of a "social construct" such as international law, is in fact false and, because of this, traditional international legal scholarship is grossly misguided. Rather than merely describing this object, international legal theory is creating an object and passing it off as "the way things are."

There is a political consequence to reification for Boyle. By inadvertently reifying its central concepts, traditional international lawyers and theorists hamstring many of the goals that the theorists themselves usually seek to promote: peace, dignity, and justice. By delineating what can and cannot be done in the name of international law, reifications construct fictitious barriers that only hinder the utopian ideals embedded in the internationalist value system that most international lawyers adhere to. Since such barriers lack any philosophical basis and play no useful role in securing the dividends that such scholars hope to achieve from a just world order, they are best abandoned.

> What I am arguing is that it was never the essential meanings of words that allowed us to do the good things we associate with the rule of law. Nor was it the essential meanings of words that caused the *Lochner* case,[33] the *Korematsu* case,[34] or any other decision. In all of these cases, inescapably political choices are made – some of them systematic, some substantive. The utopian aspect of these choices does not come from any a-political process of neutral reason, but from the struggles and ideals of courageous men and women (Boyle 1990, 351–52).

The utopian goals (that Boyle steadfastly maintains are political goals) embodied in international law are only hampered by attempts to base a theory of law upon a definition of the word "law" or the essentialism of "medieval metaphysics." Through reification, international legal scholars have built their own prison from the assumption that their ideals would be best served through a semantic analysis. It is Boyle's express aim to free us from this prison.

Koskenniemi's Critique

A third prominent postmodern critique of international law comes from a number of related scholars, but was most famously articulated by the Finnish international lawyer and diplomat Martti Koskenniemi in his lengthy and oft-cited work *From Apology to Utopia* (2005). While Koskenniemi shares many features of Boyle's skepticism and Kennedy's anthropological turn, there is enough novelty to his

33 *Lochner v. New York*, 198 US 45 (1905).

34 *Korematsu v. United States*, 323 US 214 (1943).

approach that it merits a separate discussion. While Boyle's approach is based on a general critique of reification in law that could easily apply to other legal fields, Koskenniemi's critique exploits certain structural weaknesses particular to the international legal regime.

For Koskenniemi, at the heart of international law is a contradiction, undermining any claim that it might be "law" in a meaningful sense. The dilemma that Koskenniemi points to involves two basic incompatible features of the international legal system, its apologetic character and its contrary utopian character. First, international law is a creation of states developed both through their actions and through their agreements with each other. From analyzing these behaviors, international lawyers must deduce the formal legal rules and cobble them together into a single, coherent legal system. This means that international law is in some sense a descriptive enterprise, analyzing empirical data and teasing out the norms that govern their behavior. Unfortunately, he argues, this means that international law is always going to be an exercise in apologetics: the more the law is based on observable state behavior, the more international lawyers are reduced to apologists for states of affairs that the law itself had no real voice in shaping. However, if the international lawyer ignores the actual behavior of states, she loses her connection with actual international politics and becomes increasingly more utopian and prescriptive and thereby becomes increasingly less relevant.[35] In neither cases is there law in any meaningful sense. As he describes this dilemma: "These intellectual operations do not leave room for any specifically legal discourse. The two distinctions have not been and… cannot be simultaneously maintained. Lawyer's law is constantly lapsing either into what seems like factual descriptions or political prescription" (Koskenniemi 2005, 16).

Thus, international law is forced into a contradictory state of affairs. It must prescribe behavior to states and other relevant political entities. However, unlike ethical or religious prescriptions, international law claims to be more than purely normative – it is not ethics. Rather, it purports to be an empirical *fact*, that can be discovered through observing the behavior of states and this grounding is essential to its viability as a legal system. For, "If law had no relation to power and political fact, it would be a form of natural morality, a closed normative code which would pre-exist the opinions or interests of individual States" (Koskenniemi 2005, 18). However, if it is too closely aligned with actual state behavior then it is merely a recording of what states do, and resembles empirical social science or history, not a normative field.

Traditional theorists of international law have tried a variety of strategies to overcome the *apology-utopia* dilemma by papering it over or explaining it away. It follows that much of Koskenniemi's critique as developed in *From Apology to Utopia* is not aimed at international law *per se*, rather it is a critique of theorists who deny or overlook the contradictions at the heart of the legal regime. Thus, Koskenniemi's rejection of international law is not as much a rejection of international law in the fashion of realists as a rejection of traditional ways of thinking and talking about

35 "A law which would base itself on principles which are unrelated to State behavior, will or interest would seem utopian, incapable of demonstrating its own content in any reliable way" (Koskenniemi 2005, 17).

international law. As set out in the subtitle of his work, his target is "international legal argument," not international law *per se*.

Thus, we can see that like the realists, New Stream international lawyers suggest that "law" is indistinguishable from "politics," but each has something very different in mind when they so speak. Unlike the realists, the New Stream does not merely subsume or reduce law to politics (describing international law as mere epiphenomena), but instead seeks to show that the two are so intertwined that any attempt to separate them through a conceptual analysis can only be an act of philosophical bad faith. Theories of law only hamstring efforts to realize utopian goals, *political* goals that ought to take precedence over theories and concepts. The point here is not to reject international law as such, but rather to deny the utility of any *theory* of international law. Traditional questions such as whether international law is really law or whether it is distinct from politics presuppose for the New Streamers that there is some thing called international law available for objective description, an assumption that is bound up with the dubious process of reification. Thus, like the realists, the New Streamers reject the autonomy of international law (its independence from politics), but unlike the former, they do not consider this rejection to be damning for the utopian aspirations of the law. International law is one more tool for the activist to realize her utopian goals, albeit one blessed with the faux veneer of a non-political form of legitimacy.

The New Stream scholars will have successfully rejected international law if they can show that all possible theories available for the analysis of international law entail such reification. This, then, is the most explicitly philosophical critique of international law of the three skepticisms discussed in this chapter. It is also the most radical challenge to a positive, constructive theory of international law. Insofar as the New Stream does not rest its critique of international legal theory on a highly specified definition or on the empirical analysis of actual political events, but rather on the nature and purpose of theory itself, it is involved in a deeper project than that of Austin or the realists. Responding to these charges will ultimately require delving into some heavy epistemological, metaphysical, and methodological questions regarding the nature and purpose of definitions, essences, objects, and even human society itself. This issue is a metaphysical and methodological one regarding the nature and ontology of *social objects*, that is to say the nature of the institutions, practices, and concepts that comprise human social life. If the only possible accounts of these objects entail reification, then the New Stream will have successfully proven its case and the turn towards Kennedy's anthropological approach will be justified.

However, there is an even larger issue lurking behind the criticisms of the New Stream theorists. This more abstract question revolves around the ultimate nature and purpose of theoretical inquiry. Precisely what do we hope to achieve through the formation and development of a theory of international law? Why engage in such activities in the first place? If the claim to merely describing the pre-existing phenomena that we dub "international law" is in fact fraudulent, is there nothing to be gained in an exploration into the philosophical nature of this law? (I can think of no international lawyer who would claim that law is distinct from politics, although they might disagree with the New Stream about what this claim entails.) The radical criticism of international legal theory developed by Boyle, Kennedy, and Koskenniemi, among others, requires a deep re-thinking of the nature of such a theory and its positive (and negative) roles in the construction of a world society. I will argue in the next chapter that while the New Stream gives us good reason to reflect upon the nature of such theories, it does not in fact provide grounds for rejecting these international legal theories *en totum*.

As with the broader Critical Legal Studies movement, the New Stream has not caught fire within the international legal community. While widely praised, their works have not greatly transformed how international lawyers think and write about the law. The vast majority of studies in major international law journals reflect the reified conception that Boyle attacks and do not dwell on Koskenniemi's concerns. There are reasons for this that have nothing to do with the epistemological conundrums to which these scholars refer. Rather, as I will argue in the next chapter, it is because international law is not first and foremost a political system but a social institution that these traditional ways of thinking about law remain. That is, international law is best conceptualized as the practice of a group of elite scholars, an epistemic community, that delineates the nature and scope of international law and regulates its usage. It is not the actions of states that truly matter for determining international law, but how these acts are interpreted by this community of judges, lawyers, and scholars. This is to say that international lawyers make the law, not international actors.

Conclusion

As we have seen, the critics of international law are numerous and together they have formulated some profound challenges for any constructive theory of international law. However, while they remain unified in their skepticism towards international law, they are highly fragmented in their respective agendas as well as in their philosophical assumptions and methods. The point of this chapter has not been to simply survey the criticisms that presently exist, rather to "raise the bar" for any successful theory of international law. These criticisms, where cogent, have dictated some of the criteria that a successful theory must meet or at least the objections to which any adequate theory must be able to respond. Assuming I have done my work adequately here, we now have a good grasp of what we cannot expect from a good theory of international law. That is to say that a theory that expects to succeed in describing the nature and structure of international legal norms must keep these criticisms in the forefront of analysis in order to avoid falling prey to them.

Of course, I believe that these criticisms are not the final word on the subject and are certainly not grounds for abandoning the project of constructing a positive theory of international law. In the remaining chapters I will attempt to articulate a theory of international law that will respond to the criticisms laid out here. I will respond to these theorists in a two-fold fashion: first, I will argue that beneath a number of these criticisms lie mistaken philosophical assumptions that invalidate their seemingly most persuasive criticisms. To this extent, some criticisms never get off the ground. I have provided this sort of response to a certain degree in this chapter (most noticeably with regards to John Austin's "Platonism" and Kennedy's structuralism) but I will continue this project in later chapters. Second, I will formulate a conception of international law (and international legal theory in general) that can withstand those objections remaining after such scrutiny. An adequate understanding of the nature of international law, as well as its content on a specific set of issues, will show that there is good reason to believe that international law is both a fact within international relations as well as a worthy compatriot for proponents of world peace.

Chapter 2

Conceptualizing International Law

In the previous chapter the notion of a "definition" of international law played a key role in a number of the skeptical views of this legal system. In fact, virtually all of the forms of skepticism discussed there based their criticisms upon some particular (and sometimes wholly implicit) understanding of what international law in fact is. Given this, a positive account of international law should begin with a discussion of the proper method for conceptualizing it. Such an approach will be guided by a number of different concerns, and thus I will have to carefully consider what is involved in the kind of definition I am employing before going any further. Once a satisfactory method for conceptualizing international law is provided, I will be in a better position to explicate what the law says about particular subjects in international law, the topic of Chapters 4 and 5.

A large number of factors are relevant in formulating our definition of international law, as it must serve a number of different functions. For example, the net should not be cast too wide, resulting in an overly broad definition, making it impossible to distinguish between proper and improper uses of the term.[1] On the other hand, the approach must not be too narrow, leaving important elements out of our analysis. Finally, while traditional definitions of law offered by thinkers such as Bentham, Grotius, Austin, among others may be useful guides to understanding international law properly, we should not conclude that there already exists a definitive concept of this legal system. Finally, we should keep the skepticisms outlined in the previous chapter firmly in view in developing our own positive theory. Thus, our definition of international law will be guided by a vast number of concerns that, I believe, will allow for a much richer and more fruitful understanding than those traditionally offered in the opening of a typical treatise on international law.

In this chapter I will argue for what I will call a *non-reductionist definition of international law*. Roughly put, the non-reductionist view understands international law as *the set of norms (or rules) that have a characteristically legal quality and extend beyond the boundaries of internationally recognized entities in terms of both their jurisdiction and their grounds of legitimacy.* I have labeled this definition "non-reductionist" simply because it refuses to interpret the actions or norms of one particular type of agent, such as states, as definitive of international law in its

1 For example, Hersch Lauterpacht defines international law as "the body of rules of conduct, enforceable by external sanction, that confer rights and impose obligations primarily, though not exclusively, upon sovereign States and which owe their validity both to the consent of States as expressed in custom and treaties and to the fact of the existence of an international community of States and individuals" (Lauterpacht 1970, 1). It is hard to imagine what rules would not fit under a definition of this sort.

entirety. In fact, this definition is neutral as to the ultimate sources of international law (more on this later). This distinction will become clear shortly, when I contrast this approach to the "sovereignty thesis." I will argue that such a definition, however general, serves adequately as the basis for explicating a philosophy of international law (that is, it will explicate what the nature of international law is) on the one hand, and as the basis for jurisprudence (a development of the laws *in* international law)[2] on the other.

Philosophically speaking, this definition will rest upon a conception of law as a social practice carried on by an epistemic community (in this case, international lawyers), a type of structured human endeavor that is defined by the set of rules constituting it. Jurisprudentially speaking, I will attempt to use this non-reductionist approach to explain what the best legal analysis is on several key issues (legal personality and humanitarian intervention in particular) in later chapters and ultimately how such concepts can respond to some of the criticisms outlined in the opening chapter. The primary job of this chapter will be to explicate and justify this approach to conceptualizing the law. In the next chapter, I will contrast it to other leading and, I will argue, less satisfying approaches to understanding the nature of international law.

Of course this non-reductionist approach can only be understood as a working definition of sorts. It cannot be judged in isolation, but should be evaluated only at the end of this work, when its most significant consequences have been elaborated and grasped. As this process unfolds, this definition will be modified given further insights about the social practices that it is attempting to analyze. Only if this definition allows for an understanding of international law that effectively answers the significant criticisms discussed in the previous chapter, seems to grasp the core extant international legal practices, *and* remains intuitively satisfying will the non-reductionist approach be adequate. Whether I have developed an adequate account of international law will depend upon whether I can meet these admittedly lofty standards, and this can only be adequately ascertained once the theory has come to adequate fruition in the later chapters.

This chapter will consist of three sections: first, I will approach the broadly methodological question regarding the nature of the "object" that I am attempting to describe in this work (that is, international law). This part, although admittedly abstract and removed from some of the more substantial aspects of this work, will allow me to properly respond to the objections leveled by Boyle that were discussed in the previous chapter. Then I will explicate the nature of the non-reductionist definition of international law itself, outlining some of its key features. Having completed this, I will then turn briefly to the relation of facts and values (or the "is-ought" problem) in the approach that I am advocating, as this is an important issue for my overall take on the law.

I should warn the reader that much of this chapter (and the next) will be strictly philosophical in nature and will be abstracted from law as it is familiar to practitioners. This is necessary because, as mentioned in the previous chapter, the critique that Boyle has made regarding international legal theory is a philosophical

2 I will discuss this distinction in greater depth later in this chapter.

one. Boyle does not engage with the rules of law or with the nature of global politics, but rather with the philosophical and methodological problems that arise when one sets out to conceptualize international law and theorize about it. Thus, the proper response to Boyle requires all of the tools that the philosopher has at his disposal in order to avoid his skeptical conclusions. While this will be far removed from the actual structures of international law, it is necessary for the theory of international law to get off of the ground, as it were.

The Ontology of Social Objects: Beginning to Answer the New Stream

In the previous chapter, Boyle raised some powerful objections to traditional projects aimed at grasping the essence of international law. Citing Wittgenstein among others as the basis of his critique, he asserted that any attempt to define international law was dependent upon a host of untenable metaphysical beliefs. Attempts to grasp an essence in international law as though it were susceptible to non-partisan, objective descriptions missed the fundamental ambiguity of (what Boyle refers to as) concepts. The first relevant question regarding definitions of international law is whether Boyle's fundamental criticism is correct, and this will depend upon whether I can formulate a conception of definitions that does not entail reification. I will show that throughout his argument Boyle relies upon a notion of a "concept" that is too simplistic, and that there are ways to develop a concept of law that are not metaphysical in nature. However, despite these flaws, his criticisms will provide an excellent vantage point to reflect upon the method that I will utilize throughout this work.

It is important to be careful with language before making blanket generalizations about the various projects of traditional international legal theory as well as the conception of a definition upon which each rests. Not all definitions are of a kind, not all metaphysical commitments are "medieval." It is important to delineate precisely what is involved in developing a good definition before rushing to join Boyle in his skeptical conclusions.[3] In this section, I will attempt to outline a method for constructing a "definition" of international law that avoids the pernicious metaphysical assumptions that Boyle attributes to conventional theories of international law.[4] By using some recent anti-foundationalist approaches to social phenomena found in philosophers such as Wittgenstein, Nelson Goodman, and John Rawls, I will argue that some definitions of international law can be both useful (that is, they allow theorists and practitioners to delimit proper from improper uses of the term) and defensible (avoiding the dubious metaphysical commitments to which Boyle refers). The non-reductionist approach is just such a means of conceptualizing the law.

There are numerous kinds of definitions, each with a unique set of epistemological and metaphysical commitments. Looking up a word in the dictionary is only one,

3 See H.L.A. Hart's insightful analysis of definitions (Hart 1994, 13–17).

4 I will use the terms "definition" and "conceptualization" interchangeably in this chapter. Other terms, such as "characterization" might equally apply to this approach to understanding international law.

very narrow conception of a definition. There are many other kinds. For example, if one is trying to describe a climbing expedition and uses visual cues ("this salt shaker is Mt Everest"), one has defined something (one has ascribed a meaning to something), but there is no commitment to the belief that the salt shaker represents something beyond this particular context, no grand metaphysical link between the salt shaker and the mountain (these are usually referred to as *stipulative definitions*) (Yagisawa 1995, 185–6). Similarly, one can safely define the king in chess according to the rules of chess (the rules of the game defining the nature and function of the king) without being beholden to anything existing beyond the game of chess (the king can be represented by a seashell or a mark on a paper or a piece of carved stone). In such a definition, one need not concede that there is a metaphysically permanent, unchanging "thing" called "chess" existing in a Platonic heaven in order to carry out such a procedure, only a game played by human beings that has a certain set of rules. However, the description of the king's nature is not arbitrary, it is actually essential to the game of chess (were one to begin moving the king two spaces instead of one in a single move, one would *by definition* not be playing chess). In these cases, importantly enough, the definition is neither arbitrary nor does it commit one to the belief in anything beyond the activity of playing chess.[5]

The designation of the salt shaker as Mount Everest and the king as fulfilling its proper chess role are very different from the kind of definition found in *Webster's*. They are not arbitrary (that is, they are not subject to change, given the constraints of chess or the situation description of Mount Everest), but rather denote a *social practice*, a shared collective activity that works based upon some commonly shared assumptions. These assumptions can frequently be codified or made explicit as a set of rules that give the practice its particularity and distinguish it from other types of practices. They can also change over time. The rules of chess regarding the movement of pieces, for example, distinguishes it from checkers that can be played on the same board even with the same pieces. In each case, in each social practice, there are a set of rules that more or less define the nature of the relationships presupposed by the agents involved, in part dictating the acceptable means to achieve a goal and other times defining the goal itself (a checkmate is meaningless outside of chess, for example). These rules comprise what is involved in a definition of a social practice, what it is that makes the practice what it is and distinguishes it from other types of practices. A definition for international law as a kind of practice is somewhat closer to these examples of chess and story-telling than to other forms of definition.

What Boyle has in mind is much closer to contemporary debates in the United States surrounding the morality of abortion. In these cases, how abortion is defined, whether it is seen as "the medical procedure in which a fetus is extracted from the uterus" or as "the butchering of an unborn baby" (to use some not uncommon examples) is crucial for gaining leverage in public debates. All sides of these sorts

5 As Saul Kripke has pointed out, even were there other, postulated worlds where kings were allowed to move two spaces instead of one, this would not get us out of the necessary connection between the game chess and its rules in this universe. One could say in Kripke's terms that "chess" is a kind of rigid designator. See Kripke (1980).

of disagreements hope to win the argument through definition alone.[6] Similarly, they hope to skirt any thorny moral or scientific problems (is a fetus really a baby?) by simply selecting the definition that suits their own agenda, acting as though it was obvious that it were simply "the right one," most accurately describing the facts at hand. Boyle is right in claiming that such efforts are suspect, and were the definition offered in this chapter to be of this kind, it too would not be worth serious consideration. However, these approaches to the definition of abortion are not suspect because of some omnipresent process of reification as much as they are suspect because of faulty, biased reasoning masking itself as impartiality. There is a difference between these two kinds of definitions, however, and Boyle's conflation of the two begins to illuminate some larger problems with his overall view.

I have used the example of the game of chess above in order to suggest that there are "things" that exist (sets of social practices) that do not have the metaphysical baggage Boyle attributes to medieval philosophy. International law is in fact just such a thing. Chess exists as a social practice with a clearly defined, well-understood set of rules (with scarce variation in different places) and thus lends itself nicely to a precise definition. International law, while certainly not so clearly or easily grasped as the rules of a board game, can be explicated, understood, and defined without appealing to an immaterial heaven of Platonic forms or deduced from axioms. Procedures for the definition of social practices are neither wholly arbitrary, nor are they determined independent of the practices themselves. It is not up to you or me (or any other particular person) to conjure up a definition of international law *ex-nihilo* (and thus *pace* Boyle, it is not a "concept" by any recognizable use of the term) any more than it is up to you or me to determine the rules of chess (that is similarly not a concept). Social practices are social objects, they are neither entities *sui generis*, nor are they the product of the whims of any particular person (or even a group of people).

Not only does such an approach to definitions find credence in common, everyday practices, but in addition, it has a strong philosophical pedigree stemming back to one of Boyle's own philosophical influences. Wittgenstein, in his *Philosophical Investigations*, argues that the rules and structures that guide any particular language game are not the product of any individual's conscious choices, but rather stem from shared, collective understandings that comprise what he refers to as a "form of life." Such public understandings of behavior are necessary not only for any utterance to be true or false, but more significantly, to be meaningful. In this passage of the *Investigations*, Wittgenstein confronts himself with the problem of private experiences, that what we experience is ultimately publicly unverifiable. His skeptic poses an objection:

> The essential thing about private experience is really not that each person possesses his own exemplar, but that nobody knows whether other people also have *this* or something else. The assumption would thus be possible – though unverifiable – that one section of mankind has one sensation of red and another section another (Wittgenstein 1963, 272).

---

6 Yagisawa (1995) calls this a "rhetorical definition" ("definition").

And in response to an imagined interlocutor, Wittgenstein argues that there isn't an explicit agreement standing behind the rules of a linguistic practice. That is, we don't determine meaning by explicit agreement but rather by shared agreement embodied in the practical use of language:

> "So you are saying that human agreement decides what is true and what is false?" – It is what human beings *say* that is true and false; and they agree in the *language* they use. That is not agreement in opinions but in form of life (Wittgenstein 1963, §241).

Thus, *contra* Boyle, on Wittgenstein's view the rules that define social objects (understood in my analysis as social practices) are neither subjective, nor are they the product of some explicit agreement that could be consciously changed by an individual by fiat. They are public in nature and get their meaning from the public practices themselves, whatever their ultimate rationale may turn out to be.[7]

Given that there is no otherworldly metaphysical source for the analysis of international law, the guide to a proper definition of this law must be an empirical one. This is to say that our guide to understanding international law as a social practice must be the intuitions and utterances that are taken to be international law by those who are generally understood to be in the know.[8] Just as an anthropologist must seek to understand a particular ritual (say, the Eucharist) by examining the native use of the term designating the ritual (in the practice of Catholicism as well as that of the Protestant sects that have a ritual by the same name) and from there understanding its defining features, one must look at the actual practices and understandings that guide the lawyer in her normal activities. Theological considerations may enter into a study of the Eucharist but only through the understandings of the actors themselves – otherwise this approach would likely fall back into reification (as these theologians would surely seek to put their own biases into the study). Only if international law is viewed as a sort of practice that can be studied empirically, what international lawyers *do* as members of an epistemic community rather than what they *say they do* in their theoretical endeavors, can theorists hope to escape Boyle's reification objection.[9] The validity of any theory, then, is not its logical or conceptual soundness, but its relationship to the facts as they are understood by those in the know.[10]

---

7 The point to this paragraph has not been to claim Wittgenstein's blessing on the entirety of this work, but rather to use Boyle's own influences against him, and suggest on Wittgensteinian grounds that some of the assumptions embedded in my analysis are stronger.

8 Those who are "in the know" are those who the rest of society take to be in the know. In this case, it is the judges, lawyers, scholars, and others who are recognized to be experts in their field. There will be debates around certain characters (autodidacts, for example), but regardless, the general consensus confirms the general principle.

9 To this extent, one might say that there is an "epistemic community" of international law, comprised of lawyers, scholars, and diplomats who know what international law is. For more on the notion of an epistemic community see Adler and Haas (1992) and Abiew (1999, 13–16).

10 As Verdross puts this in relation to international law, "A delimitation of an object advances knowledge only if it does not break the connection given to us by experience. It follows that neither more nor less concepts should be formulated than those necessary for comprehending the totality of phenomena" (Verdross 1949, 436).

Of course this empirical approach does not mean that every single invocation of international law will be on a par with every other. A theory cannot be expected to account for every use of the term "international law," if for no other reason than that the trained practitioners themselves disagree about the content of this law itself. "International law" is not a natural kind such as exists among biological species (cows, ducks, paramecium, and so on) where simple laws of induction require that *all* members of the species conform to a highly specific definition save a few highly specified exceptions. Just as an attempt to describe the rules of chess would have to eliminate from its definition a group of children who were moving chess pieces (consisting of "Horsies," "Castles," and so on) on a grid, but were in fact playing checkers, a good definition of international law will similarly eliminate improper uses of the term.[11] Any satisfactory and simultaneously useful definition of international law must not only be rooted in the practices and understandings of those who are in the know, but must simultaneously provide some kind of "critical bite," some manner of carving up the social practice in a constructive fashion.

This conception of law as a practice rooted in the expertise of an elite epistemic community can be helpful for understanding the relationship between international politics and international law. If political leaders wish to participate in the discourse of law, they must adopt the language and attitudes of those in the know (usually, it is the task of legal advisors to assist in this project). The political leadership does not get to decide what is or is not allowed in this discourse. They may choose to ignore the law or violate it, but they cannot make it up.

The criteria for a good definition of international law as I have set them out here are three-fold: first, this definition must fit with the current practices of those who are in the know, the international lawyers themselves. Second, it must not simply catalog the uses of the term "international law" by these people (who admittedly may disagree among themselves), but must in addition provide something "critical," something that separates the wheat from the chaff in international legal discourse. This is simply to say that it must be coherent. Finally, it must produce satisfactory results, results that have theoretical interest. Such an approach to conceptualizing international law will allow us to establish a theoretical foothold that avoids the central objections raised by Boyle.

The method that I will advocate to describe such an approach to defining international law relies upon a form of coherentist epistemology known as *wide reflective equilibrium*. According to such an approach, first formulated by Goodman and famously used by Rawls (1971), the effort to define an object (or for our concerns, a social practice) is determined by an equilibrium relationship between a theoretical model (or definition) and a set of practices or intuitions that this definition describes. Such a process conceives of definitions as an attempt to adjudicate between the objects one is describing and a set of guides or principles that capture these objects with greater or lesser fidelity. This former domain, in turn, is delineated by the common and pre-theoretical uses of a term. Rather than assuming

11 It is of course true that in many cases one will not know precisely which invocations of the term "international law" are improper until a definition has been elaborated. However, I do not see this as a serious problem.

an essence of a concept beforehand and from there judging whether this or that use of a term in common speech is appropriate (the definitional-semantic approach that I associated with Austin in the previous chapter), the essence of a thing is inferred from its common uses and subsequently captured in a constructed definition. Thus, the formation of a definition consists in a relation between a theory and that set of phenomena that this definition is purporting to describe.

In his exposition of this doctrine, Goodman usefully applies it to the analysis of our ordinary understanding of words. According to Goodman, the formation of valid inductive inferences in science is simply a special case of the process of finding the appropriate definitions for words in ordinary language:

> The task of formulating rules that define the difference between valid and invalid inductive inferences is much like the task of defining any term with an established usage. If we set out to define the term "tree", we try to compose out of already understood words an expression that will apply to the familiar objects that standard usage calls trees, and that will not apply to objects that standard usage refuses to call trees. A proposal that plainly violates either condition is rejected; while a definition that meets these tests may be adopted and used to decide cases that are not already settled by actual usage (Goodman 1965, 66).

Rather than a simple list enumerating and categorizing all of the accepted meanings of a word, reflective equilibrium offers an expression (in Goodman's sense) or definition that puts into a systematic form as many common uses of a word as possible. Thus, there is a "dual adjustment between definition and usage, whereby the usage informs the definition, that in turn guides extension of the usage" (Goodman 1965, 66). An adequate definition of a word will be one that captures a vast majority of the commonly accepted uses of a term, distinguishing cases where it should not be applied while simultaneously allowing sufficient guidance for dealing with difficult cases.[12]

Not all forms of reflective equilibrium are identical, and, as said above, my approach to international law will deploy a wide (as opposed to a narrow) reflective equilibrium in its definition. In its narrow form, all that is factored into the equilibrium, all that is taken into account in formulating the definition, are the explicit uses of the term. However, in wide reflective equilibrium "external" factors are taken into account. Our analysis of international law should not simply concern itself with the explicit uses of a term, but should factor in additional considerations such as ontological, epistemological, and logical commitments. As Norman Daniels describes this project of wide reflective equilibrium in relation to moral judgments:

> Suppose we collect, as with narrow equilibrium, a set of initial considered moral judgments. Instead of immediately settling for a "best fit" set of principles, however, we now propose alternative sets, some obviously being better fits than others. The task for the person seeking wide equilibrium is to choose between such alternatives on the basis of philosophical arguments which reveal the strengths and weaknesses of the competing moral conceptions. ... The wide equilibrium can now be characterized as an ordered triple

12 For a critique of such an approach see Stich (1988).

of (a), the considered moral judgments (b), the moral principles, and (c), the set of relevant theories invoked or presupposed by the winning arguments (Daniels 1980, 21–36).

Daniels' observation about "considered moral judgments" applies equally to expert opinions regarding international law. In both cases, coherence is not developed in a vacuum but by considering factors external to mere coherence to produce a stronger conception of the subject of analysis.[13] By saying that this definition of international law uses a wide reflective equilibrium is simply to say that philosophical concerns about the nature of political agents are relevant in formulating this definition and not merely trying to understand the social practice of international law on its own terms.

In this definition of law, I have appealed to the understandings of those "in the know," that is, practicing international lawyers, judges, and other international legal experts. However, I have chosen to ignore international legal theory proper in defining international law. This is simply because I see this approach to law as a theoretical model to compete with these others. An economic analyst or a natural lawyer may be in some sense in the know, but are irrelevant for my own analysis because they are competitors, not subjects of it. Classical international legal theorists such as Grotius, Vattel, and so on have been largely ignored on similar grounds. The domain of inquiry is narrow enough that it can effectively eliminate those people who do not engage in the social practice that I am trying to analyze. Just as one would ignore a different ethnography of the Eucharist when developing a study of the same subject (sticking to the views of the priests, believers, and so on), an analysis of international law must similarly avoid artificial scholarly analysis. This competing approach to international law must ignore other, competing definitions, stopping only to contrast itself with them.

It should be clear that this approach is in no way committed to a metaphysical realism in law, the belief that law is a pre-existing "thing" to be objectively described, as Boyle charges. Rather, reflective equilibrium looks at the actually existing usages of the term and from there develops a theoretical model (or definition) to distinguish proper from improper usage. However, neither is it subject to a naïve empiricism that uses crude laws of induction to merely describe a social practice in its entirety in this procedure. This model of wide reflective equilibrium serves to carefully distinguish acceptable from unacceptable uses on the basis of a definition. Situations where the term "international law" is used are not immediately valid, but rather they become validated through an antecedently constructed definition. With such an approach the theorist can adequately form a consistent definition of international law yet with enough normativitiy to distinguish between the proper and improper uses of the term. Through such a definition, a critical analysis of our concept is shorn of the metaphysical baggage that concerned Boyle.

---

13 Thus, legal principles that seem to be based on dubious assumptions will be given less weight than other, sounder principles with equal footing in legal practices. These philosophical assumptions, however, are *not* the same as other philosopher's conceptions of international law – conceptions that I have described here as competitors. The point is that we have certain beliefs about agents and actors and that these beliefs are relevant in understanding international law.

One of the unique aspects of linking the conception of international law with a social practice, rather than to an artificially constructed definition, is that it allows us to make a smooth transition from pre-Benthamite conceptions of global legal relations to the modern practice of international law. One of the continuous discussions in the history of international law is whether the modern era of Bentham's "international law" is in continuity with previous conceptions of the "law of nations," "cosmopolitan right," and the "*jus gentium*" of the ancient world or whether they are entirely different things.[14] A simple linguistic approach must struggle with the idea of a consistency between pre-Westphalian international legal practices with a later one that sees sovereignty as lying at its core. The question of whether they are different or identical legal regimes can be answered by simply asking whether they can be brought into a satisfactory equilibrium with each other without too drastic a transformation of either. Because the theorist is not trying to describe some *a priori* conception of international law, but rather is bound to the empirical social practice of international lawyers, theorists need not concern themselves with the formal semantics of the categories inherited from history.

Definitions and Sources

Definitions of international law are meant to do many different things. Some are meant to provide the foundations for a political theory of international law. Some are meant to provide normative foundations for the legal regime. Still others are meant to provide the foundations of a jurisprudence, a means by which one can discover the particular rules of law by referring to its sources. It should be clear by the definition that I have put forward, it is not intended to do any of these things.

The notion of a "source" of international law is obviously an important one. While most domestic legal regimes have a clearly defined interpretive principle that allows them to determine what the law is (although, the image of law as deduction has undergone withering critique over the last several decades in legal theory), this non-reductive view of law eschews any effort to develop a deep theory of sources or to provide such a hermeneutic guide. That is, it does not seek a grand theory of law rooted in normative analysis or in principles of political theory that is meant to somehow organize and prioritize existing legal rules. Rather, without an *Ur* principle behind it, its legal sources are formal and are the sources given credence by the legal community. As the analogies I have used in this chapter show, the perspective that I have taken to understand the international legal regime is closer to that of an anthropologist, sociologist, or historian seeking to grasp a social object, not a political theorist trying to justify it or a law student seeking to determine what the law says on a particular issue.

To illustrate the significance of this, I will refer Koskenniemi's distinction between "formal" and "material" sources of international law. In Koskenniemi's analysis, there are two different ways that one can conceptualize the sources of international law, each with its own assumptions and agenda. Material source theories look to

14 See Janis (1993a), Bederman (2001a) and Nussbaum (1954).

deep philosophical principles that "prove" that an utterance, act, or rule is legal in character.

> On the one hand, there is the explanation of sources as the history, cause or basis from which law "emerges". This ("material") aspect of sources seeks to provide for the law's legitimacy, pointing to its origins in a legislative process, natural reason, a principle of justice or policy that resonates with our political sensibility and that we usually take as good reason for applying the standard based on it (Koskenniemi 2001, xiii).[15]

Material theories point to some element beyond the legal rules themselves, some founding principle that one can use to search out the law. These foundations provide lawyers not only with a guide to what the law is, but why it is legitimate, compulsory, binding, and so on. Expressions of consent by sovereign states not only tell us what the law is ("x is law because the state has consented to x"), but why it is law ("the state should do x because it has consented to do x"). While I will discuss problems with this link in the next chapter, it is important to keep it in mind when discussing formal theories of law.

Formal theories, on the other hand do not rely upon some extra-legal criteria for determining law, but rather depend on the intuitions of actual practicing lawyers and other legal experts. Law is taken as a given and it is the goal of the theorist to understand what comprises this legal system, detailing its contours. This makes legal theory much more closely aligned with legal practice:

> Formalism is the *credo* of the practitioner, and with good reason... What the practitioner needs are not broad guidelines to realize "justice", to give effect to "rights", "sovereign will" or "community policy" but much more tangible linguistic unities for the justification of resolutions to actual normative problems. The normative force of an independent, practice-oriented and formal sources doctrine lies in its ability to verify or validate the argumentative *materiel* that enables the legal profession to continue to carry out its legal job without having to transform itself into a legislative agency ("realise policy") or a priesthood of right and wrong (Koskenniemi 2001, xii–xiii).[16]

The formal approach looks at the practicing lawyers' ideas of what law is and dramatically separates the existence of a law from its source of obligation.

> In this sense, there is no "fundamental" explanation for sources doctrine at all. Nor would there seem to be a need for such. Sources doctrine would appear as a kind of user's manual; a practical checklist that professional lawyers have recourse to as part of their professional task and self-image. ... For all intents and purposes, the identification of what count as sources would not be found in philosophy books but would be a function of a professional culture, a consensus among legal experts, an extrapolation of how lawyers, in fact, argue (Koskenniemi 2001, xiii).

The actual behavior of lawyers and their understanding of what the rules of international law consists in is the touchstone for understanding the law from a formal standpoint.

---

15 Footnotes in original omitted here.

16 Footnotes in original omitted here.

What Koskenniemi describes as a formal approach to the sources of international law, coupled with Wittgenstein's understanding of social practices, gives the notion of an epistemic community a more robust character and a dramatic methodological role in understanding the philosophical nature of international law. This view is neatly summed up by Anthony Carty, within the context of conceptualizing the international legal regime,

> ... International law can be reduced to what international lawyers understand by international law and how they apply it as international lawyers looking at international relations. International lawyers, unlike municipal lawyers, are a quite diverse and mobile group of individuals on the international scene. They may be professors in universities, but they also act as counselors before the International Court of Justice. These same professors may even serve on the International Court of Justice itself. This international legal community provides the recruiting pool for the foreign offices of many countries. These foreign offices then tend to rely upon what the professors in the universities say, and governments in turn draw upon this advice. This results in a kind of self-referencing discourse about the nature of international society (Carty 1993, 32).

Thus, for Carty international law is conceived as "self-referencing discourse" where political diplomacy, judicial reasoning, and academic speculations overlap. The line between those who theoretically describe international law and those who ascertain and create legal norms is a virtually non-existent one.

Thus, the approach to international law that I have set forward here does not understand the "sources" of law as extending beyond the formal sources set out by international lawyers. These are well known by everyone who practices in the field and are spelled out in Article 28 of the International Court of Justice statute.[17] These are taken to be the sources by other courts that are not beholden to the statute and become the primary method by which jurists "discover" the law.[18] Why these are the sources of law is not a particularly interesting question, what matters is that the experts who comprise the epistemic community that determines international law say that they are.

---

17 Specifically, the article says:

The Court, whose function is to decide in accordance with international law such disputes as are submitted to it, shall apply:

> a. international conventions, whether general or particular, establishing rules expressly recognized by the contesting states;
>
> b. international custom, as evidence of a general practice accepted as law;
>
> c. the general principles of law recognized by civilized nations;
>
> d. subject to the provisions of Article 59, judicial decisions and the teachings of the most highly qualified publicists of the various nations, as subsidiary means for the determination of rules of law.

18 For an example of this, see *Prosecutor v. Erdemovic*, ICTY, Judgement of 7 October 1997, Joint Separate Opinion of Judge McDonald and Judge Vorah, paragraph 40 ("The sources of international law are *generally considered* to be exhaustively listed in Article 38 of the Statute of the International Court of Justice"), italics added.

The Non-Reductionist Definition of International Law

Given these methodological preliminaries, how does the method of wide reflective equilibrium provide a robust definition of international law? As mentioned at the beginning of this chapter, I have tentatively defined international law as the set of norms (or rules) that have a characteristically legal quality and extend beyond the boundaries of internationally recognized entities in terms of both their jurisdiction and their grounds of legitimacy (pretentiously entitled "the non-reductive definition of international law"). This definition, broad as it is, is the one that I believe best results from an equilibrium relation between a theory and the understandings of those who participate in the social practice of international law. I will not engage in the actual process of equilibrium here, but rather will rely upon such a method only in the abstract as a foundation for the non-reductionist definition. In this section, I will briefly explain what such a definition of international law entails, fleshing out certain ambiguities in it.

The "rule" characteristic of this definition requires some clarification. Despite its intuitive obviousness, the view that international law is comprised of a set of rules has come under attack. Lung-Chu Chen, for example, has argued that rule-based approaches are fundamentally inadequate to the task of grasping the nature of international law. According to Chen's "policy-oriented approach" (sometimes referred to as the "New Haven School" of Myres McDougal, Harold Lasswell, and others), such a rule-based conception of law cannot account for a great deal of legal machinations and decision-making that is characteristic of the international legal sphere. Instead, he suggests that international law possesses an overarching ideal regarding the elevation of human dignity that structures the international legal system that trumps any appeal to rules.[19] As Chen himself puts it:

> Such rule-oriented approaches to international law have several inadequacies: (1) failure to grip the notions of decision (choice) in the legal process; (2) insufficient attention to the goals (policies) for which rules are devised and to value consequences of particular applications of rules; (3) failure to relate rules to the dynamic context of interaction involving the international and domestic social processes and to the ongoing process of decision making; (4) failure to grasp the normative ambiguity involved in rules; (5) failure to come to grips with the generality and complementarity involved in rules; and (6) failure to develop and employ adequate intellectual skills in problem solving (Chen 1989, 11–12).

Similar to the tradition of American legal realism before it, the policy-oriented approach to international law argues that rule-based conceptions fundamentally misrepresent the role that law plays in political relations. According to Chen, McDougal, and Lasswell, the only adequate basis for the study of international law

---

19 In contrast, Chen describes international law as bound up with policies of common interest (usually human dignity). "International law, as all law, is a continuing process of authoritative decision through which the common interest of the members of the world community is identified, clarified, and protected" (Chen 1989, 11).

is its purpose of establishing a world community of human dignity and not as any abstract, formal set of rules.[20]

The analyses of Hart and Nardin are useful for defending a rule-based conception of international law. As these theorists have pointed out, the arguments of the policy theorists and the realists grossly underestimate the roles that laws have played in judicial decision-making. Hart, in response to the legal realists, has maintained that rule-skepticism has an undue and unrealistic conception of rule-based behavior and thus harbors an unwarranted cynicism towards the behavior of judges. Whether an analysis always bears out the claim that legal decisions follow rules, he says, the rule-based conception of law stands at the heart of the legal expectations of citizens:

> [E]ven if we suppose the denial that there are rules and the assertion that what are called rules are merely predictions of the decisions of courts to be limited in this way, there is one sense, at least, in which it is obviously false... Laws function in [individuals'] lives not merely as habits or the basis for predicting the decisions of courts or the actions of other officials, but as accepted legal standards of behavior. That is, they not only do with tolerable regularity what the law requires of them, but they look upon it as a legal standard of conduct, refer to it in criticism of others… (Hart 1994, 137–48)

Thus, according to Hart, whether one can show that a rule is followed in every legal decision, there is a necessary part of our shared conception of law, what Hart calls the "internal point of view", that requires an appeal to rules. Regardless of whether there are always rules that stand clearly behind every judicial decision, a belief in the existence of rules is the *condition sine qua non* of behavior that is properly considered legal.

Nardin similarly responds to the objections of the New Haven School's critique. According to Nardin, by making legal rules subordinate to the goal of valorizing human dignity, policy-oriented theorists must presuppose a set of rules. Without such rules to adjudicate between different conceptions of human dignity and different proposals to advance this ideal, the policy-oriented analysis of international law could never get off the ground, much less flourish as a full-fledged aim of global relations. As Nardin himself puts this problem:

> [Policy-oriented theory] fails to take account of the fact that cooperation to further shared purposes presupposes agreement at the level of procedure that can be drawn upon in making and implementing agreements. It fails to grasp that the pursuit of shared purposes

20 As Chen himself puts it, his own argument "is a theory *about* international law rather than a theory *of* international law. It projects and relates international law to the living context of the contemporary world rather than to the inner or unreal world of autonomous rules and logical exercises" (Chen 1989, 14). Presumably, a theory *of* international law is an unwarranted enterprise. I will discuss this issue in further depth in the next chapter.

> itself presupposes acknowledgment of the authority of common practices and rules according to which cooperative agreements can be created, altered, interpreted, and preserved (Nardin 1983, 210).

Without such a rule-based procedure, the high ideals embodied in the policy-oriented approach remain stillborn. Even if the underlying purpose of international law were as evident as McDougal et al. believe it to be (which is questionable), it would still be dependent upon a system of rules in order to decide and develop these policies. Thus policies presuppose, and even require, a rule based theory *of* international law as a necessary condition.

The insertion of the term "legal" in my definition of international law requires further clarification as initially it seems to bear a mark of circularity. There is a lengthy tradition of differentiating legal norms from other types of norms (such as moral norms, social norms of etiquette, religious norms, and so on) and, for my analysis, all that matters is that one can distinguish between these. Hart, for example, distinguishes legal norms from those of etiquette or morality with an analysis that I myself find no good reason to question (Hart 1994, 167–80). The issue of the uniquely "legal" nature of international law (as distinct from international morality or the etiquette of diplomacy) will not be dealt with directly in this work save insofar as this issue is bound up with issues of the reality and efficacy of international legal norms. Thus, my argument has been that international law is a genre of law and while there certainly may be other kinds of norms that extend themselves internationally (norms of comity, for example) international *laws* as laws have unique properties.

International laws are rules that transcend geo-political boundaries. The term "transcendence" may mean one of several things depending upon the legal contexts, so some further discussion might prove helpful. There are two different ways that international laws transcend boundaries:

Jurisdiction

One way that international laws transcend political boundaries is in terms of their jurisdiction. This is to say that these norms do not apply to one particular state and its citizens alone, but rather to groups of states or to individuals across borders. These norms may apply to citizens of two states (such as in bilateral treaties), ten states (such as in regional law) or all states (general international law, *jus cogens* norms). It can also apply to the states themselves but they must apply to more than one to be considered valid international law – otherwise, presumably, it would be something much closer to constitutional law (that is, laws where the state determines its own behavior *qua* state). Delineating which laws apply to whom, exactly how far the scope of jurisdiction stretches, is a matter of jurisprudence and legal argument. However, the descriptive claim that international laws are laws that apply across borders seems to me to be an uncontroversial one. The origin of different laws, be they rooted in custom, treaties, or elsewhere, may additionally be debatable but in order to be considered valid international law, the scope of their jurisdiction must stretch beyond conventional geo-political boundaries.

Most international laws apply to all individuals or to all states, but not all need do so. The general laws of treaties, the laws of diplomacy, and most customary international laws apply to all states.[21] *Jus Cogens* laws similarly apply to all states and provide less room for states to exempt themselves for whatever reason. Particular treaties, however, apply to more than one state, but obviously not to those who are not a party to them. Laws against piracy similarly oblige all individuals to refrain from acts regardless of the state to which these individuals claim allegiance. The point here is that although the jurisdiction of international laws may be either extremely wide or quite narrow, they are still, by definition, international laws.

Legitimacy

For an international law to be considered legitimate, it must be valid in more than one legal system. Treaties must be ratified by more than one state in order to be considered valid international law. To assert that a customary international law exists, one must similarly show it to be based upon commonly shared international practices, not merely the acts or beliefs of one legal system. Even the unilateral declarations of one particular state are only binding because there is a larger international community that holds the state to this declaration.[22] Each political system may legitimate a rule in its own fashion, but it must be legitimized by more than one in order to be properly considered international law. In both treaties and customs then, there must be more than one political body at play, more than one state or other group involved in order to ensure a norm's status as law.[23]

Descriptions, Prescriptions, and Predictions

Such a highly specialized approach to definitions, one that self-consciously roots itself in the existing practices of international lawyers is in a unique position in many respects. On the one hand, it claims to be describing the existing understandings of the relevant agents (international lawyers, diplomats, theorists, and so on) and thus places a great deal of emphasis on being empirical. On the other hand it claims to be analyzing international law in a manner that is in some sense prescriptive, applying normative terms like "proper" and "improper" to invocations of international law by those relevant agents. Given this double duty, the non-reductionist definition of

21 The dynamics of unilateral, bilateral, and multilateral treaties is a complex issue, but a case can certainly be made that customary international law from one region or state affects customary international law globally, at least if there is not the express objection of a particular state. For an example of this see "The Asylum Case" (*Peru v. Columbia*, ICJ, 1950).

22 *Nuclear Tests Case* (*Australia and New Zealand v. France*) 1974 ICJ 253. As the Court put it: "The unilateral statements of the French authorities were made outside the Court, publicly and *erga omnes*, even though the first of them was communicated to the Government of Australia" (para. 50).

23 It is interesting to note that in federalist political systems, individual states may make treaties (on a limited number of topics) with foreign nations. Such treaties would be international laws according to this definition.

international law must be briefly interpreted in terms of the fact/value distinction. In this last section, I will briefly sketch out how this model of definitions stands in relationship to this ancient and extremely complex philosophical puzzle. Although this issue may seem removed from the nuts and bolts world of international law, legal theorists frequently founder upon this distinction, mixing empirical accounts of what international law is with prescriptive accounts of what it ought to be.

Reflective equilibrium is normative in a somewhat weaker sense than most legal theories. This is to say, that such a method prescribes the proper uses of the term and criticizes the improper uses from the standpoint of a coherent account of international law. The claim is simply that if one wishes to be participating in the practice of international law, one *ought* to follow the rules commonly accepted to be the rules of this practice. These rules, in turn, can only be discovered through an adequately articulated theory based on actual legal practices.[24] If a practice is defined by a certain set of rules and actions, then we can assert that the law ought to be understood in such-and-such a way, and that we ought to modify our behavior accordingly with a clean conscience (this, by the way, is the same grounds by which law professors judge the work of their students). The point here is that coherence is understood as a value and the constraints of coherence dictate a particular path towards development.[25]

There is a sense in which such an approach must have some predictive value. This non-reductionist approach assumes that there will be no radical breaks in the understanding of international law and that coherence is something that will continue in the foreseeable future. Were there to be radical breaks in the nature of the actual understandings of law, were all the relevant agents to suddenly abandon their existing intuitions about international law for some other, radically different conception of law, the reflective equilibrium model would seem to be in deep trouble.[26] In this context, a break would be defined as a group of uses of the term international law that cannot be brought into satisfactory equilibrium with other uses of the term, uses that are so anomalous that they defy any attempt to make sense out of the diverse uses of the term. In addition, these breaks must be so widespread that they cannot simply be dismissed as the mistaken beliefs or eccentricities of a small group. Were a case to be made that the existing material is too heterogeneous to be made coherent, my approach would seem doomed.

Indeed, the New Stream of international legal theory has sought in their own analyses to emphasize such radical breaks in the development of international law,

---

24 For an interesting and valuable discussion of the relationship between norms and the rules of a practice see Searle (1975, 120–34).

25 While there are many good reasons to expect coherence in an account of law, the most significant one is that lawyers themselves take coherence to be a virtue. Concepts such as estoppel point to the virtue of the concept and practicing jurists seek a coherent account of law when making their cases because they believe both that coherence is required by their discipline and that coherent arguments are the ones most likely to be effective.

26 Such an account of moral discourse is given by Alasdair MacIntyre in the opening of *After Virtue*, where he argues that contemporary moral discourse is so fractured as to be fundamentally incoherent (MacIntyre 1984, 1–5). It is interesting to note that MacIntyre does not evaluate a coherentist approach to moral discourse.

cases where shifts in the nature and practice of international law took place under the noses of the international lawyers themselves.[27] This view, of course, is only plausible as an interpretation of international legal history if the New Stream analyses of the relevant data are obviously superior to other analyses. That there is a consistent history stretching up to today or a series of discreet and largely incommensurable shifts in the discourse of international law is not something that can be deduced (or refuted) *a priori*, but must be the result of weighing different interpretations against the available facts as well as other considerations.[28] However, this conclusion cannot be reached on the basis of theory alone, it must instead be the result of patient research on a series of issues in international law and the analysis of the respective merits of both approaches. Chapters 4 and 5 of this work will begin to develop what I will argue are coherent and empirically viable doctrines regarding particular issues in international law, against which New Stream approaches may be compared. Whether international law may ultimately be made coherent is a question that cannot be decided here – but belongs to the individual judgment of the reader.

A coherence approach to international law, relying on a conception of reflective equilibrium, provides a great deal of the utility that can reasonably be provided by a conceptualization of international law. It escapes Boyle's objections by finding a different footing for analysis than those traditionally offered: the existing practices of those in the know. This, however, does not entail that all expert views are equally valid nor that legal analysis simply report what these experts say, but rather that in approaching international law, the theorist seeks to make sense out of their practices. This may mean, at times, rejecting some expert opinions in favor of others – or concluding that there is no prevailing consensus on a particular issue. Non-reductionists are not medievalists in Boyle's sense, but still have something constructive to say about the nature of international law as such.

Having satisfactorily defined international law (for now, at least), and provided it with a solid philosophical foundation, I can briefly turn to some of the main contenders from traditional international legal theory. In the next chapter, I will discuss two significant approaches to conceptualizing international law. I will outline their major assumptions and their significant weaknesses when contrasted with the non-reductionist approach. First I will discuss the positivist, voluntarist model of international law developed by Bentham (and continued by Austin and many others), that I will label the "sovereignty thesis,"[29] embodying the belief that international law is defined by appeal to the consent of sovereign states. Then I will discuss the natural law tradition, stretching back through Western thought to Aristotle and Plato.

27 See Kennedy (1987).

28 In addition to hermeneutical issues, there is also the pragmatic issue of whether theorists and lawyers are better off with the view of international legal history offered by Kennedy et al. Just as the validity of the New Stream approach is questionable, the ultimate value of their approach is similarly dubious.

29 Sometimes this view is equated with legal positivism. However, as Nardin has shown, the tradition is much more diverse than this (see Nardin 1988).

Having evaluated these opposing views, I will then deal more explicitly with jurisprudential issues of legal personality and humanitarian intervention, before returning to some of the skeptical arguments discussed in the previous chapter.

Chapter 3

Voluntarism and Natural Law

So far I have characterized international law according to a highly specialized definition. Because of its roots in modern analytical philosophy, its aims, goals, and assumptions are to a large extent unique in legal theory in general and among the philosophies of international law in particular. In this chapter I will attempt to highlight the uniqueness of this definition, and the entire approach to international law that stands behind it, by way of contrast. That is, I will show how such an approach to understanding international law differs from other, more conventional approaches to international law. This will allow us to see how the non-reductionist approach fares when contrasted to some of its more entrenched competitors. Once this task is complete, I will then be able to further expand upon this conception of law (the task of Chapters 4 and 5) before responding to the remaining skeptical views discussed in the opening chapter.

This chapter will stand in three parts: first, I will discuss some formal aspects of theoretical analyses, contrasting what can be described as functional accounts of international law (those frequently advocated by international relations theory) on the one hand with descriptive accounts (such as mine) on the other. Within this I will argue that functional accounts are an inadequate way to effectively approach to international law. After this, a discussion and critique of what I have labelled "the sovereignty thesis" of international law (the view, beginning primarily with Bentham, but rooted in Hobbes, that international law consists primarily in relations between sovereigns or sovereign states) will follow. This discussion will set up an analysis of Terry Nardin's (1983) views regarding international law as a "practical association" in the second part of this chapter. This in turn will lead to a brief, critical discussion of the natural law tradition of international legal theory stretching from Aristotle and ancient Stoicism up to the present day. Having thereby further justified the use of the non-reductionist approach discussed in the previous chapter, I will then move on to discuss issues of international legal personality in the next chapter.

Descriptions and Functions in International Law

A key distinction for analyzing the theory of international law is between what we may call *descriptive accounts* of international law and *purposive or functional accounts* of it. This distinction is crucially important as the confusion between these two modes or types of analysis can lead to a great deal of confusion. The former approach seeks to give an account of what a thing is, understood as distinct from its broader relations and uses. Thus, the approach is descriptive insofar as it seeks to grasp an object independent of whatever role it may play "beyond itself" in a larger whole as it were. The latter approach, however, seeks to explain why such things exist, what role they play in a broader system of nature or society, and relies heavily upon theories of the larger world. Of course, a particular descriptive account may ultimately be compatible with a particular functional account, and *vice versa*, but the two approaches can be separated for analytical purposes. In this section I will elaborate briefly on this distinction, explain its relevance for understanding international law, and argue that functional accounts are not very helpful for developing a rigorous theory of international law.

When I ask what international law is and I appeal to its uses (or lack thereof) in the international community, I am looking for a functional account. For example, if I claim that international law promotes stability and preserves peace in the hostile world of international politics, I have explained its nature by reference to a broader conception of international society beyond the law itself. Similarly, if I claim that international law is merely rhetorical wallpaper covering a structure built entirely on force or coercion, I am similarly pointing to its ideological function in world politics. In both cases, the answer given to the question goes beyond a mere description of international law itself into an explanation of what role it plays in the context of larger economic, political, or social forces. The broader context within which one places international law will be based on previous theoretical or ideological commitments (such as realism, Marxism, or constructivism) that in turn shape this functional analysis. Most international relations theory found in political science departments seeks to offer just such an account of international law.

On the other hand, if I view international law as a set of rules or norms and analyze it *independent of its broader function in world affairs* (such as was done in the previous chapter), I have analyzed it descriptively. In claiming that international law is a set of norms or rules that transcend provincial boundaries, I have said nothing about why it ultimately exists and what purposes it might serve in international society. Presumably, such a definition is compatible with a number of functional approaches to international law, at least insofar as such functional accounts would not directly conflict with the descriptive approach. Saying that X (international law) serves function Y (your preferred functional theory) says nothing about X in and of itself (unless one argued for a reductive sort of functionalism). A conception of international law as a set of norms or laws could work with a very cynical view of this legal regime, like that of the descriptive realists, as well as the most optimistically humanist view of it. In a sense, a descriptive approach is formalistic: it seeks to explicate the law independent of its various uses and contexts. In offering such an answer in the previous chapter, I have attempted to explicate the nature of the thing without appealing to any larger use or purpose to which it is or could be applied.

As mentioned above, the functional approach bears a closer relationship to conceptions of international law originating in international relations theory. Such theorists explain/describe/understand the nature of international law by appealing to its use (and misuse) by the relevant international actors and the purposes it serves in their interests. To use a contemporary example, game-theoretical analyses (of both a realist and an "institutionalist" bent) explain what international law is by appealing to the interests of artificially constructed international actors, that is, they explain its existence by describing its purposes in the international arena. If we claim that international law is the result of a compromise between self-interested, rational actors, by which they sacrifice certain interests in order to assure their survival in an otherwise hostile environment, we are appealing to a function in order to explain what international law is. Such an interpretation is obviously quite different from that found in legal textbooks and in the minds of international lawyers as they go about their business.[1] International relations theory gets its impetus from analyzing what functions international institutions such as international law might serve in the global political arena.

Both functional and descriptive approaches seek to answer the question "what is international law?" but only one, the latter, separates the thing itself from its broader social and political contexts. While one is usually inclined to view the consideration of such contexts an advantage for a given method, as it can provide a theory with a certain anthropological subtlety, the functional dimension of international law is in fact extraneous to a rigorous understanding of the law and can be misleading. There is no logical connection between an entity such as international law and the various functions ascribed to it in international relations theory. International law does indeed serve different functions in different contexts, but to claim that it is constituted by its functions is a *non sequitor*. While simple human artifacts such as chairs and pencils may be identified with their function to a large degree, complex systems and social practices are not as easily so identified. A large number of other institutions could exist in the global political arena that would fulfill the functions that international relations theory ascribes to international law, but (importantly) would not be law. One could imagine, for example, an exchange of hostages or a system of intermarriage that allowed for peace but in no way resembled international law. To claim that an institution or practice as complicated as international law is constituted or defined by its purposes or functions is to reverse the logical priorities and to confuse an item with the purposes to which it is put.

This logical disjunction is highlighted by the fact that whatever functions an institution such as international law may serve will vary widely from context to context and from practitioner to practitioner. Like all other social institutions, international law is malleable depending on the beliefs, values, and aims of those that partake in it. Given the wide array of personalities and agendas involved in

---

1 For a useful discussion of the contrast between these two persectives on the use of international law, see Lejbowicz (1999, 14–15). "Distinguons les points de vue juridique et sociologique… Une fois formulée en conformité avec les règles qui la valident, la norme est tenue par le juriste comme du droit positif, c'est-à-dire est en vigueur et s'impose si le cas étudié tombe sous sa qualification... Quant au sociologue, attentif aux conduites sociales plus qu'à la formulation de la règle, il lui importe non de dire ce qu'il y a dans les règles et les lois, mais de décrire ce qu'il en est des comportements humans en regard de ces règles." ["Let us distinguish between the juridical and the sociological points of view… Once formulated in conformity with the rules that validate it, the norm is held by the lawyer as positive law, this is to say it is in force and imposes itself if the case studied falls under its jurisdiction… As for the sociologist, attentive to the social conduct more than to the formulation of the rule, it is important to him not to say what there is in the rules and laws, but to describe that which is involved in human comportments in regard to these rules."]

international legal processes, it would be very hard to believe that there is *one* function (or even a clearly definable set of functions) that can be found throughout the practices that create the institution of international law.

To compensate for this radical diffusion of contexts and purposes, functional accounts traditionally appeal to an array of notions such as interest, security, and gain. All actors in invoking international law do so in order to serve their national interest, for example. However, while this move is appealing, it only pushes the methodological problem back one step. Because they are meant to apply to the use of law in such a wide variety of contexts and purposes, these concepts are conceptually clouded, incapable of being articulated in any rigorous fashion. This vagueness is not a small philosophical vice as it robs functional approaches of their falsifiability, and hence, their explanatory power. The elasticity of these concepts allows the theorist to discover a false uniformity among a diverse plurality of phenomena. These attempts to supplant formalistic approaches to the law by functional approaches have essentially replaced one abstraction ("the law" as a formal set of rules) for another set of even more vague abstractions. While the descriptive approach may seem open to criticisms of being unnecessarily formal, it can nonetheless claim a theoretical priority to functional analyses of international law.

Take the paradigmatic twentieth-century realist Hans Morgenthau's attempt to explain the concept of "power" as a good example of this problem. According to Morgenthau, the essence of an objective account of international relations is recognition that all international politics are driven by the pursuit of power.

> The main signpost that helps political realism to find its way through the landscape of international politics is the concept of interest defined in terms of power. This concept provides the link between reason trying to understand international politics and the facts to be understood (Morgenthau 1967, in Hoffman 1960, 56).

While Morgenthau does shortly thereafter concede, "realism does not endow its key concept of interest defined as power with a meaning that is fixed once and for all, (Morgenthau 1967, in Hoffman 1960, 59)" it remains far from clear that any definition of power *could* be offered that would meet criteria we might recognize as objective or scientific. The definitions that Morgenthau does offer, such as, "Man's control over the minds and actions of other men" (Morgenthau 1967, in Hoffman 1960, 65), simply shift the ambiguity of the word "power" onto other terms: here, "control." Control can be conceived of in such a broad number of ways (psychological control, emotional control, economic control, physical control, etc.) that on Morgenthau's grounds, *any* action can be construed as somehow an attempt to gain power, thereby robbing the concept of power of enough specificity to provide any explanatory power. Without the possibility that something could not be construed as an attempt to grab power, it is hard to see that the concept has any explanatory (and most importantly, scientific) merit.[2]

---

2 For a discussion of fallibility as a criteria for genuine scientific inquiry see Popper (1992). Specifically, in the first chapter ("Science: Conjectures and Refutations"), Popper contrasts science from pseudo-science by "the criterion of the scientific status of a theory is its falsifiability, or refutability, or testability (Popper 1992, 37). While Popper himself was largely

Turning from the realists to their institutionalist opponents, we can see that they too marshal a battalion of vague concepts in their approach to international relations. While the institutionalists disagree with the realists regarding the epiphenomenality of international law and other international institutions, they too seek to analyze international politics in terms of the interest of states.[3] Stephen Krasner explains that,

> A wide variety of basic causal variables have been offered to explain the development of regimes. The most prominent in this volume are egoistic self-interest, political power, norms and principles, habit and custom, and knowledge. The last two are seen as supplementary, augmenting more basic forces related to interest, power, and values (Krasner, reprinted in Beck et al. 1996, 175).

International norms exist for the institutionalists, but they exist as a result of the machinations of power and interest – they are their product. Thus, these thinkers start with the same assumptions as the realists, but draw more optimistic conclusions regarding international law.

While their conclusions are correct regarding the existence of international law, insofar as they rely on the same concepts as the realists, they fail to provide a satisfactory account of international relations and international law. For example, the first variable Krasner cites is "the desire to maximize one's own utility function where that function does not include the utility of another party" (Krasner, reprinted in Beck et al. 1996, 175). However, this is unsatisfying. Utilitarian concepts are unsuitable for the generation of fallible, predictive rules, as the theorists cannot adequately define utilitarianism's central notions of happiness or preference to a specificity suitable for empirical consumption. The other definitions offered by other international relations theorists reveal the same problem: the utilization of vague concepts to suggest a dubious unity to a plurality of phenomena. While the analyses of realism and institutionalism offered here are admittedly quite brief and selective, it is hard to see how the concepts deployed by such approaches to explain *the* function of international law could ever be explicated with a satisfactory degree of specificity.

Functional approaches do have a legitimate place in the natural sciences that have a very different set of methodological and metaphysical assumptions than those of legal theory, but it's far from clear that one can provide a system of functions in this context that could even closely compare to those of biology or chemistry. Philosophers of science have pointed out that functional explanations in biology can be cashed out nomologically, that is, they can be explained by appealing to universal physical laws that are missing from social-scientific models. For example, the function of a butterfly's wings providing protection can be explained by appeal to processes of natural selection, that in turn are purely causal rules of genetic mutation

---

concerned with the claims of Marxism and psychoanalysis, it is hard to see how Morgenthau's conception of power could meet any of these three criteria.

3 It has been pointed out by many that institutionalists rarely show any interest in international law *per se*, preferring to discuss "international institutions," an oversight which seems to be more a hangover from realism than any serious theoretical position (see Arend 1999, 5).

and environmental survival. Whereas natural scientists can appeal to such laws that further specify and causally explain the mechanism standing behind their functional approaches, social-scientific functionalism appeals to concepts such as "need", "interest," and "well-being," concepts that are incapable of the precision required for empirical analysis and prediction. Thus philosophers of social science have found functionalism as an approach to the understanding of social phenomena to be flawed when contrasted to its implementation in other, natural scientific, contexts (Hempel 1994).

Functional accounts, of course, are only as good as the larger functional systems in which they are placed. This is to say that the functional approaches rely upon a larger set of assumptions about nature, society, and so on, that make the attribution of functions to empirical entities tenable. If the functions that a particular entity is understood as performing, and the larger frame in which the entity is said to function, are dubious then so is the functional account of the entity. To use a trite example, the belief that my cat, Ophelia, exists in order to keep me from going insane during long, lonely hours of writing would require an appeal to a vast number of beliefs that are ultimately untenable. First, it has been noted by Hempel (1994) among others that such explanations reverse the temporal order of phenomena (I had my cat before her beneficial consequences were realized) and thereby contradicts some of the standard presuppositions of an adequate explanation. Second, it would presuppose a (perhaps divine) plan or purpose behind the order of events in my life that somehow put her in her place right now, rather than a number of causally related phenomena (that is, I found her. I brought her home, and so on). This second presupposition involves my belief in a world-view, what I described above as a functional system, that in turn stands on little beyond a faith in a teleologically constructed universe, resting ultimately on theological, not scientific grounds. My belief that my cat serves such a benevolent function obviously possesses a certain psychological appeal, but its standing as a scientific explanation of why I have my cat is noticeably flawed.

A final case worth discussing in regards to the weakness of functional approaches to international law is Douglas Johnston's avowed functionalism (Johnston 1988). In this study, Johnston asserts that there are several functions that "most will accept" in what he calls the "post-classical period of international law," and that may in turn be used to highlight the nature of international legal systems. Specifically the functions that Johnston attributes to modern international law are:

> [T]he correction of distributive injustice among nations and peoples through a restructuring of the international legal system designed to bring preferential benefits to the developing and the disadvantaged, and the planning and development of international regimes through the negotiation of interrelated treaty arrangements in response to complex institutional problems (Johnston 1988, 28).

The functions have in turn been transposed upon previous functions served by classical (pre-World War I) and neo-classical (1919 until the mid-1960s) international legal systems – presumably the roles that international law played in international society. While Johnston refrains from offering one particular function to international law, his list too remains unacceptably ambiguous and his response to the problem reveals much about the underlying assumptions of functionalist international legal theory.

The interesting element of Johnston's analysis surfaces when he applies these functions to the empirical practices of international lawyers. Johnston describes the functional approach as "an ethical position" (Johnston 1988, 57) on the one hand, and a "logic" on the other, the former is depicted as a normative project (claiming that international law *ought* to serve a set of functions) while the latter is a descriptive project (claiming that international law serves these functions). The fluctuation between these two approaches therefore allows Johnston the leeway (he believes) to consistently hold a functionalist perspective. The strategy quickly becomes clear: whenever his approach cannot make sense of international law as such (that is, international law as an empirical set of rules and practices), he reverts to talking about ethics, and how the law ought to be structured. However, Johnston does not formulate any ethical argument as to exactly why these functions are the desireable ones, but somehow assumes that these ethical norms are to be found in the law itself and thus are factual.[4] Johnston has effectively turned a social-scientific project into an ethical project, one that no longer is concerned with grasping international law as it is actually deployed by those who use it, but using a set of functions to legislate what international law should be. Thus, like other functionalists, Johnston's theory is full of holes, but whereas others try to cover over these holes with a thin paper of vague terminology, he uses normative concepts. Neither of these approaches, however, holds any water, and the problem is not with the individual thinkers themselves as much as with the underlying assumptions of a functional approach to international law.

The foregoing critique is not intended to completely dismiss functional analyses of international law, but to rein them in as it were. Such approaches have an entirely different theoretical standing if we ignore universal claims about *the* function (or set of functions) of international law and instead view these analyses as practical tools for improving the efficacy of this legal system. If one wishes to know why certain laws work and why others fail to be effective, one may look at functional theories as candidates for possible explanations, and (most importantly) apply them to a particular case. If we deploy functional analyses as guides to the study of actual events where international law comes into play, we are seeking to grasp how existing and future laws can be made better, the results of which provide useful policy recommendations for lawyers and diplomats to improve the standing of international law in the world community. Taken in such a fashion, a functional approach is both useful and valid. But when functional approaches are understood as either ontological or theoretical, telling us what international law *is*, or assigning one single function to this legal regime, the functionalists have overstepped their proper bounds, as it were.

International law according to the non-reductionist approach may be described and defined without any attempt to analyze its efficacy in any particular circumstance.

---

4 As Johnston himself puts it, "In conformity with the heritage of functionalism in political science, legal functionalism bases its ethic on the need for efficiency (effectiveness) as well as equity (justice) in international law." This, of course would only be convincing to one who was interested in maintaining this "heritage of functionalism" (Johnston 1988, 56).

The efficacy or reality of international law is ultimately (I will later argue) an empirical, not a theoretical question, one that must ultimately be grasped on a case by case basis in the comparison of interpretations and not deduced *a priori* from some speculative functional system. The means of deducing *that* international law is relevant to a particular case (a question that I will address later) is distinct from *why* it is effective in this case. Presumably, laws can be effective for a large number of different reasons, and similarly, can fail for an equally wide array of reasons, as I will argue later. The nature of international law and its efficacy are, analytically speaking, two separate questions, standing on very different epistemological footings, and the confusion of the two has led to a great deal of wasted ink.

The Sovereignty Thesis

Even a cursory examination of the leading theories of international law, both past and present, reveals the common belief that international law is fundamentally a set of rules that hold between sovereign political bodies, usually states.[5] This definition of course stands at the very heart of international law as meant by Bentham when he originally used the term to refer to "the mutual transactions between sovereigns, as such" (Bentham 1970, 327) and finds its roots in Bodin (Bodin 1992). In the first chapter of this work, such a statist conception of international law was key to Austin's skepticism towards international law and it was there that I began to express certain reservations towards this approach that I will further develop here.[6] As the sovereignty-based model conflicts with the assumptions of the non-reductionist approach advocated in this work, the Benthamite analysis merits some critical discussion. I will refer to this definition of international law and the conception of the international legal order that follows from it, common and widespread as it is, as *the sovereignty thesis of international law* (I will use this term instead of the more common term, "positivism," simply because positivism has a number of different meanings both inside and outside of legal theory and could lead to some confusion).

Of course, were we concerned with understanding the literal meanings of words alone, the sovereignty thesis would probably be the final statement on the issue. However, as discussed in the previous chapter, here we are not concerned solely with the meaning of words in an analytic sense, but are trying to understand the nature of the social practices to which the term "international law" refers. This is the only empirically relevant path to take to understanding international law and thus, in order to grasp international law as it is, it behooves us to step outside of the bare meanings

5 As Kelsen defines the term: "The thing characterized as 'sovereign.' Whether it be an order, a community, an organ, or a power, must be regarded as the highest above which there can be no higher, authority limiting the function of the sovereign entity, binding the sovereign. Sovereignty in its original sense means 'highest authority'" (Kelsen 1952, 108). See also Kelsen (1952, 439). For a brief but useful analysis of the use of sovereignty in conceptualizing international law see Verdross (1949).

6 For a concise account of the relation between Bentham and Austin see Twinning (2000), especially Chapter 1.

of words. From there, we may more profitably inquire as to whether the sovereignty thesis has a firm grip on the actual nature of international law as it is conceived by those "in the know." The question of whether this definition of international law grasps the relevant phenomena stands in need of an entirely different type of analysis than when we ask about semantics alone. It is from this pragmatic perspective that the apparent obviousness of the sovereignty thesis begins to break down. Thus, in order to really understand the nature of international law we will have to look beyond the trivial truth denoted by word meanings alone and see these words in their larger practical context.

We can distinguish between two senses of sovereignty in the field of international law. *Meta-language* sovereignty imagines sovereignty as defining and constructing the international law regime, and when we talk in this sense we are speaking in a metalanguage.[7] *Object-language* sovereignty views international law as constructed by the legal regime itself. If one defines international law as the agreements of sovereign states, one has used sovereignty at the meta-level – it creates international law, defining its essence or parameters. Thus Oppenheim's (1912, 107) characterization of international law as "the body of rules which the civilized States consider legally binding in their intercourse" is a meta-level analysis of sovereignty. Similarly, Kelsen defines international law as "a body of rules which… regulate the conduct of states in their intercourse with each other" and "the rules prevailing in the relations among states" (Kelsen 1952, 3).[8] However, if one examines a particular field of international law in terms of sovereignty (what are the legal rights and duties of sovereign states *vis-à-vis* each other?), one has conceptualized sovereignty at the object level as a part of the system. There, sovereignty is seen as a construction of law, not a constructor of law.

What are the connections between these two notions of law? If one assumes that sovereignty is operative as a meta-language, in theory at least, this would "trickle down" to the object level, structuring the legal discourse in such a way that sovereignty would be the "trump card" of international law. If an individual invokes sovereignty *within* the legal discourse, say, in a doctrinal analysis, this is going to be structured by this bedrock legal principle: sovereignty is unquestioned (of course, as critics have pointed out, this makes international law effectively useless as a sovereign state may change its mind at any moment). All other rules would get their legitimacy from state sovereignty and only sovereign states would be legal actors. However, if one rejects the meta-language claim of sovereignty as essential to international law, then it follows that international law need not bow before sovereignty as such a trump card. Sovereignty would mean something in international law, but it is not central to it: it is a card that can be played (perhaps an effective one), but is not a trump card. In such a case, sovereignty would be a legal construction, but not a foundational one.

It comes as no surprise to anybody who has made even a superficial analysis of the actual practices of international law (law at the object level) that the sovereignty

7 For more on the concept of meta-language in international legal theory see McDougal et al. (1981, 53).

8 Janis (1984, footnote 14) lists numerous versions of such a conception of international law.

thesis is unsatisfying. There are some important reasons for this. As Mark Janis has noted, Bentham's influential definition showed little resemblance to the actual practices of international law even at his own time (Janis 1997, 409). For example, Janis cites the status of individuals in cross-border disputes, not considered the exclusive domain of one state's domestic law even in Bentham's own time, a fact the philosopher himself must have been aware of. Bentham's attempt to capture the essence of international law through appeal to the notion of sovereignty misses key elements of international law as it has been construed throughout history, throwing the validity of his definition immediately into question.

Whether or not his definition was actually valid in the European political climate of the 18th century, its status as a definition of modern international law is undoubtedly false. The diffusion of international law at a variety of levels that do not require recourse to the state have made Bentham's approach even less tenable than it was in his own time. Cases that have had increasing influence since the Nuremberg and the Tokyo tribunals and the status of individuals in international criminal law (and the various international criminal courts) further this phenomenon of legal diversification that undermine Bentham's analysis. While we will discuss this issue in much greater depth in the next chapter, suffice it to point out now that the analysis of existing international law and international legal practices conjures up strong suspicions regarding the transactions of sovereigns as the essence of this law. Given the facts of the practice of international lawyers (and others in the know), there is no reason to immediately accept the claim that "the mutual transactions of sovereigns as such" is somehow definitive of international law as it is.

However, it is worth noting that in Janis' view, Bentham himself intended the term to be normative, how we *ought* to think about international law, and not referring to what the actual legal practices were. This would mean that he does not claim to be merely describing international legal practices, thereby saving him from the objections I have raised above. In regards to Bentham's divergence from actual legal practice (and Blackstone's more empirically grounded account) Janis concludes, "We should expect as much. Bentham was attempting mostly to reform the law, Blackstone mostly to restate it." In his definition of international law, Bentham relied upon what he called "censorial jurisprudence" rather than "expository jurisprudence"; that is, he described what law ought to be rather than what the law is. Such an interpretation would fit well with Bentham's self-styled reformist utilitarianism, but in turn would involve him in a host of different philosophical problems.

As a normative prescription regarding how international law should be understood, rather than a descriptive definition, Bentham's analysis of international law would have to stand on an entirely different (presumably moral) footing. As a normative prescription for the understanding of international law, Bentham's view stands or falls on the merits of Bentham's own utilitarianism, an issue that we are (mercifully) justified in side-stepping here. Because his approach is normative, we should not see ourselves as bound to Bentham's analysis or his definition in trying to grasp international law as an empirical social practice. Purely normative approaches to international law have of course a rich history, and it is not entirely implausible that Bentham himself meant for his analysis to be thoroughly grounded in his broader utilitarian morality. However, and paradoxically, Bentham, and Austin in his footsteps, would then hold views much closer to natural lawyers than the paragons of legal positivism. Both Bentham and Austin would be describing how international law *ought* to be, not how it is. That makes their views seem more akin to ethics or natural law views about the status of unjust laws. This in turn raises the question, why should we view the sovereignty thesis as paradigmatic of a moral world order especially with the dubious moral history of the nation state and its claim to untrammeled sovereignty? While reform in international law is certainly a valid topic for discussion, Bentham's approach masks its normative agenda behind a definition that is so narrow that it has had damaging effects on international legal theory from its initial formulation.

We must then cast a skeptical eye towards the sovereignty thesis not only if we wish to escape Austinian objections to international law, but also if we wish to give an accurate account of the social practice of international law as it actually exists at the object level. As an analysis of the meaning of the words "international" and "law," the sovereignty thesis is true, but only trivially so, it tells us nothing insightful about the reality that the terms are meant to describe. As there is necessarily something transcultural about international law, we should not see ourselves as completely beholden to the somewhat arbitrary English designation, which is only one among many. We will see as the non-reductionist analysis unfolds in succeeding chapters that there are a vast number of aspects of international law that the sovereignty thesis fails to capture.

The idea that the realities of global politics suggest that the only international laws that work are those closely tied with the notion of state sovereignty is an empirical claim about which laws are effective, not a theory about the nature of international law itself. As a concept that seeks to capture the essence of international law, the notion of sovereignty is incomplete at best. As we will see in later chapters, international law properly understood inflicts a large number of constraints upon the concept of state sovereignty, and further, international law is created in a vast number of ways that do not rely upon the consent of sovereign states (either explicit consent through treaties or implicit consent through custom). Additionally, there are a vast number of legal principles and legal agents that do not rely upon the transactions of sovereign political bodies in order to establish their existence *qua* principles and agents; their legal standing is effectively independent of the consent of sovereigns. Thus, the bare linguistic analysis of international law as based upon the consent of sovereign states will be shown to be misleading when international law is viewed through the lens of the non-reductive definition.

Nardin on International Law as a Practice

My conception of international law as a practice bears some resemblance to that given by Terry Nardin in his book *Law, Morality, and the Relations of States* and it is worth some effort to highlight the distinctions between the two. In the opening paragraph of his book, Nardin argues that international law should first and foremost be understood as a kind of common practice with a set of shared rules:

> I want to defend the view that the practices of international law and international morality constitute the indispensable foundation of all durable international association. To the extent that the relations of states achieve a significant degree of permanence, rising above the level of mere episodes in the separate histories of isolated political communities, they must be understood as taking place on the basis of common, authoritative practices and rules (Nardin 1983, ix).

As in the analysis offered here, international law, for Nardin, is based upon a set of authoritative practices shared by a particular group of agents (for myself it is the practitioners of international law, while for Nardin it is states who create international law through their acts [Nardin 1983, 272–74]). For Nardin, what makes these practices unique is that they are distinct from the norms of any particular political or cultural institution such as a religious worldview or a political ideology that would justify these legal norms. The central idea here is that the rules of international law are only based on the factual rules that structure the actual behavior of states, and not on any other normative scheme (such as the moral precepts of natural law).

Relying on Michael Oakeshott's analysis of social behavior in *On Human Conduct*, Nardin argues that practices as a technical concept denote a sub-species of human associations, distinguished from others by the unique aims and purposes of this association. Nardin defines such an association as

> The circumstances within which transactions take place and provide the rules on the basis of which they can be carried on... A practice is a set of considerations to be taken into account in deciding and acting, and in evaluating decisions and actions. Practices therefore always reflect an ideal conception of the activities out of which they grow and of the agents engaged in them…

Beneath this meta-concept of a practice is the subordinate notion of a "practical association" defined as the principles that guide human relations, idealized through a set of formalized rules presupposed by the relevant actors, and without roots in some overarching goal or telos. "Practical association… unites those engaged in the pursuit of different and sometimes incompatible ends through their recognition of the worth of those ways of life constituted by the authoritative practices that apply to them as moral agents or as members of a political community" (Nardin 1983, 11). These practical associations denote the broadest form of rule-governed human association and it is in terms of this genre of association that other associations must be understood.

According to Nardin, other kinds of rule-governed human relations must presuppose practical associations in order to "get off the ground" as it were. In order for groups of agents to interact in any meaningful way, they must initially be guided to some degree by a set of common practices that in turn may be formulated as a set of rules or practical associations. Relations that Nardin calls "purposive relations," – "relationship[s] among those who cooperate for the purpose of securing certain shared beliefs, values, and interests" (Nardin 1983, 14) – are just such a kind of relation insofar as this cooperation must (presumably, logically) rely upon a set of rules and behavior guided by such rules. At times Nardin refers to practical associations as "the condition for the pursuit of all purposes" (Nardin 1983, 309) and elsewhere he argues, "Rules cannot serve as an instrument for the achievement of shared purposes unless those united for the joint pursuit of these purposes are willing to defer to rules" (Nardin 1983, 209). For Nardin then, the authority of rules, *qua* rules, underlies any other type of rule-governed behavior, and while purposive relations, guided by substantive aims, may be more common, beneath each sits a practical association of sorts.[9]

The rule-governed dimensions of international relations (specifically international law and international morality) are based upon a conception of international society that differs from religiously motivated international alliances (and other forms of political relations based on substantial moral doctrines) on account of their status as a practical association. For Nardin, the basis of international relations is one wherein states that do not share an overarching moral goal or comprehensive world view (most certainly a reality in world politics), nonetheless consent to follow a set of rules on account of a larger shared interest in promoting stability. "International society, according to the practical conception, is constituted by the forms and procedures that states are obligated to observe in their transactions with one another" (Nardin 1983, 15–16). This common interest is only compelling to states in the weak sense that it is an interest in what states have to gain through a law-governed relation with others. International law is a kind of practice with a set of presuppositions, but these presuppositions are not moral in any strong sense, only the formal recognition of the worth of the rule itself compels states to follow it. Beyond the unique ethos of a law-governed association, there is little that is shared among those operating within the framework of international law, and therefore international law is a weak, but ultimately functional form of human association.

For Nardin, international law has values in it, but only in a weak sense that it seeks to mediate and maintain relationships between states that share no overarching conception of what political philosophers refer to as "the good." As Nardin himself describes it:

> The values of practical association… are those appropriate to the relations among persons who are not necessarily engaged in any common pursuit but who nevertheless have to get along with one another…
>
> Values such as legality, morality, and justice are therefore best regarded not as ends to be produced as an outcome of collective action but as values embodied by the constraints governing all action, values that can only be realized by acting within those constraints (Nardin 1983, 13–14).

---

9 If this is viewed as a logical argument, and not an argument about the realities of world politics, it seems dubious. It is certainly not incoherent to argue that in some societies with strongly shared values, there could be a purposive association without the existence of a practical one. This is to say that there can be purposes and rules which guide these purposes without reference to the conditions for a practical association (namely, that people consent to follow rules independent of any notion of a common purpose). The underlying question here is whether a society functioning according to rules presupposes the elements of a practical association which Nardin describes, or at a minimum, precisely what Nardin means by the word "presuppose." Nardin's argument seems to conflate the existence of any rules with a certain kind of social arrangement.

And elsewhere:

> Durable relations among adversaries presupposes a framework of common practices and rules capable of providing some unifying bond where shared purposes are lacking. Such practices are embedded in the usages of diplomacy in customary international law, and in certain moral traditions ... [B]y prescribing restraint, toleration, and mutual accommodation according to authoritative common standards of international conduct, they make it possible for states pursuing different ends to coexist (Nardin 1983, 5).

The values found in the practices that comprise international law are only strong enough to guide relations between those who have to maintain relationships despite remaining in constant competition with each other. This overarching need to maintain some ordered relations produces values that are autonomous to a large degree from the substantive moral doctrines of these diverse societies.

However, despite the fact that he explicitly distinguishes practical associations from purposive associations, both are analyzed in terms of their respective use in international society. The former we may say serves a kind of pragmatic or utilitarian function, it allows agents with competing interests to secure their shared overarching interest of stability while simultaneously pursuing their particular (sometimes conflicting) agendas. This stability is even useful when their larger moral conflicts are undermined by the obligations of the rule of law. Thus, while Nardin claims to distinguish the ends of a purposive association from the values inherent in a practical association, he analyses both forms of association functionally. He seeks to explain why international law as a practical association is valuable (either for humanity in general or to the states themselves) and not what international law is, *qua* empirical object. Nardin's analysis of both purposive and practical associations seeks to define human conduct by answering the question "why do human beings associate in this particular way?" The difference between the two is in the answer given for each case, not the nature of the analysis itself.

While there is no strong notion of shared values standing behind international law in Nardin's view, it should be noted that he isn't always consistent through *Law, Morality, and the Relations of States* on this issue. At times he seems to assert that states follow international law because it is there (and presumably authoritative) and other times seems to be claiming that international law is based upon a mutual recognition of the utility of a shared code of conduct. In the first view, law is authoritative because it is the law without recourse to any larger scheme or purpose for this law. Following the law (and the values of "legality, morality, and justice") is an independent moral good whether in the long term it leads to any further end. Closely akin to Hart's conception of "obligation" in *The Concept of Law*, according to this view the law prescribes without any direct reference to further gains following said law (Hart 1994, 83–4). In this second view, the law is authoritative not simply because it is authoritative, but rather for some other, additional reason (namely, "getting along with each other").[10] Nardin's apparent equivocation on this issue suggests that he himself is unclear about the nature of his analysis, whether

10 For an interesting discussion of these different conceptions of authority see Kierkegaard (1989).

international rules are best analyzed functionally (in terms of their goals) or by some other, perhaps deontic or otherwise non-functional account.

At first it may seem perplexing why Nardin is so insistent that his own approach to international law does not impose some broader purpose to international law, despite the fact that he is so clearly giving a functional account of international law that must presuppose some kind of goal or telos. However, a survey of much of the political theory of international relations to which Nardin is responding reveals that the notion of purpose that is read into international law is often so crude that Nardin's is unique. Nardin's intellectual foils are groups such as Marxists and others who seek to read into the international legal system a set of strong and highly contentious moral or political norms. Against these kinds of analyses, Nardin's view does look so weak, such that it may indeed seem to be of a different category. However, the conception of common good that he articulates at the basis of international law is still a highly normative theory – one that seems to bear little resemblance to extant legal practices. Like the realists and the institutionalists, Nardin has confused the question of why legal norms are effective (a functional question about what purpose this law may serve in the international community) with what international law is (a descriptive question that remains neutral to function issues). What makes Nardin unique is that he uses the distinction between purposive and practical associations to bludgeon his opponents without conceding that he himself is imposing a purpose on international law.

In addition, it is unclear precisely who uses international law to the ends that he attributes to it. It is an open question whether those who actually practice international law recognize Nardin's criteria of practical associations as being definitive of international law. Like game theoretical and rational choice analyses of international relations, it is hard to see precisely what the connection is between the actual practices of international law and the functions that Nardin attributes to it.[11] One can analyze and define an object or social practice to a vast degree without ever making reference to its functions, and there may be vastly different views regarding its functions among those who prescribe to the legitimacy and authority of said practices (thus distinguishing the functional analysis of social practices different from the functional analysis of other types of entities, biological organisms for example). Nardin concedes as much when he maintains, "the essence of any practice is to be found in the conditions it recommends or imposes on the conduct of agents pursuing self-chosen purposes" and *not* the functions that such a purpose serves in broader society (Nardin 1983, 8). The problem of course is that a vast amount of the data, vast swaths of what international lawyers believe to be international law (for example, treaties) would be

11 This is especially true insofar as he has explicitly disavowed giving a normative analysis of international law. "This is not a work of science – of 'empirical theory'... But neither is it a work of 'normative theory,' if by that is meant an inquiry aimed at justifying or recommending conduct... My own engagement... is with a mode of inquiry that would appear to be excluded by the current empirical/normative dichotomy. To theorize about morality and law, I would argue, is above all to be concerned with understanding the character and presuppositions of moral and legal conduct and argument" (Nardin 1983, xi). None of this, however, requires the kind of functional analysis which Nardin offers and the question remains however as to *who* such a practical association analysis applies if it is neither empirical nor normative.

rejected as they fall off his theoretical map.[12] The definition of international law that I have justified above does not seek to explain why we have international law (simply because the answer to this question would be very different depending upon who we ask[13]), but rather seeks to explain what those in the know believe international law to be and thereby differs from Nardin's approach.

Natural Law and the Metaphysics of Definition

One considerable challenge in defining international law worth consideration comes from the natural law tradition. Natural lawyers seek to understand the nature of law by pointing beyond any positive law and towards a larger normative structure, be it theological, scientific, or moral. From the perspective of these higher rules, the lawyer can thereby determine the legitimacy of any particular positive law and then decide whether to follow or ignore this putative law. Judges may choose to invoke "higher principles" in ignoring statutes and rendering a decision, and individuals may feel free to break these alleged laws and ignore the broader consequences for their act within the framework of natural law. The principle *lex iniusta non est lex* stands as the guiding light of natural law: An unjust law is no law at all.[14] In this section, I will briefly outline this view and some of its more significant problems in relation to the analysis of international law.

This history of the natural law tradition stems from the ancient world, but finds its most rigorous and systematic adherent in St. Thomas Aquinas. For Aquinas, there were four kinds of law (that he defines as "a dictate of practical reason") (Aquinas 1996, Questions 90–97), ultimately stemming from God: Eternal Law (the law by which God created the universe), Natural Law, Divine Law (the law found in scripture), and Human Law. Natural law or the dictates of practical reasoning are the means by which finite, human beings participate in the divine law:

> Now among all others, the rational creature is subject to Divine providence in the most excellent way, in so far as it partakes of a shore of providence, by being provident both for itself and for others. Wherefore it has a share of the Eternal Reason whereby it has a natural inclination to its proper act and end: and this participation of the eternal law in the rational creature is called the natural law (Aquinas 1996, 15).

---

12 For example, Nardin dismisses treaties as genuine international law (1983, 124) – or at least argues that treaties do not make law – as they do not fit with his theoretical model. Again, on p. 171: "The international legal system is ultimately a system of customary law because the existence of international custom is logically prior to the particular rules created by treaty." This understanding, however compelling from a functional standpoint, seems to do injustice to what international lawyers actually do in their practices and how they conceive of law.

13 Here again Nardin's view seems to rely upon a statist conception of international relations (that is, that the agents whose answers are relevant in deciding why international law is valuable are states). This answer, although sound within the context of his own theory, seems to rely upon too many psychological assumptions about states (I will have more to say about this issue later).

14 For a short history of this tradition, see Verdross and Koeck (1983).

The dictates of right reason point the way to natural law and the law of nations, in turn, is derived from this natural law "as conclusions from premises" (Aquinas 1996, 84). The God-given ability of human reason to participate in eternal law, and from there to recognize natural laws, be they domestic or international, and thereby judge human laws is the cornerstone of Thomistic natural law.[15]

Grotius "secularizes" natural law doctrine, moving it from the realm of the expressly theological to a modern, secular context. While not wholly original in this claim, Grotius systematically argued for the rational, and not theological basis for a natural legal order.[16] After laying down his fundamental premises regarding natural law, he concludes, "what we have just said would have validity, even if we granted what cannot be granted without great wickedness, that there is no God, or that he has no care for human affairs" (Grotius 1949, 5). Thus, Grotius' arguments for the natural law of human sociality (a "care to preserve society") (Grotius 1949, 5) appeal to animal behavior, psychology, literary history, but not expressly to revelation. Shorn of its theological underpinnings, the model of natural law played a key role in the development of modern international law, by appeals to purposes and rules that rational inquiry discovers through the analysis of nature and history.[17]

Independent from this oft-cited tradition of Western legal thought, the claims of natural law can be viewed formally as a claim about the nature of law in relation to morality and other normative concepts (such as justice).[18] The most general claim is that there is a difference between what we may believe to be law, and what the law is in truth.[19] That natural lawyers make a distinction between our social practices of law and the real (natural) law then is the key assertion that distinguishes natural law from the non-reductive approach I outlined in the previous chapter. If one can really offer a plausible natural law theory, then we would have little reason to turn to the social practices of those "in the know" as definitive of international law. It is this formal dimension of natural law, the claim that there exists a two-tiered structure of "real law" and "apparent law", and its consequent challenge to the non-reductive approach that primarily interests me, and not any particular conception of or justification for this natural law.

For natural lawyers the extant practices are to a large degree irrelevant in deciding whether a rule is really to be regarded as law. A larger normative structure, be it religious, metaphysical or otherwise, defines genuine law, regardless of what practicing lawyers in a positivist mode may believe to be the case. The point is not that the dictates of morality are superior to the rules of law and thereby should trump

15 "Laws framed by man are either just or unjust. If they be just, they have power of binding in conscience, from the eternal law when they are derived…" (Aquinas 1996, 94).

16 I say "not wholly original" because some have maintained that this view is first found in Suarez. See Schneewind (1988), pp. 66–70.

17 For more see D'Entrèves (1970), pp. 53–7.

18 While natural law is frequently associated with Western history, there is no reason to believe that non-Western legal ideals such as the Muslim law of Shariah are not forms of natural law.

19 As John Finnis puts it: "A theory of natural law claims to be able to identify conditions and principles of practical right-mindedness, of good and proper order among men and in individual conduct" (Finnis 1980, 18).

legal concerns when the two conflict, but rather that norms of justice, discovered by reason, *define* the true essence of law. One may say perhaps that the claims of natural law theory are ontological (dealing with the nature of the law) and not simply normative, or that natural law argues for the inseparability of these two categories. Thus, the project of defining international law (and law in general, for that matter) stands on entirely different footing than does the non-reductionist approach advocated here.

The natural law approach to defining law rests in turn upon what we might call a "moral metaphysics," a way of situating our conception of justice within a broader philosophical framework such as God, nature, or human reason. Most often, natural lawyers follow Grotius, pointing to larger purposes found in nature, and maintain that real human laws must fit within the broader order of nature to truly deserve the title "law." Thus Aquinas puts human laws within a hierarchy of laws, the sum total of which emanate from God, and Grotius points to the natural ordering of the world. Each has a larger whole that provides the context of natural law and any laws passed by humans that conflict with this whole are mere pseudo law. Regardless of where a particular legal theorist derives her normative structure, for purposes of justification (explaining why X is a legitimate law), the laws remain wholly independent of present understandings and justification mechanisms of positive law.[20]

To support their view, natural lawyers frequently cite cases where legal practices are so divorced from what would commonly be morally acceptable that one bristles at the claim that such practices deserve to be described as legal.[21] Famous cases, such as the trials of war criminals in Nuremberg and Tokyo after World War II, have invoked principles of a higher law to prosecute war criminals whose evils might have gone unpunished in a positivist legal system. In his famous defense of natural law in the context of the segregated South, Martin Luther King Jr reminds the reader that, "everything Hitler did in Germany was 'legal' and everything the Hungarian freedom fighters did in Hungary was 'illegal'" (King 2000). The appeal of a natural law approach is precisely this inflexibility in highly esteemed concepts such as "right" and "justice" and our view that somehow these concepts trump the corrupt practices of particular governments. The moral metaphysics outlined above provides a bedrock of sorts, preventing the rule of law from sinking to depths that would shock the moral conscience.

Given the metaphysical backdrop to their theories, natural lawyers also initially seem to have a theoretical edge over other approaches to international law when dealing with the problems of political and cultural difference endemic to international law. If the natural lawyer can outline correct metaphysical principles, by their very nature these principles would transcend political borders (after all, there is only one metaphysical reality), and if our legal principles are based upon this metaphysics, then it follows that these real laws always transcend domestic politics

20 This is not to say that positive law must be wholly distinct from natural law, but the reason why a rule is valid law has nothing to do with conventionally positivist forms of justification (that is, that it was passed by this or that legislative body), but rather with the overarching moral metaphysics.

21 See Hart (1958), along with Fuller (1995).

and the plurality of culturally-bound conceptions of the good.[22] On this account, Aquinas can announce with confidence that since there is only one reason there is only one natural law that "is common to all nations" (Aquinas 1996, 64). Similarly, natural laws oblige all rational persons independent of their cultural background and political affiliation. Just as a moral metaphysics trumps the laws of a corrupt political institution, they also trump appeals to cultural difference that the relativist (from Chapter 1) might use to reject international law, at least when viewed from a purely logical standpoint.

Over the centuries there have been numerous cogent objections to natural law, and I have few original ones to offer here. However, I would like to suggest that some of the problems endemic to natural law approaches in general become particularly acute when we examine such theories at the level of global legal relations. Specifically, some of the pragmatic and epistemological concerns that arise from a conception of law rooted in a moral *weltanschauung*, problems that pose difficulties for natural lawyers in any context, undermine its appeal as an approach to international law. Thus, my brief criticisms of natural law approaches to international legal theory primarily highlight the weaknesses of natural law when contrasted to the approach offered in this work.

Natural law approaches to international law gain a very strong normative basis for their conception of law at the expense of the utility of such theories in comprehending existing practices. If we define international law through recourse to a moral metaphysics, we *may* be able to give compelling accounts of why norms *ought* to be applied to a set of agents and transactions, but this may (and often does) bear little resemblance to the actual practices. There is no direct, theoretical link standing between international law as it is practiced by those in the know and natural law as expounded by the philosophers and theologians who formulate it. Theoretically, this may be an acceptable consequence, but nonetheless seriously weakens the relevance of natural law for understanding the modern legal world to a degree that I expect most natural lawyers would find unsatisfactory. This is what Koskenniemi means when he refers to the "ethical dimension" of international legal theory and its pernicious "utopianism" (Koskenniemi 2005, 46–8). Grotius surely recognized this, and in response claimed that the proof of a law of nations is found in customary international law as it actually takes place, and not solely through the reasoning of philosophers.[23] But this connection is tenuous at best. A normative system of rules gains much of its appeal precisely because it seems superior to the messy facts of the real world, but this also means that the connection between these rules and existing practices must remain weak.

However, if natural lawyers wish to step outside of a purely prescriptive approach and in turn have something to say about existing legal relations, a host of problems

22 It has been pointed out that this works both "horizontally" (that natural law applies cross-culturally) as well as vertically (that natural law applies to all rational beings within each culture – independent of their status within that culture). See Friedman (1998).

23 "The proof for the law of nations is similar to that for unwritten municipal law, it is found in unbroken custom and the testimony of those who are skilled in it" (Grotius 1962, 44).

arise. Boyle has pointed out that there is an unwarranted circularity embedded in natural law approaches to international law once they involve themselves in an empirical exercise. He points out that in order to achieve such a goal, natural lawyers must vacillate between law as it is practiced and law as it ought to be practiced, claiming to have something substantial to say regarding both.

> [T]he natural lawyer must walk a narrow line between saying that this normative deep-structure is already clearly evidenced by the actions of states (and thus implying that whatever states do is legal) and saying that deep-structure is *not* evidenced by what states do (and thus implying that it is hopelessly irrelevant) (Boyle 1990, 337).

While Boyle's stark contrast between emptiness and irrelevance is too extreme (for it is certainly possible to believe that whatever most states do *most*, but not all, of the time is legal), he does have a valid criticism regarding the empirical utility of natural law theory, if not its theoretical cogency. Either the natural lawyer must cut herself off from any relationship to actual legal practices and stick to international law as it ought to be ideally, or she must claim that within the domain of empirical law itself there is a rational moral structure at the core of political relations – a suspicious claim. Additionally, this empirically discoverable rationality would have to be developed through an analysis of extant law in itself, an approach that would seem much more like positivism than natural law. Thus while natural law is a tempting fall-back position for a definition of international law, it runs the risk of abstracting so far from actual legal practices that it loses much of its power and is ill suited as the foundation for an analysis of international law.

Problems of cultural difference also make life difficult for natural lawyers at the international level. While the inability for natural lawyers to give any robust account of the rules of natural law that is accepted beyond the small circle of natural lawyers themselves is a minor difficulty in discussions of domestic law, the problem becomes particularly acute when we step into the global arena. The wide variety of traditions, faiths, and metaphysical beliefs throughout the world would make the development of the universal moral metaphysics that natural law requires a difficult, if not impossible project. The deep pluralism of values makes the consensus that international legal norms require to be effective (for after all, a natural law must be recognized by all rational creatures according to Thomas' definition) all but impossible when one steps outside of the Western tradition and into the global legal setting. Even if a theoretically cogent argument could be made for a natural law approach to defining international law, there nonetheless remains the difficult (and perhaps impossible) task of developing a set of principles upon which lawyers and diplomats from vastly different backgrounds could agree.

Finally, legal concepts from a non-naturalist tradition may serve a vast number of the functions for which natural law gets credit. Concepts such as *jus cogens*, peremptory legal norms that may not be obviated by states, regardless of their desire to do so, function in a manner similar to natural law but without any of its metaphysical baggage.[24] Like natural law, *jus cogens* rules certainly trump extant

24 According to Janis, *jus cogens* is "rather close" to natural law but is nonetheless distinct from it and elsewhere as "a modern form of natural law." While he is not specific regarding the

legal practices, but it does not entail that one step outside of a traditional conception of law in order to demonstrate the existence and validity of such norms.[25] Similarly, the general principles of civilized nations, cited by the International Court of Justice as a legitimate source of international law, and discussed in the previous chapter, can fill a number of roles that natural lawyers sought in invoking reason and a divinely ordered world. Even the advantages that natural law is believed to provide can be satisfied without appeal to the dubious metaphysics underlying natural law, and more importantly, with few of its practical impediments.

Thus it seems that a natural law approach to international law suffers from a number of different practical, if not theoretical faults. Pragmatically speaking, it is difficult to see the utility of a legal system that does not connect directly with the extant practices of the international law community. Moreover it is hard to imagine a set of moral principles upon which members of all cultures on the planet could agree. Finally, concepts from a more positivistic conception of international law, such as *jus cogens*, can serve the same functions without the need to appeal to a larger moral metaphysics. While these arguments will surely not convince a devout natural lawyer, they certainly make appeals to natural law as definitive of international law unnecessary.

Yet despite these criticisms, it is certainly possible to conceive of a positive role for natural law to play. If we don't look at natural law as an attempt to grasp law as such, but instead as part of an ongoing debate about the rules and aims of a just world order, it is very valuable. Natural law may not explain what rules there are in international law, but instead help those "in the know" to understand what rules need to be changed and what the new rules ought to look like. Finnis, in his own attempt develop a natural law approach, has nicely articulated this role:

> A theory of natural law need not be undertaken primarily for the purpose of thus providing a justified conceptual framework for descriptive social science. It may be undertaken, as this book is, primarily to assist the practical reflections of those concerned to act, whether as judges or as statesmen or as citizens (Finnis 1980, 18).

The point here is that natural law can be used to evaluate existing law in relation to larger moral ends to which we hope these laws will aim, as well as to articulate what these moral ends are themselves. Just as the functional approaches discussed above can help develop strategies to strengthen the role international law plays in global politics, natural law approaches can help to articulate the just world order towards which many international lawyers strive. Neither of these approaches is without merit, but neither of them can be justly viewed as providing the best theoretical foundation for the analysis of international law as such.

---

differences between these two genres of law, one key difference may be their philosophical foundations. Natural law rests upon a conception of reason and a moral metaphysics, while *jus cogens* avoids such claims (see Janis 1993a, 62–6).

25 Here I am interpreting the term "positivism" as somewhat more rich than it is usually taken to be when it is construed to refer solely to the rules to which states consent. For a discussion of the various forms of positivism in international legal theory see Nardin (1998).

Towards Jurisprudence

The point of this chapter and its predecessor has been to argue that the rules of the practice of international law lend themselves to a non-reductive view. This is to say that the best way to understand the nature of international law is to turn to the understandings of those "in the know", those authorities considered competent to understand it, rather than to some artificially constructed theory of international law. In addition, we have circumscribed the philosophical method underlying this approach, articulated its primary assumptions, and defended it against some of its major competitors. Thus we have carried out some of the philosophical "spade work" and constructed a foundation from which we may continue to build. Now that we know what our foundation looks like, what international law consists in, we can proceed to construct the edifice itself, the specific rules of international law. This entails developing the non-reductive analysis of international law as a jurisprudence, discussing how this approach would understand important issues within international law itself. The beginnings of such a construction are the themes of the next two chapters.

As said in the previous chapter, the non-reductive definition of international law will only be vindicated when its full scope and implications have been articulated. Now this model of international law will finally be put to the test, and in the next two chapters, the analysis will shift to the level of what may be considered jurisprudence proper: the study of what international law says on particular topics. While I will (obviously) not be unable to use this model to develop a complete jurisprudence of international law (this will not be a textbook), I will seek to outline what international law has to say on a few crucial issues within international law. In the next chapter, I will apply the non-reductive approach to the analysis of legal personality in international law. After this I will turn to the problem of state sovereignty in the context of humanitarian intervention. Finally, having briefly outlined international legal doctrine on these two important issues, I will return to a more theoretical plane in many of the remaining chapters to address the issue of the "reality" of international law.

Chapter 4

International Legal Personality

This chapter moves away from the theory *of* international law and into a more substantial analysis of the rules *within* the law by asking the following series of connected questions: "Who makes international law?"; "If international law obliges anyone, who does it oblige?"; and finally, "Who has international legal rights and the ability to bring grievances before international legal bodies?" These questions traditionally fall under the heading "international legal personality" and the answers to them will rely upon the non-reductionist definition of international law I have already sketched out. It is here, then, in the context of a theory of international legal personality, that the foregoing analysis is put to the test and its results evaluated.

In this chapter, I will show that both philosophical and legal scrutiny undermine the assumptions embedded in the sovereignty thesis discussed in the previous chapter. There, the sovereignty thesis was understood and criticized largely as a definition of international law (that is, that the sovereign state marked the line between genuine international laws and other kinds of rules), whereas in this chapter I will interpret it in terms of the problem of personality (the delineation of the agents of international law). Here, too, I will charge that it is inadequate. Put more precisely, the view that the only international legal actors are sovereign political bodies while other types of corporate entities *and* (biological) individuals have only a derivative status, will be found wanting on several accounts.[1]

To say that this approach will undermine the sovereignty thesis of international law is not to say that sovereignty does not exist as a part of international law. Rather, the issue is the nature of sovereignty and its role in the field of legal personality. Returning to the meta-language/object language distinction as it was developed in the previous chapter, we can see that the sovereignty thesis as a *meta-theory* of international law would entail significant consequences for our traditional thinking about international legal personality doctrine. If one believes that international law is a creation of sovereign states, then it follows that the sovereign state would have a central role to play in the doctrinal construction of international legal personality. The personality of the state would presumably be preeminent and unquestioned and all other entities in international law would gain their personality in a derivative

1 For an illuminating discussion of the history of sovereignty-based approaches to international law see Okeke 1974, 9–19. While some thinkers (for example, Brierly) that define international law as the creation of states do not hold such a narrow conception of international legal personality, it seems to me to be difficult to consistently view international law as the creation of states and at the same time maintain that other entities have an independent legal existence. My reasons for this should become clear as this analysis of legal personality unfolds.

fashion: they have personality insofar as it is granted to them by sovereign states and without this there is no legal personality for such entities. Moreover, in many, if not most contexts, non-state actors would have no personality whatsoever.

As was mentioned in the previous chapter Oppenheim laid the modern foundation for such a conception of international legal personality. According to him, while it is clear that states are the central legal persons, the *dramatis personae* to use Cassese's term (Cassese 2001, 46), the relation of states to the rest of the international legal order isn't completely clear.

In lieu of this traditional conception of legal personality, I will argue for an analysis where states are but one type of legal actor among many, each with its own respective personality. Other types of agents, including the UN, other intergovernmental organizations (such as the International Labor Organization), quasi-states (Liechtenstein, The Holy See), regional groups (such as the European Union), as well as individuals (you and I), are not only passive objects of law, but also active subjects, participating with greater or lesser degrees of independence within, as well as having greater or lesser degrees of impact upon, the international legal community. In addition, I will argue, there is no reason to believe that in the future there will not be different kinds of agents, with completely new forms of legal personality. While each of these different agents has (and will have) a different form of personality with different ramifications for the international legal order, these non-state international political agents play a genuine role in international law nonetheless.

Terminology

In order to avoid any unnecessary confusion, it is worthwhile briefly clarifying some of the relevant terms before proceeding. Like so many other aspects of international legal theory, the language surrounding legal personality is rife with ambiguities that can undermine a careful discussion of the issues. This problem is only compounded for this study in that a number of these legal terms have meanings that differ dramatically from their equivalent words in other disciplines. Thus, it is important to carefully distinguish and clearly explain the various relevant concepts we will use before continuing. While this terminological map may only fit awkwardly onto some existing uses for the same terms (in both law and philosophy) it will nonetheless be useful to clear the ground before proceeding further.

Entity – An entity is any physical thing, whether animal, vegetable, or mineral.

Agency – I will use the terms "agency" and "agent" in a non-legal sense, to refer simply to those whose entities possess the capacity to act. This is the conception of "agent" as understood by most mainstream ethical philosophers. This capacity to act consists in the possession of beliefs, desires, intentions, as well as the capacity to carry them out with some degree of rationality (here, simply meaning that their chosen means are likely to achieve their goal).[2] Later, I will claim that agents are

2 See Fotion (1968, 17–18).

beings whose actions can be understood using certain explanatory criteria (which make up what I will later – in Chapter 6 – refer to as "rationalizing explanations"). For now at least, we need not concern ourselves with who is an agent, whether individuals, animals, machines, Martians, states, or international bodies are rightly so considered, and what the ascription of agency could mean in the broader scheme of things (however, I take the individual, sane, adult human to be the paradigm for agency). In addition, at this point we should not concern ourselves with the question of whether all agents possess legal personality or if all legal personalities are best understood as agents. This issue will be discussed later in this chapter.

Physical Persons – These are physical, biological agents, human beings who are still alive (in addition, when I use the term "person" without the prefix "legal", then I am referring to physical persons).

Legal Objects – A legal object possesses no recognized legal personality by itself, regardless of whether or not it is an agent. An object cannot bring cases before a court, it cannot enter into treaties with others, nor can an object establish any legal precedent. They may have certain rights, but they cannot assert them in a legal forum. An object may be an agent, but a piece of property may also be an object (from a legal standpoint, there is no difference between them when they are both considered as objects). Thus, objects of law are effectively inert: they cannot make law *per se*, they are not accountable for their violations of international law, nor can they bring complaints before legal bodies. Individuals in the context of the International Court of Justice (ICJ) are clearly examples of legal objects as they have no standing before this court.

Legal Personality/Legal Personhood – This is the broadest of all the specifically legal concepts I will discuss in this chapter. It is intended as a broad "umbrella concept" under which different kinds of agents can be analyzed and discriminated (provided that they are not legal objects, and thus possessing no legal personality). A very simple and useful definition of legal personality in general comes from Judge Giuseppe Marchegiano:

> We may consider as "international persons" all those entities whose juridical situation is governed, whose rights and obligations are determined, and whose competency is extended or restricted by public international law… [I]nternational personality exists in every association or collective entity clothed with recognized international competency[3] (Marchegiano, in Bederman 1996, 337).

This is clearly not a complete definition and bears the mark of circularity. Any further substance we give to the concept of legal personality will stem from the further legal and philosophical distinctions developed below.

---

3 "'[P]ersonality' as a term is only short-hand for the proposition that an entity is endowed by international law with legal capacity. But entity A may have the capacity to perform acts X and Y, but not act Z, entity B to perform acts Y and Z but not act X, and entity C to perform all three" (O'Connell 1982, 82).

We can break down our taxonomy of international legal personality in the following manner:

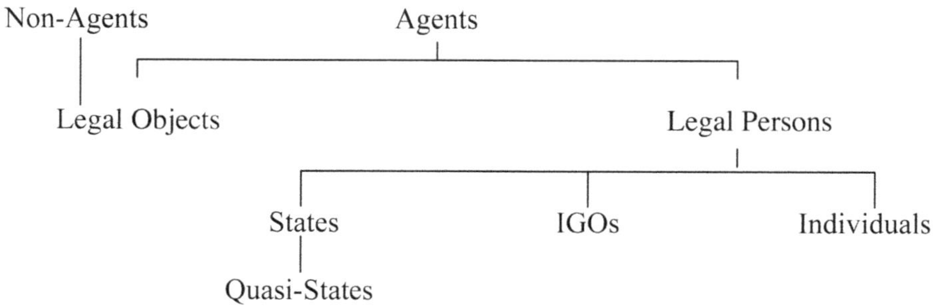

Figure 4.1 The structure of international legal personality

Legal Subjects – A legal subject is an entity that has a legal personality of some sort. The two terms are effectively interchangeable (Malanczuk 1997, 91). As Brownlie (2003, 57) puts it: "A subject of law is an entity capable of possessing international rights and duties and having the capacity to maintain its rights by bringing international claims."

International Legal Personality

The notion of legal personality, and the privileges and duties that arise out of it, is complex and multifaceted. However, there are three primary dimensions of legal personality, three results that stem from an agent occupying the juridical position described by Judge Marchegiano: *legislation*, *standing*, and *obligation*. I will discuss each in turn.

Legislation – The first dimension of legal personality is the capacity to make rules of law via an array of legislative tools (treaties, custom, declarations, and so on). Subjects in this sense are endowed with the capacity to play a role in the international legislative process.

Standing – This second dimension of international legal personality refers to the capacity of legal persons to seek remedies before judicial bodies or arbitrational tribunals. International legal persons are not mute when they perceive themselves as harmed, and may use the rules (that they often played a role in fashioning) to seek redress. The standing of a particular agent may differ from context to context, of course. Individuals may bring cases before the European Court of Human Rights, for example, but not before the International Court of Justice. In addition, some legal persons may have the capacity to seek redress without the capacity to make law, and *vice versa*.

Obligation – The final dimension of legal personality is closely related to standing and is its passive correlate. Only a legal person can be a defendant in a legal action.

If an agent has no obligations (such as a physical person in the context of the ICJ) she may not herself be the subject of complaints, but another legal person must stand in her place (usually her home state, but perhaps the international organization of which she is a member).

In addition to these three primary elements of legal personality, there are a large number of subsidiary aspects, such as the ability of a state to give its citizens diplomatic privileges, its right to issue passports, and the right to have ships fly under a national flag, and so on. Although the importance of such secondary attributes of international legal personality should not be underestimated in analyzing international law and the political context in which it functions, they are not essential to our discussion here.

We should also note that these three dimensions of international legal personality work in two directions. On one hand, they are the effects of possessing this personality. That is, they result from being considered a legal person by the international diplomatic and legal community. On the other hand, they are also indicative of an agent's possessing personality when this may be in dispute. An agent that is seeking to make a case for its legal personality can point to its having standing in certain contexts, its activities being cited as indicative of law, and (perhaps strangely) its being a defendant in a legal situation as proof of its possessing personality.[4] Thus an agent whose legal personality is questioned gains something fairly substantial from being sued by another legal person, their legal personality has been affirmed.[5] That is, these dimensions of international legal personality are as much *performative* as they are *constative*. They imbue an agent with legal personality as much as they are a product of possessing this personality (Austin, 1962).

The State

The most obvious international legal subject is the traditional state. This creature has existed in its modern form since at least the Peace of Westphalia, signed by the dominant European powers in 1648, and has held hegemony over conceptions of global politics ever since.[6] The rise of the state as a modern political reality in turn dramatically changed the landscape of international law and international legal personality to the extent that many scholars argue that the existence of a system of sovereign states is the necessary and sufficient condition for the existence of international law. After Westphalia, so the story goes, the political reality of the

---

4 Although this last issue is debatable. The United States' State Department has special requirements that a plaintiff must fulfill in order to sue an unrecognized government in federal court, for example.

5 Thus Israel, when sued by the UN in the *Reparations* case, had mixed feelings. On the one hand it was the object of a lawsuit, but on the other the suit itself validated the existence of the Jewish state at a point where this was questioned by many in the international community.

6 Although for a critical reading of this traditional reading see Kennedy (1988, 14). Although there is good reason to believe that a "state system" existed in other times and in other places. See Bederman (2001a, 16–21).

sovereign state became a logical necessity for the existence of international law, that is, international law became defined by figures such as Austin and Bentham as the legal rules guiding the relation between autonomous states (and any other paradigm for international law, such as natural law, was thereby rendered obsolete). Thus, the political reality of the state changed the legal realities that developed from it and thereby the nature and structure of international legal rules.[7]

While we have dealt with the issue of state sovereignty to a certain extent in the preceding chapters, the analysis here will simply seek to understand how the sovereign state fits into a broader theory of international legal personality (assuming that I have already dealt with these stronger conceptions of the role of the state in the previous chapters). None of these previous discussions ought to be seen as somehow arguing that states are irrelevant to international law. On the contrary, they are extremely important for understanding the modern international legal system. However, their role is not fundamental or axiomatic in the sense understood by sovereignty theorists like Austin and Bentham. But, even if we reject the sovereign state as the foundation of international law, it is clear that the international legal personality of states stands as the cornerstone of any discussion of modern international legal personality, so it is only natural that we begin our discussion here.

For the vast majority of states, their status within the three dimensions of personality described above is clearly delineated under modern international law. Their privileges and capacities as legal persons can be summarized by the notion of *sovereignty* (Brownlie 2003, 287; Krasner 1999, 14–20). All states (especially those who have signed the Charter for the UN) have a high legislative capacity (at least insofar as they can create laws that bind themselves and that their actions may be seen as indicative of the existence of customary international law),[8] an almost unquestioned standing before international courts, and they may be sued in almost any international legal forum. Whether there is a *de facto* equality of states in the international political realm (in terms of their respective economic and military power), in virtually all areas of international law, sovereign states are juridical equals (Brierly 1963, 37–40). Bolivia's standing before international legal bodies is the same as that of the People's Republic of China, the United States is the legal equal of Zimbabwe. Thus, for our purposes (of providing a simplified schema in which to understand international legal personality), we can assume that all states possess roughly the same legal personality in terms of both quantity and quality.[9] This equality of the capacities inherent in legal personality is the full-blooded meaning of the common notion of the "sovereign equality of states."

7 Hedley Bull describes a system of states: "a group of states, conscious of certain common interests and common values, form a society in the sense that they conceive themselves to be bound by a common set of rules in their relations to one another, and share in the working of common institutions" (cited in Bederman 2001a, 16–17).

8 See Article 38 of the Statute of the International Court of Justice.

9 Anthony Arend has shown that in customary international law, this is frequently not the case as larger and more powerful nations have stronger legislative capacities than other states, but I leave this issue aside for now. See Arend (1999, 87–103).

The modern sources consulted by international lawyers to determine whether a state actually exists are primarily the Montevideo Convention on Rights and Duties of States, written in 1933, and the Charter of the United Nations of 1945 (Brownlie 2003, 70). The former is particularly valuable because it specifically elaborates upon the notion of statehood in international law and lists three specific criteria that give a state international legal personality:

> The state as a person of international law should possess the following qualifications: (a) a permanent population; (b) government; and (c) capacity to enter into relations with other states.

These "Montevideo requirements" have been used both by the ICJ and its pre-UN incarnation, the Permanent Court of International Justice, to determine when, and to what extent, a political body may be granted international legal personality. For example, the free city of Danzig was denied international legal personality (specifically, the ability to independently join the International Labor Organization) in 1930 as a result of its special relationship with Poland.[10]

In addition to Montevideo, Articles 3–6 of the UN Charter lays out several explicit and widely accepted criteria for determining the existence of a state. While these requirements are more political than those in the Montevideo Convention (insofar as the UN is first and foremost a political body and only secondarily a legal one), their general acceptance makes them valuable for understanding the sources of the international legal personality of states.[11] Aside from the founding states (mentioned in Article 3),

> Membership in the United Nations is open to all other peace-loving states which accept the obligations contained in the present Charter and, in the judgment of the Organization, are able and willing to carry out these obligations.

In addition to these normative requirements – normative in the sense that they set out the criteria prescribed by the UN – stand several sometimes difficult procedural hoops that an aspiring state must jump through in order to become a full-fledged member of the UN: permission from the Security Council and a vote in the General Assembly.

The recognition of other states, sometimes through the UN, sometimes independent of it, plays a central role in the attribution of legal personality to would-be states. Scholars have debated for years over whether recognition is constitutive of statehood or whether *de facto* sovereignty is sufficient for jurists to declare statehood. While not wishing to delve too deeply into the hoary distinction between "constitutive" and "declaratory" theories of statehood, we should perhaps note that recognition is not entirely necessary for a political agent to create international law and be bound by international legal norms.[12] To cite Henkin:

---

10 *The Free City of Danzig and the International Labor Organization*, PCIJ, Advisory Opinion No. 18, August 26, 1930.

11 However, statehood may perhaps be distinguished from legal personality.

12 I here refer to them as agents in order to distinguish them from full-fledged states, for whom international recognition is not a problem.

> It is clear that an entity that meets the conditions of statehood cannot, because of the lack of recognition, be denied its rights or escape its obligations. "Its territory cannot be considered to be no-man's-land; there is no right to overfly without permission; ships flying its flag cannot be considered stateless, and so on." Nor can such a non-recognized entity evade the duties of states under international law (in fact, non-recognized states are often charged with violations of international law and are the object of international claims by the very states refusing recognition) (Henkin et al. 1993, 245).[13]

Thus, while we should not dismiss the importance of recognition to the establishment of international legal personality, its formalities should be placed in the context of real-world diplomatic and legal practice. Although there would certainly be dramatic consequences to a widespread and deeply entrenched denial of recognition (we may suspect that the capacities of legislation, standing, and obligation will be significantly weaker for states that lack a universal recognition perhaps to the point where the state could no longer properly function), this does not affect the capacities afforded to states as international legal persons to any great degree.[14]

Article 3 of the Montevideo Convention furthers this realist claim that *de facto* sovereignty contributes a great deal (although admittedly not everything) to the *de jure* attribution of international legal personality to states. Here the document explicitly separates diplomatic recognition from "the political existence of the state." Under this notion of existence are several features that we would recognize as elements of legal personality as set out at the opening of this chapter. To cite the text of the Convention:

> The political existence of the state is independent of recognition by the other states. Even before recognition the state has the right to defend its integrity and independence, to provide for its conservation and prosperity, and consequently to organize itself as it sees fit, to legislate upon its interests, administer its services, and to define jurisdiction and competence of its courts.

The process of recognition is a notoriously prickly and politicized affair, one where certain states withhold recognition from what are obviously genuine states for a number of reasons. Even when its existence is assured, the determination of the representative government is equally problematic.[15] Therefore, states that go unrecognized by others are still able to claim some measure of personality, if for no other reason than the obviously troublesome consequences of denying recognition to a state whose power has been established.

---

13 Internal citation is from Mugerwa (1968, 269).

14 See the Arbitrational Opinion of William Howard Taft regarding British claims against the government of Costa Rica for acts of the previous, unrecognized Tinoco regime. "When recognition *vel non* of a government is by such nations determined by inquiry, not into its *de facto* sovereignty and complete governmental control, but into its illegitimacy or irregularity of origin, their non-recognition loses something of evidential weight on the issue with which those applying the rules of international law are alone concerned."

15 The United States refused to recognize the People's Republic of China as the legitimate government of China for over two decades after it attained *de facto* control of the Chinese state.

Whether a state has international legal personality can best be seen as a combination of the Montevideo requirements (many of which comprise *de facto* personality), membership in the UN, and the recognition of other states. This can be a long and delicate political and diplomatic affair, but once complete, the agent becomes a state, one among equals, juridically speaking and may begin to assume all of the functions that any other state may fulfill in the international arena. They may negotiate treaties, create custom, haul others before international tribunals, and be brought before the same. While its government may change, the state itself will continue to exist as an autonomous legal person.

A new trend in recent years for determining whether a state exists and is a recognized legal person in the international community is its adherence to international human rights norms. Governments with a political status that meet the formal criteria set out by the Montevideo Convention and the UN Charter, but routinely violate the rights of their citizens have met stiff resistance, largely from Western governments, in their requests for full international personality. This has led some scholars to describe a set of states, states that meet the Montevideo requirements but do not represent their people, as not truly legitimate (Roth 1999). While one cannot easily state that human rights standards are a necessary condition for the attribution of legal personality to states, one could perhaps make a clear case for optimism that the future trajectory of the law of international legal personality points in that direction. Again, keeping in mind the limitations of the notion of recognition in granting states legal personality, the question of whether states must respect human rights in order to be legal persons is, strictly speaking, unnecessary for our analysis.

Parasitic on the international legal personality of states is the personality belonging to quasi-states. These problem cases are agents that appear to share many common features with established states but are not the masters of their own house, so to speak. Sometimes, as in the case of the free city of Danzig prior to World War II, they are special protectorates set up to serve a particular function for nearby communities. Other times (such as in the cases of the Western Sahara and Liechtenstein) they are political agents that, for whatever reason, are unable to be complete members of the international community. Still others (such as Taiwan) are in such volatile circumstances that the political consequences of giving them statehood could be disastrous. These agents usually do not meet all of the Montevideo requirements and their legal personality, while not completely nonexistent, is thereby notably diminished in important ways.

The Holy See is perhaps the most well known of these quasi-states, and the limits of its legal personality highlight some of the relevant features of this concept for quasi-states (Aufricht 1943, 220; Brownlie 2003, 63). In the Lateran treaty and Concordat of 1929, Italy recognized the rights of the Holy See as a sovereign international person. Although clearly not a state (and not an international organization), the Vatican has entered into numerous treaties, such as telecommunications treaties and multinational conventions, some of which are open only to states.[16] Similarly, it has become a full member of agencies of the UN, such as UNESCO, the WHO, and the ILO. However, its status in the UN is only that of "Permanent Observer" and not

16 See Fitzmaurice (1956).

that of a full member of the General Assembly, a position that would be available to any full-blooded state. While the Church itself claims that its legal personality does not stem from its possession of territory (Vatican City, inside Rome) but rather from its spiritual position, international law scholars have largely kept the spiritual and secular personalities of the Holy See distinct.[17]

Intergovernmental Organizations

Perhaps the most interesting place to study non-state agents as subjects of international law is to look at the status of intergovernmental organizations (IGOs) as legal persons. In this case, there is neither the political obviousness of the legal personality that is afforded the nation state (that is, nobody seriously doubts that states are international legal persons), nor the metaphysical obviousness that underlies the status of the human being (that is, it is clear that human beings are agents and should have *some* kind of legal status). However, despite these apparent weaknesses (and perhaps, to some extent, because of them), there is a well-articulated international legal jurisprudence regarding these agents. The legal status of IGOs along the three axes described above is clear at least in its outline. Further, this doctrine is accepted by most, if not all, practicing international lawyers, thereby qualifying it as genuine law according to the non-reductionist definition described in Chapter 2.

IGOs are agents that come into existence through treaties negotiated between states. While they may physically be located in one particular country (and thus subject to its domestic legal jurisdiction on a number of matters – such as criminal behavior committed on the organization's grounds or contracts made with local businesses) they are not, strictly speaking, under the legal control of these states. They should not be confused, however, with Nongovernmental Organizations (NGOs) as international agents that do not owe their political allegiance to a particular state such as Amnesty International and Human Rights Watch, but that are created through the activities of individuals. States have found intergovernmental organizations useful to handle problems that are of common concern for a group of states. They have proven quite effective, and their number has dramatically expanded over the last half-century, largely under the patronage of the UN.

Intergovernmental organizations are genetically beholden to the states that are party to its charter, and to this extent are derivative personalities, and thus not truly legal subjects at all. This means that, unlike states, they are not *sui generis*. They did not rise out of the primordial ooze of power politics and ethnic identity in the domestic sphere, autonomously asserting their presence in the global order. States come and go largely based upon their internal dynamics (excluding the now rare cases of conquest or dissolution), and do not lose their personality as a result of the acts of their political peers. This is different for dependent agents like intergovernmental organizations, who are born from the womb of the political and legal relations of states who freely choose to constitute the organization as a political agent. In some ways, this has given intergovernmental organizations a tenuous existence: should the

17 See Okeke (1974).

states that are part of a treaty abandon their agreement, the organization would cease to exist as a legal person.[18]

In theory then, this would make the outlook for intergovernmental organizations seem rather grim. However, in actual legal practice the status of these agents as international legal persons becomes significantly more complex and dynamic than their derivative origins would make it seem. As Cassese has argued, intergovernmental organizations have a foot in each of two different aspects of international law:

> First of all, a distinction should be drawn between the rights conferred and the duties springing directly from the instituting *treaty*, and those deriving from general international law. The former are normally provided for in the "constitution" of the Organization. Of course, they give the institution a status in relation to member States only…
>
> As to *general* rules, the international practice which evolved after the Second World War shows that at least a handful of international rules do confer rights on Organizations in relation to non-member States on condition that the former are sufficiently autonomous from the latter and have a structure enabling them to act in the international field (Cassese, 1986, 86).

Cassese's point here is that the standing of IGOs as legal persons is not *merely* dependent. The organization's charter is not only a contractual relation between states, but is also subject to broader principles of international law, principles that transform the legal status of this organization. They may, if conditions are right, claim a legal personality of their own that is independent of its charter.

There are several significant cases that address the status of IGOs as distinct legal persons illustrating Cassese's assertion that intergovernmental organizations can be independent entities. Among these, the *Reparation for Injuries Suffered in the Service of the United Nations*,[19] an Advisory Opinion of the ICJ, is by far the most well known. The assassination of a UN envoy (Count Folke Bernadotte) in Palestine opened up the question as to whether the organization could seek reparations from Israel for the death of their agent. The General Assembly of the UN posed the question to the court:

> In the event of an agent of the United Nations in the performance of his duties suffering injury in circumstances involving the responsibility of a State, has the United Nations, as an Organization, the capacity to bring an internal claim against the responsible *de jure* or *de facto* government with a view to obtaining the reparation due in respect of the damage caused (a) to the United Nations (b) to the victim or to persons entitled through him?

This opinion put the legal personality at the forefront of international law and the future of the UN hinged upon the Court's decision in many significant ways.

---

18 This is the unfortunate fate of the League of Nations, which was dissolved in 1946. As Bowett puts it: "Since the creation of this separate personality had been by the will of the member States, expressed in treaty form, it was obvious that those states could bring an end to the personality by a similar method" (Bowett 1963, 19).

19 1947 ICJ 173.

If the sovereignty model of international legal personality had been the most appropriate way to understand the law, the answer would have clearly been a "no" – the prerogatives of the sovereign state would not trump the derivative personality of IGOs. The only legal option available to the organization to seek remedy for the harm inflicted by the Zionists would be to seek reparation through the Count's home state of Sweden. This, in turn, would have dramatically undermined the ability of the UN to work independently of the wishes of its constituting states (and in areas openly hostile to its presence), making it a weak and wholly subordinate entity. The overarching issue of the *Reparations* decision, then, is whether intergovernmental organizations have any independent existence in international law, whether they have legal personality, or must they remain legal objects, functioning as a thin skin covering the real legal relations existing between states.

The court examined the UN's Charter and determined that in order to carry out its goals the organization required a good measure of legal personality. The Charter (and the charter members' lofty ambitions for the organization) would have been meaningless without the legal personality required to carry out its mandate.

> In the opinion of the Court, the Organization was intended to exercise and enjoy, and is in fact exercising and enjoying, functions and rights which can only be explained on the basis of the possession of a large measure of international personality and the capacity to operate upon an international plane. It is at present the supreme type of international organization, and it could not carry out the intentions of its founders if it was devoid of international personality. It must be acknowledged that its Members, by entrusting certain functions to it, with the attendant duties and responsibilities, have clothed it with the competence required to enable those functions to be effectively discharged. Accordingly, the Court has come to the conclusion that the Organization is an international person.[20]

While quickly thereafter asserting that while, "This is not the same thing as saying that it is a State", the court nonetheless concludes that the UN "is a subject of international law and capable of possessing international rights and duties, and that it has capacity to maintain its rights by bringing international claims." Here, the court concludes what had been a more or less developing doctrine for the preceding half-century, that international organizations have some form of genuine international legal personality.[21]

The opinion in *Reparations* is far reaching in its scope (Amerasinghe 2005, 86–92). The Court concludes that legal personality can be deduced from the function of an international entity and the requirements necessary for this agent for carrying out its assigned duties. Thus, giving the UN standing before courts is necessary for the Organization to carry out the duties mandated by the charter. This is what is sometimes referred to as the "implied powers" doctrine taken from American constitutional law (Arangio-Ruiz 1997), that is, the UN has powers that are not expressly stated in the Charter but are implied by the practical necessities of carrying out the purposes mandated by Articles 1 and 2 of the Charter:

---

20 At 179.

21 For a brief history of the development of the legal personality of intergovernmental organizations prior to the *Reparations* decision, see Bederman (1996).

> It must be added that the Organization is a political body, charged with political tasks of an important character, and covering a wide field, namely, the maintenance of international peace and security, the development of friendly relations among nations, and the achievement of international cooperation in the solution of problems of an economic, social, cultural or humanitarian character (Article 1); and in dealing with its Members it employs political means. The "Convention on the Privileges and Immunities of the United Nations" of 1946 creates rights and between each of the signatories and the Organization (see, in particular, Section 35). It is difficult to see how such a convention could operate except upon the international plane and as between parties possessing international personality.

While not a state, international law provides the UN with a number of the capacities normally given to states, in order to properly carry out its work.

Whereas this language is somewhat specific to the work of the UN, other parts of the opinion are formulated in much more general language (and set against the *locus classicus* of international legal personality, the state):

> Whereas a State possesses the totality of international rights and duties recognized by international law, the rights and duties of *an entity such as* the Organization must depend upon its purposes and functions as specified in its or implied in its constituent documents and developed in practice.[22]

While the UN is in many ways a unique intergovernmental organization, this uniqueness is not such that it requires that we treat its legal personality in a manner that is fundamentally different from other organizations. The fact that it is an intergovernmental body that serves as an umbrella for many other intergovernmental organizations and whose broad mandate is "to maintain peace and security" does not completely divorce it from other intergovernmental organizations with a more modest mandate. The UN is at bottom just one intergovernmental organization among many others.

Given *Reparations*, what does the personality that international law provides intergovernmental organizations look like, and how does it fit onto the legislation-standing-obligation schema outlined at the beginning of this chapter? Intergovernmental organizations can and do enter into treaties with states that in turn impose legal obligations upon both parties (Schneider 1963). The UN is at present party to numerous treaties and contracts with private industry. Similarly, other organizations such as the ILO work to form treaties that will be effective and enforceable. These treaties are legal by most standards of international law and have had some effect in legal disputes.

This fact entails that these international organizations have a legal personality that allows for at least some legislative capacity. This customary reality has in fact been formalized into a treaty. The Vienna Convention on Treaties Concluded Between States and International Organizations or between Two or More International Organizations states specifically that the treaty-making abilities of these bodies are "governed by the relevant rules of that organization."[23] The International Law

22 Emphasis added.

23 Article 6.

Commission, in commenting upon this treaty, has specifically argued that the treaty-making capacities of international organizations should be understood as limited by the powers given to the international body in its founding treaty.[24] Just as the UN's capacity to seek redress for its slain diplomat was given to it by the ICJ on the basis of the powers implied in the UN charter, the legislative capacity of other organizations, too, is charter (and context) dependent. While we will see shortly that the notion of "objective legal personality" has made this issue somewhat more complicated (and led some legal scholars to reinterpret the *Reparations* decision), it does not undermine the broader fact that most intergovernmental organizations have the capacity to legislate through their ability to formulate treaties.

The standing of intergovernmental organizations is an equally complex issue. The *Reparations* decision clearly asserts that the UN and similar organizations may seek remedies for damages done to it or its members, but *where* precisely it may seek these reparations is a tricky matter. While this organization has been a party to cases in other forums, it is restricted from access to the World Court. Article 34 of the ICJ is unambiguous: "Only states may be parties to cases before the court," denying this avenue to the UN. The only organizations with the capacity to ask the court for advisory opinions (according to the charter) are the UN General Assembly, and the Security Council. The Headquarters Agreement between the United States and the United Nations (allowing the UN to build its headquarters in New York City) provided for arbitration where disputes between the two persons develop. This said, the UN is greatly limited in its ability to seek redress in international courts. There is reason to be even less optimistic about other intergovernmental organizations with a less robust legal personality.

The responsibility of intergovernmental organizations is fairly well spelled out in international law. Since these organizations can be plaintiffs in international disagreements, it (logically, at least) entails that they can be defendants, a conclusion shared by most courts. They can be sued by others (including by individuals) in a variety of forums,[25] and it is interesting to note that the states that created the organization are frequently immune from responsibility for the behavior of the independent organization (and its "objective international personality").[26] In United States' law, members of the UN have special immunities that protect its employees and diplomatic personnel, but the organization itself may be sued in certain contractual cases. While the UN cannot be placed before the ICJ, it may be brought before arbitrational tribunals according to its Headquarters Agreement. For the majority of intergovernmental organizations then, their privileges and immunities are spelled out in their charter.

The question of legal personality for intergovernmental organizations is further complicated when we consider "organic" conceptions of legal personality. As the metaphor implies, organic approaches to legal personality assert that an organization's

24 Ibid., p. 358.

25 See Jenks (1962).

26 See *J.H. Rayner Ltd. v. Dep't of Trade and Industry* (1989) where various banks sued the International Tin Council, and the states that created the ITC, before the British Law Lords.

personality is independent of the constitutive treaty. Specifically, in the *Reparations* case, the court argued that the practices of the General Assembly, the Security Council, and the Secretariat are distinct from the acts of the members.

> Practice – in particular the conclusion of conventions to which the Organization is a party – has confirmed the character of the Organization, which occupies a position in certain respects in detachment from its Members, and which is under a duty to remind them, if need be, of certain obligations.

The point here is that the existence of the UN is not reducible to the will of its individual members, but possesses its own, corporate identity as a necessary (albeit implied) condition for carrying out its mandate. There is an ontological separation between (A) "the organization as an embodiment of the agreements of sovereign states" and (B) "the organization as an actor on the international legal scene." (A) is a *functional* legal person while (B) is an organic person.

In 1949, at the time of the *Reparations* decision, the state of Israel was not a member of the UN, and thus the court was required to consider "whether the Organization has 'the capacity to bring an international claim against the responsible *de jure* or *de facto* government…' when the defendant State is not a member of the Organization."[27] The question dealt with whether its personality is merely real for those who have accepted the UN Charter or extends to all states, UN member or otherwise. This additional question changes the quality of the legal personality given the UN, insofar as its standing may extend beyond those who have accepted its jurisdiction, making it an "objective" international person (as opposed to a "subjective" person that has personality only for states that choose to accept its personality).

The ICJ was emphatically in favor of viewing the UN's international legal personality as full-blooded enough to make claims against those who have not ratified the Charter. In essence, the failure of the State of Israel to recognize the authority of the UN is irrelevant for the organization's standing in courts and its ability to seek reparations from Israel.

> On this point, the Court's opinion is that fifty States, representing the vast majority of the members of the international community, had the power, in conformity with international law, to bring into being an entity possessing objective international personality, *and not merely personality recognized by them alone*, together with the capacity to bring international claims.[28]

While the court's reasoning as to what dimension of international law ratifies the objective international legal personality of the UN is left somewhat obscure, the conclusion is not. This objective personality is in no way parasitic upon the consent of individual states, but rather must find its ground in the common will of the vast majority of international agents.

---

27 Internal quotation is from the request for an advisory opinion given to the Court by the General Assembly.

28 Italics added.

Several cases have arisen since *Reparations* to further define and strengthen the international legal personality of the UN. By holding a strict separation between the "internal" mechanisms of the organization and its "external" actions (in this case the ability of the General Assembly to legitimately allocate peacekeeping troops without the permission of the Security Council) the *Certain Expenses of the United Nations* case further expands upon the "organic" metaphor described above.

> If it agreed that the action in question is within the scope of the functions of the Organization but it is alleged that it has been initiated or carried out in a manner not in conformity with the division of functions among the several organs which the Charter prescribes one moves to the internal plane, to the international structure of the Organization. If the action was taken by the wrong organ, it was irregular as a matter of that internal structure, but this would not necessarily mean that the expense incurred was not an expense of the Organization. Both national and international law contemplate cases in which the body corporate or politic may be bound, as to third parties, to an *ultra vares* act of an agent.

The point of this decision is to solidify the view of legal personality first set out by *Reparations*: legal persons are, analytically speaking, distinct from the views, choices, and so on, of their individual members.[29] By maintaining a strict separation between an internal decision-making processes of a non-state international person, and its engagements with the world, the ICJ has further highlighted the distinction between the body itself and the members that comprise it – (A) and (B) described above. Far from being a fluke, the precedents set out by the *Reparations* decision have had a lasting influence on the international legal doctrine of legal personality.

Unlike intergovernmental organizations, Nongovernmental Organizations (NGOs) such as Amnesty International and Human Rights Watch are largely private in character and lack the requisite political credentials to establish themselves as legal persons before international law. This lack of personality stems from one central (and good) reason: these organizations, however noble they may be, are not democratic and do not represent the will of a particular group of people (save those who support its ideology). They tend to represent interest groups with a common ideology spread across political borders. This strength of ideological conviction is admirable and quite useful when they play an advisory role in providing intergovernmental organizations with reports on their respective fields. However, their lack of democratic accountability and ideological unity (preventing them from the requirement of moderation in pursuit of their agendas) provide good grounds for being skeptical about advocating providing them with the benefits of legal personality.

The sole source of legal personality that has been afforded to NGOs at the present time is the consultative arrangements provided for them by certain treaties. Organizations such as the International Committee of the Red Cross have been given a special status and the ability to give authoritative reports on certain issues on the domestic affairs of certain states in several treaties. These treaties have afforded certain NGOs a good deal of legitimacy in the international legal community

29 This is also enforced by the Law Lords' decision in the International *Tin Council* case already discussed.

(specifically with regards to human rights). While one may in turn perhaps give an argument similar to that presented by the court in *Reparations*, that powers that these treaties require for the NGOs to pursue their assigned tasks would necessitate some form of personality, to the best of my knowledge, no such argument has been explicitly offered by any jurist that I have found (and it is doubtless that such an argument would go far, at least at present). Regardless, were such an argument made (and accepted), the personality afforded to the respective NGO would be very limited and very weak.

The overall significance of this discussion should be clear: although the states themselves were in many cases essential to the formation of intergovernmental organizations, genetically speaking, these legal persons are neither logically nor legally dependent upon their creators. The utility that these organizations provide for the international legal community, coupled with the personality required by these organizations to carry out their mandates will most likely lead to the continued multiplication of intergovernmental international legal persons. These new agents will further modify the terrain of international law in general and the nature of international legal personality in particular. Cases like *Certain Expenses* and *Reparations* have laid the groundwork for an understanding of the legal persona that is more nuanced than that offered by the sovereignty thesis. International legal personality extends further than the borders of the Westphalian nation-state and into the realm of the modern intergovernmental organization.

Individuals

As for the international legal personality of physical persons, legal doctrine is less clear and more controversial than in other, more established domains of international legal personality. Historically, their personality has been weak to non-existent in many areas of international law. On the other hand, in the metaphysics of agency (in establishing who – or what – is an agent), the agency of individuals is, of course, unquestioned. This seemingly trivial point, that people are agents, becomes decidedly untrivial when we seek legal accountability for behavior (especially criminal behavior). There is something unsatisfying about finding an abstraction such as a state or intergovernmental organization responsible for horrifying crimes such as genocide or torture. The human need for justice is not satisfied by punishing mere abstractions (Durkheim 1997). This tension between the metaphysical certainty of human agency, the natural desire for human moral accountability, and their relatively impoverished legal personality accounts for a good deal of the ambiguity surrounding their international legal personality. The uncertainty of this dimension of legal personality will allow me to engage in a certain amount of speculation along with a healthy dose of policy discussion at the end of this section.

Historically, individuals have played only a marginal role as international legal persons, remaining subordinate to more established agents (Janis 1984; Brownlie 2003, 65). However, there are some important exceptions. In areas such as the law of piracy, there has been a long-standing recognition that individuals may be tried *as individuals* for violations of the law of nations (Kelsen 1945, 345–6; Paust et al. 2000,

1039–49). International criminal law has similarly made the individual accountable *qua individual* for particularly horrendous crimes such as genocide, crimes against humanity, or war crimes (Ratner and Abrams 2001). Since Nuremberg, it has been commonly accepted that egregious activities perpetrated by individuals, regardless of the flag under which they serve, are subject to punishment as individuals.[30] The Nuremberg precedent for individual accountability has been further bolstered by the development of international criminal law in treaties such as the Genocide Convention and institutions like the International Criminal Court (Fichtelberg 2007). While the record of the prosecution of war criminals globally is at best uneven, and frequently accused of "victor's justice," the doctrine that individuals are accountable for their behavior in wartime has a strong standing among international lawyers.

These developments, while dramatic, are not entirely unprecedented. Twentieth-century institutions establishing the accountability of individuals before international law were foreshadowed by many cases in foreign and American domestic legal practice. Mark Janis cites the case of *Respublica v. De Longchamps* (an eighteenth-century American case involving the assault on the Consul General of France), holding an individual accountable to the law of nations, among others concluding:

> All of these examples – *De Longchamps*, *Paquete Habana*, the Nuremberg Trials, the European and American human rights systems, the European Economic Community, and *Filartiga* – demonstrate that a large and important part of international law practice establishes individual rights and obligations and provides international and municipal procedures for enforcing these rights and obligations... It is wrong, both in terms of describing reality and in terms of preferential expression, for the theory of international law to hold that individuals are outside the ambit of international law rules (Janis 1984).

Independent of the drafting of human rights documents, Janis concludes, individuals are valid international legal persons, and have been for quite some time. The ICC denotes a further evolution of existing law, not a dramatic departure from it.

While the obligation axis of international legal personality is relatively well defined for physical persons, the standing of individuals in international law is significantly hazier. The development of human rights has given a certain legal standing to individuals but there are few (if any) forums in the international sphere where these individuals may assert their rights against a state, particularly when this state is their own. As was previously noted, the ICJ is the exclusive domain of states (and the General Assembly may ask it for Advisory Opinions) and is off limits to individuals. An individual must find a state sponsor to press a claim in

30 Here the court argued:

It was submitted that international law is concerned with the actions of sovereign States, and provides no punishment for individuals; and further, that where the act in question is an act of State, those who carry it out are not personally responsible, but are protected by the doctrine of the sovereignty of the State. In the opinion of the Tribunal, both these submissions must be rejected. That international law imposes duties and liabilities upon individuals as well as upon States has long been recognized... The principle of international law, which under certain circumstances protects the representatives of a state, cannot be applied to acts which are condemned as criminal by international law (International Military Tribunal (Nuremberg) Judgment and Sentences 41 A.J.I.L. 22–221).

most international courts. While there are many justifiably famous international documents that provide individuals with inalienable rights, these same laws provide paltry resources for these individuals to assert their rights as individuals.

However, the standing of individuals is much less bleak when we turn from international law writ large to the various regional systems. Most regional legal systems have acknowledged that individuals have a standing before international legal courts. The European Court of Human Rights specifically allows individuals to lodge complaints against their own governments regarding their treatment and it has been a very busy institution. While this ability is not immediately available for all who have grievances against their home state (specifically, plaintiffs must have exhausted local remedies before they can continue their fight in the international arena), nonetheless, their standing before these courts is an established fact of law. Given these developments, an international human rights court where individuals have standing is not unimaginable.

Finally, domestic courts can frequently serve as a *locus* where individuals have *standi*. Individuals may sue foreign governments and foreign individuals in a number of states, applying domestic or international legal standards. *Filartiga v. Pena-Irala*, a US federal case, asserted the rights of torture victims to seek damages for harm committed overseas by government officials. "We hold that deliberate torture perpetrated under color of official authority violates universally accepted norms of the international law of human rights, regardless of the nationality of the parties". *Filartiga*, and cases similar to it, have established a domestic legal context where individuals can seek damages for violations of international law that has opened up dramatic new possibilities for those interested in enforcing human rights. Although domestic courts are frequently at the mercy of the foreign policy of their government (and these courts frequently submit themselves to the foreign policy of the state), they nonetheless provide a valuable tool for the individual to assert herself, albeit indirectly, using the tools of international law. Despite its domestic context, this represents an important form of standing available to individuals in international law.

At present it is obvious that individuals have no legislative capacities as individuals in international law. Any abilities they may have they receive solely as representatives of the state. Foreign ministers have the ability to make treaties or unilateral declarations of law, but only do this under the legal fiction that they are a part of the state. Contracts that they make are only private agreements. This means that the only forms of legislating that may be done by the individual are either through the formation of precedents (when they argue cases before international bodies) or as representatives of states.

At this point in its development, it is perhaps best to view the legal personality of individual persons in international law in general as existing in a state of flux. In a few years, the regional courts may opt to sharply rein in the abilities of individuals to assert their rights against their government (or more frequently defer to the plaintiff's home state). Similarly, the fallout of the *Pinochet* case and similar international criminal prosecutions, along with the perilous future of international criminal law (and the permanent International Criminal Court, that holds individuals responsible for their behavior) will further decide whether individuals will continue to be obliged by international law. Finally, the current diplomatic battles over the permanent International Criminal Court have similarly left the international legal personality of individuals in the air. While I have tried my best to delineate the contours of international law at present, the reader should not overlook its precariousness (save in established domains such as the law of piracy).

Given this ambiguity, it is not unwarranted to briefly discuss whether strengthening the legal personality of individuals would ultimately be a good thing. The central concern of those who wish to limit the legal personality of individuals usually stems from "prudential diplomats" (recalling a term from Chapter 1) who fear that a legal system that further expanded the role of individuals in international law would ultimately undermine peace and stability in international politics. States have a large number of complex tasks to deal with and inevitably they must violate the rights of some of their own people to preserve the happiness of all. Should states be required to answer to individuals for their behavior, their ability to carry out their policies could be severely hampered (as the argument goes). In addition, states can cynically manipulate these processes bringing up embarrassing, perhaps fictional violations of individual rights in order to embarrass their opponents.

While one should certainly be concerned about the abuse of institutions such as the International Criminal Court, it is a mistake to believe that the strengthening of the international legal personality of individuals would easily lend itself to such problems. Aware of these concerns, states have successfully put up safeguards to prevent the abuse of international courts by states and organizations seeking to make trouble for their more influential peers. While I will discuss this issue in further detail when I take on the prudential diplomat in Chapter 7, suffice it to suggest that widening and strengthening the forms of obligation that individuals have as legal persons would produce more good than ill. Naïve idealists are rare among practicing international lawyers (and judges). The vast majority of those involved in international criminal law and human rights law are well aware of the diplomatic and political complexity of their work.

There are additional, less moralistic reasons for supporting the strengthening of the legal personality of individuals. With the continuing complexity of international business and the development of technology that can render traditional borders (and traditional jurisdictions) meaningless, it makes sense to support effective legal tools for dealing with new forms of international criminal behavior. Developing and further articulating the legal personality of individuals in international law would give law enforcement agencies a new set of tools to effectively deal with modern international crime. Strengthening the legal personality of individuals will not only allow for these individuals to assert their basic rights in the international legal forum but will also create new avenues through which states can assert their own rights against individuals. Should the individual remain on the back benches of international law, states will suffer as much harm as the individuals that are presently at their mercy.

The significance of the expansion of the aspects of legal personality for individuals is important. While many of these aspects of individual personality can be traced back to the consent of sovereign states (and thus, in some sense cohere with sovereignty), others do not. Just as the objective legal personality of IGOs like the UN challenges the sovereignty thesis's account of legal personality, many features of the legal personality belonging to individuals cannot easily fit into that model. For example, the prohibition against torture, the right of individuals not to be tortured is often described as a *jus cogens* (non-derogable) right (De Wet 2004). If more human rights norms or norms of international criminal law are given such status, then the ability of states to restrain the legal personality of individuals would be seriously compromised and attempts to deploy sovereignty as the foundation of this field of international law will be increasingly weakened (Meron 1986).

The Future of International Legal Personality

Like everything else in this work, the analysis of international law developed here is bound to the present circumstances of international law. This means that future transformations in the international community could alter international legal personality in some dramatic ways. This is unfortunate for us as the present international system is showing an unprecedented dynamism that augurs what may be dramatic new developments. Such changes could, in turn, have a profound impact upon the matters discussed in this chapter. The three axes of legislation, standing, and obligation, though abstract, are probably useful enough that they could still be applicable to a very different international context. However, it is worth our time to briefly speculate about the road ahead for international legal personality and how these changes could modify the analysis offered here.

Hedley Bull has suggested that international society is transforming itself into a radically new form of political arrangement, in which international law plays a significant part. This new phase, that he labels "neomedievalism," would resemble Europe's feudal period in many ways, "a secular reincarnation of the system of overlapping or segmented authority that characterized mediaeval Christendom" (Bull 1977, 264).[31] Here, international power would be diffused into a vast number of different local, regional, and global organizations all of which are interconnected and none of which has the exclusive right over human beings. The state would probably still exist in such a system and would have some form of international legal personality, but would be only one player among many, and would most likely be substantially weakened when contrasted to its present position. Regional systems would overlap with national governments, both of which would compete with intergovernmental organizations and transgovernmental groups (such as religious and ethnic groups) for the allegiance of the people of the world. Such international political systems would radically change the legal structures that undergird it in such a way that all of the non-state actors discussed in this chapter would have more robust and clearly defined legal personalities.

Of course, Bull's analysis is purely speculative. It is certainly possible that the sovereign states will succeed in maintaining their strength and their exclusive legal and political privileges, weakening the role that intergovernmental organizations and individuals play in the international legal community. This would, in turn, limit the

31 Cited in Arend 1999, 172.

development and articulation of the legal personality afforded to non-state actors like the UN. However, there is no *a priori* reason why legal personality must stay in its present form, just as there is no necessity to the hegemonic role played by the sovereign state in legal personality. No deductive argument, such as given by many sovereignty theorists, can show that international law in general and international legal personality in particular is wedded to state sovereignty. International politics will undoubtedly change in many unpredictable ways, giving new actors entirely new roles in international law, the point of international legal theory is to grasp and study these changes, not dismiss them because of their failure to cohere with theory.

Conclusion

As we can see even from this very brief discussion of international legal personality, there is much more to this concept than can be offered by the sovereignty thesis alone. The best, that is, the most empirically accurate approach to international law recognizes that there is a stratification of types of legal persons, each of which possesses a different amount of the three primary elements of international legal personality described at the opening of this chapter. While certainly this part of international law is at present developing rapidly (especially with regards to the legal personality of individuals), it is clear that legal personality encompasses a much wider set of agents than is afforded by a strict sovereignty view.

Returning to the "meta-language/object language" discussion of sovereignty that was mentioned in the previous chapter and at the opening of this one, we can see that the implications of a meta-language conception of sovereignty don't seem to pan out. While sovereign states are clearly important parts of the field of international legal personality, they do not serve the foundational role that one would expect them to serve if they defined international law. The robust personality ascribed to nonstate actors as well as the objective legal personality of intergovernmental organizations and the development of international criminal law shows that the state is not the only important legal actor in the international field. International society and its law may not be "medieval" in its structure at present, but neither is it purely Westphalian.

In the next chapter, we will discuss the related issue of the international law of humanitarian intervention. There is a logical connection between sovereignty as a theory of legal personality and sovereignty as a theory of legal right. Hand in hand with the view that states are the only actors on the stage of international law, the sovereignty thesis asserts that states have untrammeled freedom within their own borders to govern themselves they see fit. For the sovereignty thesis, the make-up of international politics is atomistic, comprised only of indivisible units each with absolute dominion over its own territory. If states are the only persons in law, and these states have equality before the law, it follows that no state is in a position to violate the space and integrity of any other state without their permission.

But with the diversification of legal persons, as outlined in this chapter, the hegemony of state sovereignty has been eroded, in at least one of its forms. If the sovereign state is not the only legal actor on the international scene, as I have argued here, perhaps the latter claim, the impenetrability of the sovereign state, is not sacrosanct either. To what extent can the boundaries of a state be *legally* violated, either by other states or by an international organization like the UN? This question, part of the ongoing and highly contentious debate surrounding the legality of the violation of a state's sovereignty (especially when the motives for it seem wholly benevolent), is the subject of the next chapter.

Chapter 5

Humanitarian Intervention

This chapter, a study on the present state of the international law of humanitarian intervention, stands in close relation with the previous one for two reasons. Both seek to explicate important aspects of international legal doctrine, as opposed to the more abstract, theoretical questions of Chapters 1–3. More significantly, however, they both share the agenda underlying the larger view set out in this study: the critique of traditional, state-based conceptions of international law. The preceding analysis of legal personality revealed that the sovereign state is not the sole actor on the international legal stage (which has become increasingly crowded). This effort was intended as the first assault on the sovereignty thesis, an attack that will take on a second front here. In this chapter, I will also study the present rules and practices in international law with an eye towards understanding the nature and strength of the legal boundaries of the sovereign state. Thus I am also explicating the rules of international law rather than dealing with philosophical speculation regarding the foundations or functions of this legal system. Further, both this and the previous chapter apply the non-reductive definition of international law described in Chapter 2.

The purpose of this chapter is to show that under the present international legal regime the walls of state sovereignty are not impenetrable. In certain (admittedly extraordinary) circumstances, the veil of sovereignty may be pierced by other states and by the international community in a direct and forceful manner in order to protect human rights. This means that at certain times the international community (or individual states acting unilaterally) may use force against a state or other organization in order to protect individuals who are suffering from severe, unjust oppression. What was at one time considered to be inviolable, and the lynchpin of sovereignty (the rights of a state to govern its people) is now sharply limited by human rights norms and by an increasingly interconnected and interdependent global society.

Of course, any study of international laws dealing with the use of force must discuss the Charter of the United Nations in significant depth. I will do this by developing my discussion of humanitarian intervention along three different tracks, each of which corresponds to a separate principle set out by the Charter. The first two will be indirect arguments for a "mixed" humanitarian intervention, pointing out the consequences of domestic atrocities for the international system as grounds for intervention – seeing humanitarian intervention in terms of self-defense. The first of these will involve interventions justified in terms of the natural (or "inherent") right of states to self-defense as cited in Article 51 of the Charter. This will include a discussion of the 1971 war between India and Pakistan over atrocities committed in Bangladesh and the Vietnamese intervention in Cambodia in 1978. After this, I will turn to the functions of the Security Council as defined by the Charter, focusing on its obligations under Chapter VII to uphold peace and security. This will lead to a brief discussion of the US intervention in Haiti in 1994 to stop the latter's oppressive military dictatorship. Finally, the last section will look at the human rights components of the Charter and in other parts of international law as possible justifications for "purely" humanitarian interventions (that is, interventions where the *sole* justification for the use of force is humanitarian). It is my ultimate aim to show that international law allows a limited right to humanitarian intervention in both a mixed as well as a pure form, both within the UN system and from outside.

Before proceeding, however, it is perhaps worthwhile to characterize what humanitarian intervention is and, equally important, what it is *not*. I can preempt a number of objections by carefully circumscribing our object of study and then seeing whether such interventions can be accommodated under the present international legal regime. Fernando Téson's influential study, *Humanitarian Intervention: An Inquiry into Law and Morality* provides an adequate working definition of humanitarian intervention:

> I define human intervention as the transboundary help, including forcible help, provided by governments to individuals in another state who are being denied basic human rights and who themselves would be rationally willing to revolt against their oppressive government (Tesón 1997, 5).

Throughout the rest of this chapter, this will be the definition of intervention that I will be seeking to justify within contemporary international law.

Tesón's definition is particularly useful because of what it includes as well as what it leaves out. First, it does not require that the intervener have "pure intentions" in carrying out their acts or that their acts be justified *solely* on humanitarian grounds.[1] As I will show, both in theory and in fact, states always have some kind

1 This likewise separates Tesón's approach from others such as Wil Verwey who defines intervention as: "[T]he threat or use of force by a state or states abroad, for the sole purpose of preventing or putting a halt to a serious violation of fundamental human rights, in particular to the right to life of persons, regardless of their nationality, such protection taking place neither upon authorization by relevant organs of the United Nations nor with permission by the legitimate government of the target state" (Verwey 1992, 114). This definition is flawed insofar as it removes any role for the UN in intervention (and as I will show, many interventions commonly described as humanitarian happened with some Security Council approval) and it expects that the purpose of the intervention be solely humanitarian. This also is part of an unrealistic portrayal of real interventions.

It also conflicts with Beck and Arend who assert that true humanitarian intervention cannot be performed under the Security Council as such would be better described as "collective uses of force" and "to describe… United Nations undertaking[s] as a 'humanitarian intervention' is to deprive the term of its traditional core meaning" (Arend and Beck 1993, 113). Unfortunately, they do not provide further justification for this limitation on the notion of intervention and its "core meaning." Suffice it to say that cases such as Haiti where intervention did take place under a Security Council Resolution for partially humanitarian reasons is proof that Arend and Beck's view is unnecessarily dogmatic.

For another interesting analysis of the issues involved in defining humanitarian intervention, see Brownlie (1973).

of national interest (however that concept is conceived) when they intervene in the affairs of another state – we live in an interdependent world and domestic policy is never hermetically sealed within a state's borders. Second, it excludes incursions by one state into another in order to rescue one's own nationals – such as Israel did in Uganda in 1976.[2] Third, it excludes mercenary attempts by one state to undermine another, without just cause (such as with US support of the Contras in Nicaragua in the 1980s or Germany's occupation of Bohemia and Moravia).[3] Finally, it is limited to actions committed by governments against other governments, and does not consider interventions by other actors such as guerilla movements or wars of national liberation. These conflicts are important and merit significant discussion, but as they can be distinguished from humanitarian intervention, I will ignore them for this discussion.

The topic of humanitarian intervention is significantly more controversial than the issue of international legal personality, and many lawyers are more willing to object to intervention, than to the precedents set out in the *Certain Expenses* and the *Reparations* opinions. This means that I will have to make a much more involved case to prove that there really is a law of humanitarian intervention and what this law entails. I also add that critics, wishing to rid international law of the notion of humanitarian intervention will find more resources to make their case than they might have found on other topics.[4] This does not necessarily impugn my overall views regarding the law. Practicing lawyers recognize that their arguments are *always* contentious, but this does not impugn their conviction about their arguments. The harder the *prima facie* case is to make, the more resourceful the attorney making it must be. But no case is impossible to make. This chapter should perhaps be seen in this light, as a legal brief of sorts, a controversial point of law where opposing views will be submitted before the courts of professional legal opinion and practice.

Further, the general points made about the law here are only useful when applied to the messy facts of real world cases. If even a small wedge can be forced under the barrier of the sovereignty thesis, then there may be a future case where the facts can follow this wedge. Past cases are only partial templates to apply to future ones and we search through the available precedents for law that could be used in a different case that shares similarities with its precursor. The former may be only a partial fit

2 See Ronzitti (1985: 17–20). This does not necessarily mean that the Israeli commando actions in Uganda were necessarily illegal, but rather that it was not a humanitarian intervention, strictly speaking.

3 In his Proclamation on the German Occupation of Bohemia and Moravia of March 1939, Hitler referred to "assaults on the life and liberty of minorities, and the purpose of disarming Czech troops and terrorist bands threatening the lives of minorities" (*Docs. on British Foreign Policy 1919–1939*, 257. Cited in Brownlie [1963, 340]).

4 As the UK Foreign Office Policy Document No. 148 asserts: "The best case that can be made in support of humanitarian intervention is that it cannot be said to be unambiguously illegal… But the overwhelming majority of contemporary legal opinion comes down against the existence of a right of humanitarian intervention" (UK Foreign Office Policy Document No. 148, cited in Harris [1998, 918]). Harris points out that in later documents, the Government asserted that "international intervention *without* the invitation of the government of the country concerned can be justified in cases of extreme humanitarian need" (1998, 921).

onto the later case, but it is this part that is relevant and a clever attorney cobbles together different aspects of past cases that provide rules to apply to a future case. Thus, if I can show that there *could in principle be some kind of legally authorized humanitarian intervention* then it is merely a matter of finding the appropriate case and applying to it the norms of a legal humanitarian intervention.

The Question of Motive

Many opponents of humanitarian intervention assert that the intentions behind such interventions are inevitably more sinister in character than the rhetoric of humanitarianism reveals. Seemingly benevolent acts by states are often mere dressing for baser national interests of some kind or another. Such critics are quick to point out the ulterior motives of political and military leaders when they respond to atrocities in other states: these interventions are just masks for power, kind rhetoric concealing military conquest. Fighting oppression abroad can be a great pretext for weakening or destabilizing an enemy state, installing a friendly government, or even acquiring the territory of a neighboring state. As Brownlie states:

> Examination of state practice in relation to this form of intervention is rendered difficult as it is frequently a subsidiary justification for an intervention which is an expression of purely national policy. Moreover, the jurists have tended to *ex post facto* classification of interventions which were justified without reference to any specific doctrine of humanitarian intervention (Brownlie 1963, 339).

And further,

> The state practice justifies the conclusion that no genuine case of humanitarian intervention has occurred… With the embarrassing exception provided by Germany [cited above], the institution has disappeared from modern state practice. As a matter of international policy this is a beneficial development (Brownlie 1963, 340).

This historical fact, the skeptics assert, undermines the idea that there is such a thing as *humanitarian* intervention – simply because truly humanitarian intentions are non-existent among those who commit them. No state possesses the benevolence implied by the label, and those well-meaning idealists who support the idea of legalized intervention are buying into a lie that can do a great deal more harm than good. Any attempts to legitimize such interventions play into the hands of hegemonic powers.

While I will address this issue further in the next chapter, I should comment here that one must be careful about the unwarranted import of psychological language designed to explain individual behavior into complex political situations involving entities of a very different sort. States are not individuals and their foreign policies are very rarely, if ever, the product of one person with clearly definable motives, intentions, and interests. The reality is that foreign policies are constructed by numerous people from both within a government and from without and carried out with a number of different objectives in mind. Foreign ministries and heads of state consider a broad number of issues in their calculations: ideological, economic, political, and yes, moral concerns do play a role in their decisions and affect different groups in different ways. Corporations and investors at home and abroad impinge upon the schemes and plans of politicians and diplomats, as do citizens with more provincial concerns (in democracies, small groups of highly organized voters can have a big impact on the development of a foreign policy). Sometimes it is extremely difficult (from the outside) to discern what motives guide a dramatic policy decision as important decision-making processes are kept from the public eye. To point to one possible motive for an international act (say, an economic one) and then to assert that this motive somehow explains a particular act dramatically oversimplifies human political life.

The point here is that psychological questions, such as whether a state has "good intentions," are not as helpful for understanding the formulation of foreign policy as they might seem. This general truth of the analysis of political behavior is even more relevant in relation to the vast complexities of humanitarian intervention. As I will show below, there are many different issues that contribute to a decision to intervene – some are moral, some not. What a state's intentions are and whether they are "pure" is something that cannot be concluded by looking at one person, one political party, or the taking of a poll of a state's populace.[5] Critics can always exploit the complexity and secrets of foreign affairs in order to concoct a theory explaining why this or that humanitarian intervention isn't quite so benevolent.

Sovereignty

In the previous chapter I interpreted the sovereignty thesis as a claim about the subjects of international law (that is, the belief that states are the only real legal subjects) and it turned out that this model did not fit the legal facts. In this chapter, sovereignty is interpreted in two somewhat different ways. Here, I am not concerned so much with the quantity of agents in international law as much as with their quality. Specifically, I will ask the question: "How sacred is the inviolability of the state in contemporary international law?" This question in turn relies on a deeper one regarding the role that sovereignty itself plays within the international system. If the sovereignty thesis (as it was described in Chapter 2) is correct, presumably the state is an atomistic, conceptually indivisible entity – at least when seen through the prism of international law. From this inviolability it obviously follows that nobody may legally set foot within a state's borders against the will of the state, much less dictate how a government should treat their own nationals. Hall clearly sets out this view in relation to humanitarian intervention:

> In giving their sanction to interventions of the kind in question jurists have imparted an aspect of legality to a species of intervention, which makes a deep inroad into one of the

5 This view directly contrasts with the views of Arend and Beck who assert that intentions are important to understanding intervention as being humanitarian: "International legal scholarship has long recognized that state motives must be taken into account in legal assessments of state practice. For there to be a genuine 'humanitarian intervention,' we have suggested, the intervening state's objective must be essentially *limited* to protecting human rights" (Arend and Beck 1993, 119).

> cardinal doctrines of international law (viz. that it is concerned only with the relations of States to each other) (Hall 1904, 290).

Under the sovereignty theory of international law then, humanitarian interventions are illegal *a priori*, as indeed are all efforts to coerce a state to change its policies against its own people. If this view of the law is wrong, however, and I believe that it is, then (theoretically at least) humanitarian intervention can be made compatible with the present international legal regime.

There is a deeper connection between the diffusion of legal personality on the one hand and the development of the doctrine of humanitarian intervention on the other. If agents other than states have legal personality and thereby possess some rights, then it is reasonable to claim that these rights must be protected in some way. If states are the only legal persons in the international legal system, then it follows that other entities have no particular rights – which is clearly not the case in international legal doctrine. This gives non-sovereignty-based models of international legal personality an advantage in conceptualizing humanitarian intervention. As Abiew puts it:

> The context of interventionary practice has changed; thus, the principle needs reformulation and some coherence to take account of developments in international relations. The identification of international law with society conceived in terms of states emerged largely with the growth of positivist theories and the ascendance of the nation-state as the predominant actor in the global arena. This development is rapidly changing with the emergence and influence of non-state actors in international relations. Modern practice does demonstrate that individuals have become increasingly recognized as participants and subjects of international law. They possess certain rights as against their states, and states are subject to international scrutiny regarding their human rights practices. If the increase in and growing concern about violation of human rights is taken into account which the principle of non-intervention fails to take into account, then a justification for reformulating the principle will be in order and of the utmost importance (Abiew 1999, 72–3).

Abiew's point here is that the sovereignty thesis must be rethought with the modern diffusion of international legal personality – that the quantitative multiplication of legal persons has a qualitative effect on legal personality as such. That individuals have rights (as legal persons) entails that state sovereignty cannot be absolute in relation to these individuals.

The view of the sovereignty thesis that I will attack in this chapter asserts that the integrity of the state is inviolable on purely conceptual grounds. If the states themselves, through their wills create international law, then this will of sovereigns is definitive of international law. There is no higher legal authority than the act of state on this reading. Humanitarian intervention (as opposed to other kinds of intervention – such as peacekeeping – that will be discussed in greater detail later in this chapter) goes against this same will of the sovereign state asserting that there are legal norms that trump this agenda. Thus it is a logical contradiction to say that "the will of the sovereign state defines international law" on the one hand, and on the other assert that "at times international law may violate the will of this state."

While some reject the idea of humanitarian intervention on these conceptual grounds, others admit the legal possibility of intervention, but question whether such ideas can be made to cohere with the bulk of international law. Thus, humanitarian intervention is both legal and illegal in modern international law: a paradox. According to Bederman, the legal values of human rights and principles of sovereignty, while both legitimate, clash at their core. This conceptual conflict has bequeathed us a paradoxical doctrine of humanitarian intervention. For human rights to be effective it is sometimes necessary that one override the will of sovereign states, but:

> How this ultimate enforcement mechanism of human rights norms (the physical invasion of the offending State and the removal of an abusive government) can be reconciled with other international law rules promoting international peace and security is perhaps an unsolvable riddle in international law today (Bederman 2001b, 109).

While I agree with Bederman's analysis regarding the legality of humanitarian intervention, as a matter of law, his skeptical conclusions are probably unwarranted. Humanitarian interventions have taken place and some of these have found political and legal sanction. I will argue in this chapter not only that international law allows for certain humanitarian sorts of interventions, but also that they can fit into a largely coherent conception of the international laws regarding the use of force.

A large number of theorists who hold a version of the sovereignty thesis read it as denying the possibility of a legal humanitarian intervention. Often, such international lawyers assert that it is impossible for a state to consent to having its territory violated against its will, as sovereignty is an inalienable right. Thus, the "right" of humanitarian intervention becomes an oxymoron. For example, Jianmeng Shen has argued:

> The non-intervention principle is a necessary derivative from the principle of state sovereignty. Every state is sovereign *vis-à-vis* every other. Being an equal sovereign, a state is not subject to any form of foreign interference in its own domestic matters except where international law or treaties permit it by consent (Shen 2001).

This traditional argument has appeared in a variety of forms, almost inevitably coupled with the more practical concern that a legal principle justifying humanitarian intervention undermines international peace and stability:

> There is no commonly acceptable standard of what humanitarianism means and what human rights embrace in the sense of international law. In the absence of common understanding, the concepts of "humanitarianism" and "human rights" are *bound to be abused* if the international community is to allow humanitarian intervention, or to simplistically attach superiority to individual human rights over national sovereignty. The consequences of this kind would be too dreadful to contemplate (Shen 2001, 5).[6]

---

6 As Brownlie puts it: "There is a great deal of useful circumstantial evidence which suggests both that the law does not recognize humanitarian intervention and also that the prognosis for such action as a genuine instrument for the benefit of mankind is not good" (1973, 146).

That these odious consequences have resulted from the actual interventions of states on humanitarian grounds is debatable. I will show in the two instances of humanitarian intervention discussed below that they did not produce results that dramatically destabilized the international regime (or at least created no more damage and havoc than continued atrocities would have done). Regardless, the traditional argument from state sovereignty asserts that international law cannot (by its very nature) validate international humanitarian interventions in sovereign states.

The UN Charter

Any serious attempt to understand the international laws governing the use of force must begin with the UN Charter, the source of most modern international laws governing the use of force. This means that how the Charter is read will dramatically influence how one thinks about the laws regarding the use of force and by extension, how one conceives of any possible legal basis for humanitarian intervention. In this section, I will develop three different themes found in the UN Charter. The first two are more congenial to the notion of sovereignty (and the sovereign equality of states) while the third, dealing with the promotion and protection of human rights, is a direct challenge to sovereignty. Each, however will provide some legal basis for humanitarian intervention in certain contexts as part of a larger sense of the nature and purpose of the UN (I should note that some of this discussion will be *very* basic, intended for the non-lawyer).

When looking at the UN Charter, the case against legalized humanitarian intervention has much to rely upon at first glance. At the forefront of this interpretation stands Article 2(7), categorically asserting that states have an absolute power over certain (undefined) internal matters. Thus, the limits of international legal authority are defined by the notion of "domestic jurisdiction":

> Nothing contained in the present Charter shall authorize the United Nations to intervene in matters which are essentially within the domestic jurisdiction of any state or shall require the Members to submit such matters to settlement under the present charter.

This article limits the concerns of the organization to those that affect the external relations of states and the threats that they create for the international order. This means that all interventions, whether armed or political, limited by the ability of states to rule their people largely as they see fit. Further, Article 2(4) asserts that all uses of force must be constrained by the purposes of the Charter:

> All Members shall refrain in their international relations from the threat or use of force against territorial integrity or political independence of any state, or in any other manner inconsistent with the Purposes of the United Nations.

On this reading, the Charter is rooted entirely in the conception of international society as a group of sovereign states ruling within their borders as they see fit and who are immune from international criticism (much less armed attack) for their domestic policy.[7]

The Charter is not the only source of this principle of non-intervention in contemporary international law, of course. One can easily find other, subsidiary legal statements in the UN regime regarding the inviolability of state sovereignty and the irrelevance of domestic policy for international affairs. For example, the Declaration on the Inadmissibility of Intervention in the Domestic Affairs of States and the Protection in the Domestic Affairs of State and the Protection of their Independence and Sovereignty adopted by the General Assembly in 1965 asserted:

> No State has the right to intervene, directly or indirectly, for any reason whatever, in the internal or external affairs of any State. Consequently, armed intervention and all other forms of interference or attempted threats against the personality of the State or against its political, economic, or cultural elements are condemned.[8]

(While General Assembly declarations are not international law *per se*, they nonetheless are not meaningless in establishing a legal principle of non-intervention.) These documents are backed by some important cases that reaffirm the legal value of non-intervention as a customary norm.[9] Similarly, Security Council resolutions, make routine references to the principles behind Articles 2(4) and 2(7). Thus the UN Charter, the General Assembly, the World Court, and the Security Council have all in some ways sought to foreclose the possibility that one state (or a group of states) may interfere with the domestic affairs of another. At least they assert this with one side of their collective mouth.

To further complicate the notion of intervention are those situations where the appropriate characterization of the conflict is either unclear or controversial. How a war is characterized will dramatically affect the legality of intervention. The war in Vietnam is a classic case and the analysis of hinges upon whether one saw it as a civil war within the single state of Vietnam (making the US role in the war an intervention of sorts) or as an international conflict between two different Vietnams. Whether the US intervened in a domestic affair or lawfully defended the state of South Vietnam (in accord with its SEATO obligations) will dramatically change how a sovereignty

---

7 As Shaw describes the international legal system, the UN Charter marks a change from a previous legal regime which allowed for such interventions to one that clearly does not. As he puts it, humanitarian intervention "has some support in pre-Charter law and it may very well have been the case that in the last century such intervention was accepted under international law. However, it is difficult to reconcile today with article 2(4) of the charter unless one adopts a rather artificial definition of the 'territorial integrity' criterion in order to permit temporary violation" (Shaw 1991, 724).

8 Res. 2131 20 UN GAOR Supp. (No. 14) (1965). Cited in Abiew (1999, 69). See also, the "Declaration on principles of International Law Concerning Friendly relations and Co-operation Among States in Accordance with the Charter of the United Nations", Res. 265 UN GAOR Supp. (No. 28) 25: 121 (197).

9 Among others see *Military and Paramilitary Activities Against Nicaragua* (*US v. Nicaragua*). For a critique of this judgment, see D'Amato (1987, 101–85). See also: Roberts (2001, 785). For a brief history of intervention see Chesterman (2001, 22–40).

theorist would understand the legality of the war.[10] As many interventions with a humanitarian element have been wrapped up with secessionist movements (such as in East Pakistan) or domestic civil conflict (such as with Haiti and Cambodia), the issue of whether the intervener is actually intervening in the domestic affairs of a sovereign state or protecting a nascent state from a foreign power further complicates the issue. Simply asserting a blanket principle of non-intervention fails to respond to a common issue in humanitarian operations: who is the object of intervention?

Sovereignty and Self-Defense: Article 51

Of course, the sovereignty thesis as set out by the Charter and the subsidiary legal sources does not completely rule out the right of a state to use force against another state, simply when it is justified solely by reference to the state's behavior towards its own citizens. Self-defense as a basis for intervention has been a long-standing principle of international law, articulated by figures no less august than Grotius and the Scholastics among others. To ensure their existence is a natural right for sovereign states, and is understood in Article 51 of the UN Charter as a legal norm standing separate from other legal principles. Article 51 asserts in part that,

> Nothing in the present Charter shall impair the inherent right of individual or collective self-defence if an armed attack occurs against a Member of the United Nations, until the Security Council has taken measures necessary to maintain international peace and security.

While sovereignty theorists may debate the exact scope of this "inherent" right of self-defense (Does it include anticipatory self-defense? How much violence is legitimate under the law of self defense? etc.), and whether there are any exceptions to this right (such as the right of the apartheid government and other unrecognized states to defend themselves), Article 51 nonetheless sits squarely at the heart of modern international law conceived in terms of sovereignty.[11] One sovereign state may intervene in the affairs of another if its own sovereignty is at stake.

Of course mass violations of human rights frequently have international repercussions that can undermine a neighboring state's internal stability. This can happen in numerous ways. Horrible, widespread human rights violations can frequently create large numbers of refugees, who quickly overwhelm a neighboring state's resources. This results in economic hardship for the receiving state and unrest from disgruntled refugees left to linger in crowded camps. These refugees can then easily become involved in internal disputes in the state that receives them. Additionally, the oppressive regime may intervene to pursue these refugees. Thus,

---

10 See for example, Henkin's subtle interpretation of the Vietnam war in *How Nations Behave*. As he states the issue, "What international law would say about US involvement in Vietnam depends on disputed questions of fact, even more on debatable characterizations of those facts. The lawyer seeking to apply norms needs first to decide what was going on" (1979, 306).

11 For a discussion of the "inherent" nature of the Article 51 right, see Asrat (1991, 208–11).

in many ways, a state's internal policies can intensify regional problems to the point where the neighboring state may justly claim self-defense in order to intervene against an oppressive regime. In this vein, I will briefly discuss two examples of humanitarian interventions that were carried out (partially) in the name of a state's innate right to self-defense.

The 1971 Pakistan–India conflict

A clear case of such overlap between humanitarian concerns and the right of a state to defend itself is found in the brief December 1971 war between India and Pakistan. While this conflict is frequently characterized as a form of humanitarian intervention (Franck and Rodley 1973; Abiew 1999), such analysis of the conflict misses some of its important aspects. In particular, the legal justifications given by Indian authorities for their war with Pakistan and their support of Bangladeshi independence combine humanitarian concerns with Indian self-defense.

Beginning with the 1969 coup in the west, the independence-minded Awami League's rise to power in the east, and Pakistan's subsequent butchering of the League's civilian supporters, Indian security issues were tightly bound up with the events inside the borders of Pakistan, both east and west.[12] The massive wave of Bangladeshi refugees into India threatened a delicate balance that existed in the northern and eastern provinces of India for a quarter century. Indian and Bangladeshi communists, in league with the Chinese Communist Party, a major threat to stability in India, were quick to exploit the situation and sought to give the Chinese time to cultivate centers of power within Bangladesh. The Indian government saw these political challenges as serious threats to the unity and ultimately the viability of the secular, multi-ethnic Indian government.[13] While the moral outrage of the Indian people against the Pakistani government for butchering innocent civilians was a further aspect of their decision to go to war, the security concerns were probably foremost in the minds of the Gandhi administration.

Additionally, the influx of Hindus and Muslims from Bangladesh placed a heavy financial burden on India. Experts estimated that feeding, housing, and care for the

---

12 As the International Commission of Jurists described the events around the Spring of 1971:

> The principle features of this ruthless oppression were the indiscriminate killing of civilians, including women and children and the poorest and weakest members of the community; the attempt to exterminate or drive out a country a large part of the Hindu population; the arrest, torture and killing of Awami League activists, students, professional and business men and other potential leaders…; the raping of women; the destruction of villages and towns; and the looting of property. All this was done in a scale which is difficult to comprehend.

International Commission of Jurists, *The Events in East Pakistan, 1971* (cited in Abiew 1999, 114, 26–7.).

13 Additionally, any chance to undermine Pakistani power was appealing as the Muslim state was undoubtedly India's biggest enemy. However, as I will argue in the next chapter, such realist analyses are not incompatible with the notion of law-determined behavior in international politics.

refugees would come to £290 million and the country had received little more than a third of that in foreign aid (and only about £30 million in hard currency) (Mani 1972, 85). These financial issues provided fuel for Communist rebels as peasants, toiling in desperate poverty saw that (or at least believed that) Bangladeshi refugees sequestered in camps received free food, shelter, and health care from the Indian government. Those who were able to leave their confinement along the Bangladeshi border went to the cities where they increased the ranks of the urban unemployed. It was clear that the economic and political burdens that the refugees placed were beyond the Indian government's capacity regardless of the support offered by the international community. Had Pakistan not struck first, experts now believe that India had every intention of securing the refugees' return by military means (Sisson and Rose 1990, 4).

An examination of the speeches made by Indian leaders before the world shows that for India, their right to defend themselves was intimately bound up with halting atrocities as well as facilitating the return of the refugees to Bangladesh. Prime Minister Gandhi asserted before her own Parliament on 24 May that the forced immigration of the refugees was not a problem limited to the confines of Pakistan's borders:

> What was claimed to be an internal problem of Pakistan has also become an internal problem of India. We are therefore entitled to ask Pakistan to desist immediately from all actions which it is taking in the name of domestic jurisdiction and which vitally affect the peace and well-being of millions of its own citizens. Pakistan cannot be allowed to seek a solution of its political or other problems at the expense of Indian soil. Has Pakistan the right to compel at bayonet point not hundreds, not thousands, not hundreds of thousands, but millions of its citizens to flee from their homes?[14]

Gandhi's words show the confluence of human rights, mass-immigration, and the self-defense of states when it comes to the behavior of Pakistan in Bangladesh. In asserting its entitlement to stop the flow of refugees, Gandhi established what she saw as the legal right of India to involve itself in the affairs of another state strictly within the framework of Article 51 of the UN Charter.

Samar Sen, the Indian ambassador to the UN made similar statements. On 4 December 1971, he equated the influx of refugees into India as a form of aggression against India by Pakistan (Weisburd 1997, 148). On 12 December he further highlighted the dramatic problem the refugees presented and India's determination to address it:

> [A] massive exodus into India of the people of Bangla Desh commenced on the night of 25 March, which still continues. This is an exodus unprecedented in known history across

14 Cited in a speech by Samar Sen before the United Nations Security Council on 7 December 1971.

an international frontier. The threat to our security, stability and economy by what has been called the massive civilian invasion of refugees into India cannot be determined in tangible terms.

Further, Sen argued that Pakistan had an obligation to make the safe return of the refugees possible:

> The voluntary return of the refugees to their homeland under conditions of dignity and honour, with guarantees of rehabilitation and resettlement in their homeland, and the discontinuation of the military repression of East Bengal by the Government of Pakistan are directly interlinked.[15]

Clearly, India felt that it had certain legal rights in relation to the domestic affairs of Pakistan because of their geographic proximity and the fact that the effects of internal policies impacted upon India so dramatically.

Finally, the Indian motivations had a humanitarian element to them, and they made these motives explicit before the various organs of the UN.[16] The Indian representative made several public statements condemning the Pakistani government in the context of the Indian war:

> [T]he reaction of the people of India to the massive killing of unarmed people by military force has been intense and sustained... There is intense sorrow and shock and horror at the reign of terror that has been let loose. The common bonds of race, religion, culture, history and geography of the people of East Pakistan with the neighbouring Indian state of West Bengal contribute powerfully to the feelings of the Indian people.[17]

And further before the Security Council:

> We are glad that we have on this particular occasion nothing but the purest of motives and the purest of intentions: to rescue the people of East Bengal from what they are suffering.[18]

Thus, the motives of the Indian government were clearly mixed. They felt that their intervention was justified in terms of self-defense, but additionally cited human rights violations as partial grounds for intervening. The UN Security Council responded in kind: Resolution 307 refused to fault India for violating the sovereignty of Pakistan.

---

15 Sen (1971).

16 As I have already shown, Prime Minister Gandhi asserted that Pakistan did not have the right to force Bangladeshi people from their homes – seeing this as a separate issue from the impact of this policy upon India.

17 26 U.N. G.A.O.R. 2002th, UN Doc. A/PV 2002 (1971). Cited in Tesón (1997, 207 ff.).

18 26 U.N.S.C.O.R. 1606th mtg. 26, UN Doc S/PV. 1606 (1971) at 18. Cited in Tesón (1997, 207 ff.).

The Vietnamese intervention in Cambodia

The atrocities of the Pol Pot regime in the late 1970s are well known. When the Khmer Rouge rebels seized power, they unleashed a wave of death that can only be compared with Nazi Germany and Stalinist Russia. Arbitrary executions and brutal, forced migrations were central elements of state policy. As Sir Robert Jackson, the Under Secretary General and Senior Adviser to the United Nations described the situation, Cambodia was a nation of...

> Ceaseless killings ... torture, persecution, iron discipline, ruthlessly imposed, hunger, starvation, deprivation of even the most elementary essentials of life. Some of the methods of torture and execution were, if anything, more obscene than those practised by the Nazis and degraded the human mind and body in ways never before known... rarely in history has the entire population of a nation been subjected to such bestial and inhuman treatment as that endured by the Kampuchean people under Pol Pot (Jackson in Klintworth, 1989, 6–7).

In less than three years, as much as one third of the population of Cambodia (approximately two million people) had been murdered by government forces. Clearly, if there was any post-World War II situation where forcible humanitarian intervention was called for, it was Cambodia under the Khmer Rouge.

However, as the atrocities were made public, moral outrage was in short supply, especially among the permanent members of the Security Council. Consumed with cold-war rivalries in a particularly sensitive part of the globe, the international community was unsympathetic to the suffering of the Cambodian people. However political and military tensions developed between Cambodia and its neighbor, Vietnam over numerous issues which resulted in armed conflict. In January 1979 Vietnamese forces invaded Cambodia and in a military rout, quickly seized control of the country, installing the head of a Vietnam-backed Cambodian exiles organization, the United Front, as their new leader. The mass killings were stopped, the Khmer Rouge fled, and Pol Pot ultimately died in the Cambodian jungles some two decades later.

Just as with Bangladesh, this intervention is not a "pure" one. There was more to Vietnamese mobilization than preventing senseless slaughter. The harm being done to Vietnamese citizens near the Cambodian border was more than a minor irritant to the country. Nonetheless, the Vietnamese government included humanitarian justifications in defending their actions. In debates before the UN Security Council, the Vietnamese delegation set out two different grounds for the invasion of Cambodia: self-defense and humanitarian intervention.[19] As Ronzitti describes the rationale of the Vietnamese forces:

> Vietnam's official position – such as it transpires from the United Nations Security Council debate – is as follows: the Kampuchean affair was made up of two distinct conflicts, the conflict between Vietnam and Kampuchea and the civil war itself in Kampuchea. Vietnam had been attacked by Kampuchea. It had therefore, reacted by exercising its right

---

19 For a short analysis of the competing claims about the origins of the conflict between Vietnam and Cambodia in the context of Article 51, see Klintworth (1989, 15–28).

> to self-defense. As far as the second conflict is concerned, it sprang from the inhuman conditions in which the population of Kampuchea was being kept by the régime in power. The people had rebelled by forming a United Front and had managed to overthrow the Pol Pot régime.
>
> Vietnam never claimed to have given military help to the rebels, nor to have intervened to re-establish human rights in Kampuchea (Ronzitti 1985, 99).

The Chinese defended the claim that the Vietnamese government acted out of self-defense. However, it is mistaken to suggest that these two conflicts are isolated: Vietnam trained and supported the United Front in camps along the Cambodia border. Their support for the exile army in the conflict is a form of intervention into the domestic affairs of Cambodia. Thus, in part at least, the Vietnamese invasion of Cambodia had a humanitarian basis to it.

The international reaction to the Cambodian intervention ranged from open hostility to faint praise, largely dictated by the strategic interests of cold-war *realpolitik*. A noteworthy exception to this general trend were the comments made by the American senator George McGovern who called for the use of force to stop the slaughter:

> I am wondering under these circumstances if any thought is being given, either by our Government or at the United Nations or anywhere in the international community of sending in a force to knock this Government out of power, just on humanitarian grounds.[20]

As Richard Butler, the Australian ambassador to Thailand asserted, the Cambodian intervention was "understandable."[21] That said, there have been a number of experts and diplomats who have offered guarded praise for the humanitarian aspects of Vietnam's war against the Khmer Rouge. Others, such as Beck, Arend, and Tesón refuse to characterize Vietnam's invasion as a humanitarian one at all, despite admitting a general satisfaction that the Khmer Rouge were dislodged from power (Arend and Beck 1993, 122–3).

Peace and Security: The Security Council's Chapter VII Powers

As previously discussed, Article 2(7) sets up a strong roadblock that prevents any easy case for intervention save in the context of the inherent right of states to defend themselves outlined in Article 51. However, there is another exception to the rule of non-intervention: following swiftly on the passage of Article 2(7) is an important caveat: "but this principle shall not prejudice the application of enforcement measures under Chapter VII." The reference to Chapter VII of the Charter points

---

20 See Indochina: Hearings before the Subcommittee on East-Asian and Pacific Affairs of the senate Committee on Foreign Relations, 95th Congress, 2nd Sess. (1978). Cited in Ronzitti (1985, 198).

21 See Klintworth (1989, 69) and Abiew (1999, 130). It is worthwhile to note that several scholars who are sympathetic to the doctrine of humanitarian intervention refuse to characterize this conflict as such.

to the enumerated powers and mechanisms of the Security Council in responding to threats to international peace and security. These enforcement measures are defined primarily by Article 39 of the Charter:

> The Security Council shall determine the existence of any threat to the peace, breach of the peace, or act of aggression and shall make recommendations, or decide what measures shall be taken in accordance with Articles 41 and 42, to maintain or restore peace and security.[22]

This second fundamental limitation on the sovereignty of states is their ability to threaten international peace. While still clearly limited to inter-state transactions, the UN Charter recognizes that there are good reasons to restrict the right of states to conduct their affairs as they see fit. While I have yet to justify humanitarian intervention via the UN Charter, I have laid its foundation in the aims of the UN itself (from Article 1): "To maintain peace and security."

These Chapter VII powers have been used to justify humanitarian interests as well as the right to intervene in a state's domestic affairs. In relation to the conflict in Yugoslavia, for example, the Security Council recognized that the ethnic conflict in the former Eastern Bloc country fell under the provisions of Article VII in Security Council Resolution 808:

> Expressing once again its grave alarm at continuing reports of widespread violations of international humanitarian law occurring within the territory of the former Yugoslavia, including reports of mass killings and the continuance of the practice of "ethnic cleansing",
>
> Determining that this situation constitutes a threat to international peace and security,
>
> Determined to put an end to such crimes, and to take effective measures to bring to justice the persons who are responsible for them,
>
> Convinced that in the particular circumstances of the former Yugoslavia the establishment of an international tribunal would enable this aim to be achieved and would contribute to the restoration and the maintenance of peace.

While not advocating the principle of humanitarian intervention (the resolution only validated the creation of an international criminal tribunal for the former Yugoslavian territories), Security Council Resolution 808 asserts that human rights and humanitarian concerns more generally (such as war crimes) in a domestic context are legitimate cause for invoking Chapter VII powers. Similarly, Security Council Resolution 688 (dealing with the suppression of the Kurdish minority in Iraq),

> *Demands* that Iraq, as a contribution to removing the threat to international peace and security in the region, immediately end this repression.[23]

---

22 Articles 41 and 42 outline the peaceful or forceful methods that the UN may use to maintain or restore international peace.

23 A similar line of reasoning was cited to justify UN intervention in Somalia in 1992 "acting under Chapter VII of the Charter of the United Nations."

In both of these cases, the rights of sovereign powers to determine their domestic policies were severely curtailed by their impact on the rest of the world. Here the line between domestic affairs and international affairs in relation to human rights becomes blurred even under the hard-nosed values of realism: peace and security.

Thus, even within the context of the UN's goal of protecting international peace and security, the right of states to be left alone to run their domestic affairs is not an absolute one (we could also discuss the prohibition of genocide under the Genocide Convention in this context [Schabas 2000, 1–14]). Just as humanitarian interventions may in part be justified by the inherent right of self-defense in Article 51, the rights entailed by Article 2(7) are limited by their impact on international peace and security. With the approval of the Security Council, states and other international organizations may intrude upon the sovereignty of a state to protect suppressed citizens. Of course, these powers of the Security Council are not absolute – they are constrained by other parts of the Charter, but clearly there are many cases where humanitarian intervention may be justified under the Chapter VII powers. In this context I will now discuss the American intervention in Haiti and its relation to both international peace and security as well as to the notion of humanitarian intervention.

Haiti

The overthrow of the democratic government of Haiti, headed by President Jean Bertrand Aristide, in the fall of 1991 by a military junta precipitated numerous events, culminating in preparations for a US invasion of the island government.[24] The lengthy gap (almost three years) between the appeal for assistance made by President Aristide to the UN and the actual mobilization of US and UN forces reveals the political difficulties involved in implementing such a doctrine. This intervention was carried out under Security Council Resolution 940 passed on 31 July 1994, which appeals to the Council's Chapter VII powers. There, the Council,

> Acting under Chapter VII of the Charter of the United Nations, authorizes Member States to form a multinational force under unified command and control and, in this framework, to use all necessary means to facilitate the departure from Haiti of the military leadership, consistent with the Governors Island Agreement, the prompt return of the legitimately elected President and the restoration of the legitimate authorities of the Government of Haiti…

The wording of this resolution is important because the Council had initially refused to confront the matter as it was first deemed to be purely domestic. As the *New York Times* reported, "The president of the Security Council had informed [a Haitian official] that a majority of the delegations felt there should not be a meeting on what was seen as 'an internal matter'" (Friedman 1991). Of particular note in this respect are China and Cuba, neither of which welcomed the idea of intervention based upon principles of human rights.

24 For a history of the downfall of the previous Duvalier regime, the succeeding juntas, and the rise, fall, and return of Aristide see Malone (1998).

There were numerous factors that transformed the minds of the Security Council members between the fall of 1991 and the summer of 1994. First, there had been several attempts to reach a negotiated settlement with Haiti's *de facto* military dictators Lt. Gen. Raoul Cedras and Brig. Gen. Phillipe Biambay. There was also a voluntary embargo carried out by the Organization of American States (OAS) and a UN General Assembly Resolution denouncing the coup. Then, in June 1993, the Security Council adopted Resolution 841, implementing a compulsory embargo under its Chapter VII powers, preventing any states from engaging in trade with the illegal regime. The embargo forced the dictatorship to consent to the Governor's Island Agreement, which was to reinstate the Aristide government, thereby causing the Security Council to lift the sanctions. This Agreement collapsed and UN troops were prevented from landing in Haiti as the agreement stipulated. As a result, in October 1993, the Council passed Resolution 873, reinstating the original embargo.

In Resolution 940, the UN were authorized to halt the brutal suppression of the democratic Aristide supporters and force the military to relinquish power. However, there are conflicting analyses of the meaning of the Council's invocation of Chapter VII in this resolution. For Tesón, it confirms his view that human rights violations in and of themselves entail a threat to peace and security, regardless of whether their effects spread beyond their borders. Here, he contrasts the Security Council's approach in Resolution 940 with Resolution 767 on Somalia, which explicitly stated that, the "situation in Somalia constitutes a threat to international peace and security."[25]

> In contrast with the case of Somalia, in this resolution, the Security Council *did not* determine that the situation in Haiti constituted a threat to international peace and security, while at the same time asserting that it was acting under Chapter VII of the Charter. Thus this case strengthens the [thesis]… that the practice of states has accepted serious violations of human rights as ground for action by the Security Council under Chapter VII (Tesón 1997, 253).

As Malone asserts (and Tesón concedes), the US motivation was not altruism. The flow of refugees into the United States and other nearby countries stemming from the Haitian dictatorship's oppression was clearly an annoyance for America and had caused political repercussions for President Clinton. Thus, "this knowledge makes it difficult to pigeon-hole comfortably the Haiti case as primarily a humanitarian intervention" (Malone 1998, 182).

What is to be made of the Security Council's invocation of Chapter VII in Resolution 940 then? Tesón admits that there is an interpretive ambiguity in the resolution (and its relationship to the previous Security Council pronouncements), but, somewhat unfairly, asserts that any attempt to read peace and security concerns into Resolution 940 is simply a dogmatic appeal to sovereignty. According to Tesón, the true meaning of the resolution *must* be found in the modern human rights regime.[26] However, this either–or dichotomy oversimplifies the legal matters at hand.

---

25 Cited in Tesón (1997, 242), see also Murphy (1996, 217–42).

26 As he describes it, "And again, the answer [to this reading] is that this is stubborn adherence to the noninterventionist thesis even when it flies squarely against the facts. No one

If the analysis of this section of the Chapter is correct, interventions may be *both* humanitarian in character *and* be aimed at a more conventional reading of Chapter VII powers. They are not mutually exclusive possibilities. Had there been a refugee crisis in Haiti without a coup, there probably would have been no intervention (after all, there have been many refugee crises in the world, especially in the United States, such as the Cuban flood in the 1960s, none of which provoked a military response), and had there been a coup without a refugee crisis the justification for the intervention *would have to be found outside of Chapter VII* (this is the topic of the next section). Thus, rather than seeing it simply as an act in the national interest of the US government, or a primarily humanitarian endeavor, one can see Haiti as a case of overlap between humanitarian concerns and the maintenance of peace and security as dictated in Chapter VII of the Charter. Both motives were relevant to the intervention and neither is tarnished by the presence of the other. Thus, Resolution 940's invocation of peace and security was both a response to the flood of foreign refugees into the United States *and* a condemnation of the regime that precipitated this crisis in the first place.

This brief discussion should make it clear that even under the sovereignty thesis, there is still a limited right of states to forcibly intervene in the affairs of other states for reasons that are quasi-humanitarian in character. Whether carried out in the name of self-defense, or under the banner of international peace and security, interventions of one state or group of states into another have taken place in history and have been justified within the body of international law.

But this argument is clearly not enough. There are certain cases, cases where the principles underlying Article 2(7) cannot be marshaled to defend a humanitarian sort of intervention. None of these arguments justify a "purely humanitarian intervention," that is, an excursion into another state where there is no direct or vicarious threat to any other state. Similarly, these arguments do not adequately confront a threat whose scope does not go so far as to be a threat to international order. This hypothetical problem becomes more acute, and much less hypothetical

can seriously argue that the Haitian situation posed a threat to international peace and security in the region. A more accurate reading of Resolution 940 is that the previous reference to threat [*sic*] to peace in the region in Resolution 841 was unpersuasive because it reflected neither the facts nor the normative context of the Haitian situation. For that reason the Council, in Resolution 940 sensibly abandoned the reference to the language of article 39." While this is certainly an interesting reading of Resolution 940, it ignores the fact that under Article 39, the Security Council is given the sole power of determining "the existence of any threat to the peace, breach of the peace," the threshold for this determination however, is not spelled out by the Charter. This power may not be unlimited given the constraints of Article 2(7) – although this too is debatable (see the *Lockerbie* case presently before the ICJ), the Council may decide that mass refugees do constitute such a threat. If so, then Tesón falls prey to his own objection of confusing psychological motivations for legal ones – by assuming that the motivations were *not* those of Article 39 despite the Council's legal pronouncements to the contrary (Resolution 940). As Justice Kooijmans (among others) has asserted, the Security Council has "complete discretion… with regard to the interpretation of the three concepts 'threat to the peace', 'breach of the peace' and 'act of aggression' which – once their existence has been determined – may unleash the régime under Chapter VII" (Kooijmans 1993, 111).

when we recognize that many of the controversial interventions to have taken place were done outside of the UN system, sometimes ignoring the dictates of the Security Council. While I have not discussed it here, the NATO bombings of Yugoslavia in response to "ethnic cleansing" in Kosovo come to mind as just such a case. In order to make this next step, to justify a purely humanitarian intervention, one must look beyond the Charter, to some other central texts of modern international law, those that comprise the International Bill of Rights.

Human Rights and Intervention: Article 1(3)

The rights of self-defense in Article 51 and the goals of international peace and security in Article 2(7) are not the only normative ideals set out in the Charter. These two values stand in sharp contrast with another stated goal of the organization: the promotion and protection of human rights. Among the purposes of the UN set out in Article 1 of the Charter is "promoting and encouraging respect for human rights and for fundamental freedoms for all without distinction as to race, sex, language, or religion." Reading the Charter and the related legal documents and through Article 1(3), an alternative picture of the Organization begins to emerge, one in which human rights stands, if not at the forefront, at least *near* the front of the word polity.

A few brief but important articles of the Charter set out the relevance of human rights to the international body: Article 55, part of Chapter IX of the Charter, asserts, "The United Nations shall promote: ...universal respect for, and observance of, human rights and fundamental freedoms for all without distinction as to race, sex, language or religion." Following closely upon this, Article 56 asserts that, "All Members pledge themselves to take joint separate action in co-operation with the Organization for the achievement of the purposes set forth in Article 55." This means that one of the central goals of the UN is to promote the rights of individuals, and this may be taken to be relevant in considering possible legal justifications for the use of force. If this human rights reading of the Charter can be rendered plausible, it will have significant impact upon the international law of humanitarian intervention, possibly creating a different justification for international interventions into states in order to protect the rights of individuals inside of the nation's borders.

Along with Articles 1(3), 55, and 56 of the Charter, are the documents that comprise the so-called "International Bill of Rights," particularly the Universal Declaration of Human Rights, the International Covenant on Civil and Political Rights, and the International Covenant on Social and Economic Rights. These documents lay the foundations for further treaties on the rights of children,[27] the rights of women,[28] and the elimination of discrimination among others.[29] It is frequently asserted by lawyers that these documents are not run-of-the-mill treaties, more trappings of a state-oriented legal system, but rather represent a dramatic turn in the

27 Convention on the Rights of the Child, G.A. Res. 44/25.

28 Convention on the Elimination of All Forms of Discrimination Against Women, R.A. Res. 34/180.

29 International Convention on the Elimination of all Forms of Racial Discrimination, 660 UNTS 195.

nature of the international legal system: by emphasizing the rights of individuals as a central value of the international legal system, these values challenge the legal primacy of sovereignty as well as the sometimes violently oppressive peace that this sovereignty is intended to provide (at least within the framework of the UN Charter). Regardless of whether these human rights treaties constitute a genuine revolution in international law, there is no mistaking the fact that they further flesh out and bolster this third reading of the UN Charter, one grounded in Article 1(3). The wide-spread acceptance of, and acquiescence to this international bill of rights makes it a viable, if developing lens through which to read the UN Charter and the international legal system stemming from it.

Along with the treaty-and charter-based foundations for the international human rights regime are the legal norms of human rights that have arisen through other means. Customary rules and *jus cogens* norms further substantiate the legal matrix of the human rights regime and the alternative reading of the UN Charter. Whether a state has acceded to the International Convention against Torture, there is widespread acknowledgment that torture violates a firmly established rule of customary international law. Even more strongly, *jus cogens* prohibitions against genocide oblige all parties (states or otherwise) independent of their will. They cannot derogate from the international law against genocide, and a treaty in which two states agree to carry out such acts of genocide is on these grounds not a real law. When these and similar rules are placed alongside the documents of the international bill of rights, the notion of human rights emerges as a basic element of public international law. If human rights (inside and outside the UN Charter) are a real part of international law, then while they may not trump other legal values, at a minimum they stand in competition with the goals of international peace and security and its primary component, the respect for the sovereignty of independent states, in the international legal regime.

Article 2(7) gets a profoundly different reading when seen through such a human rights reading of the Charter. While this article precludes interventions "in matters which are essentially within the domestic jurisdiction of any state," the word "essentially" takes on an entirely different meaning here. Human rights treaties, customary practice, and *jus cogens* norms of international law each circumscribe a much narrower conception of domestic jurisdiction than is commonly understood and substantially reduce those aspects of political dominion that are "essentially" a domestic concern. Human rights violations – even when limited to the confines of a particular state become an international matter. Whether the full gamut of human rights norms fall within the international domain (much less potential legal grounds for the use of force), and thus are no longer "essentially within the domestic jurisdiction of any state", it is clear that at a minimum torture and genocide (two prohibitions commonly accepted to be *jus cogens*) are no longer purely domestic matters. In the human rights reading of the Charter, there is no reason to accept that the principles articulated in Article 2(7) pose any great roadblock to humanitarian interventions in the face of egregious violations of human rights within a state.

Such a reading requires reinterpreting the Security Council's Chapter VII powers in a new light. The question now becomes: to what extent the notions of a "breach of the peace," "threat to the peace," and "act of aggression" are strictly international issues, relating the interactions between sovereign states, and to what extent they are defined through the lens of the International Bill of Rights. If these acts of aggression can only be acts of one state against another, then it is clearly the case that there is no right of humanitarian intervention within the framework of the United Nations. However, if a government commits breaches of peace or acts of aggression against its own people (or such acts are committed by one ethnic group against another), then it is clear that the UN, through the Security Council, could authorize the intervention into the domestic affairs of one state.

In none of the cases that I have examined were the interventions predicated *entirely* on humanitarian concerns, entirely within the legal discourse of human rights. In each example the states made recourse either to a principle of self-defense (such as in Vietnam's invasion of Cambodia and India's war with Pakistan), or to the Security Council's mandate to uphold peace and security along with citing the atrocities in the subject state. However, and this is important, *in every case human rights violations were considered relevant for the interveners*. While Cambodia is a notable exception to this principle (as the Vietnamese claimed that it was not them, but the Cambodians themselves who were out to overthrow the Khmer Rouge), in each case the states involved cited the atrocities committed in the oppressor state in discussing their grounds for intervention. In all of these cases, these arguments were relevant to understanding the legal justification for the act, and in some of these cases, the arguments were accepted by other states (or, as with the Indian intervention, they weren't rejected). This means that humanitarian concerns are in principle relevant for understanding the legitimate use of force under modern international law.

What does this reading of these events, coupled with the analysis of human rights described in this section entail? Namely, that human rights violations are a legally relevant aspect of international affairs even when they are kept within the confines of a particular state and are also relevant when states or international organizations seek to justify the use of force against others. If they were not relevant, they would not have been mentioned in the public, *legal* pronouncements of agents whose utterances have a legal dimension to them. The fact that they are routinely mentioned in the relevant legal documents means that they are legally significant for determining the right to intervene. They may not have the sole justification for intervention in previous cases (and given the realities of world politics, it is unlikely that they would *ever* be the sole reason for intervention), but this does not mean that as a point of law they cannot serve as a sufficient condition for the use of force. International human rights laws are an important part of determining if and when force should be applied (either unilaterally, or under the umbrella of an international organization) and there is no reason to believe that they could not serve as they sole ground for intervention. Thus Article 2(7) must be read in terms of both Article 1(3) of the Charter as well as the previous practices of state parties and other international persons with a legislative capacity.

Where can one find these references to human rights as part of the international laws of armed force? As Sydney Bailey has shown in his work *The UN Security Council and Human Rights* (1994), the Council has dealt with human rights matters in a number of different contexts, some of which have been relevant to the use of force. Along with Resolutions 808 (Yugoslavia) and 688 (Iraq) cited above, there are a number of cases where the Security Council has taken human rights concerns under consideration. For example, Resolution 361, dealing with the conflict in Cyprus, "*Calls upon* all parties to do everything in their power to alleviate human suffering, to ensure the respect for human rights."[30] Security Council Resolutions 733 and 794 called for humanitarian intervention into Somalia, suggesting that there was an international basis for intervention in this failed state, despite the fact that the problems in Somalia were largely limited to the domestic plain.[31] Thus there have been numerous cases where the Security Council has considered the matter of human rights relevant to international law in the context of the use of force or other kinds of intervention. In each of these cases, the Security Council has established a precedent for human rights to be a justified use of force in international law.

Outside of the Security Council there has been less willingness to allow for a legally justified *unilateral* humanitarian intervention, but there is some reason to believe that it is there. As Tesón shows, the international response to India's intervention, while far from laudatory, nonetheless had aspects to it that recognized the legitimacy of India's efforts to rescue the people of Bangladesh:

> It is true that the dominant concern of states who participated in the UN discussion was the restoration of peace, rather than the condemnation of one of the parties. But even these statements and the wording itself of General Assembly Resolution 2793 (XXVI) show that nations were also concerned with "the restoration of the conditions necessary for the voluntary return of refugees", an ultra-euphemism to urge Pakistan to renounce its genocidal policies... [T]he majority did not react by flatly condemning India for a violation of article 2(4). Rather, the majority implicitly acknowledged that the normative force of that principle is attenuated where acts of genocide are concerned (Tesón, 1997, 208–10).

In cases like this, cases where states (partially) justified their unilateral uses of force by reference to human rights and this reason was (partially) accepted by the international community, they created a benchmark – or more precisely, they have set a precedent. This precedent, rooted in the human rights reading of the charter outlined above shows that at times when extreme acts of violence take place inside a state, and international bodies do not act, a state may unilaterally use force to stop it themselves.

As Beck and Arend, two critics of a legal conception of humanitarian intervention, put their view: "If humanitarian intervention is to be legally permissible, then it is the task of states to render it so" (Arend and Beck 1998, 136). The resolutions cited above, where the Security Council considered human rights as part of the basis for the legitimate use of force, did so. The arguments given by India and Vietnam for their interventions, when they cited human rights violations, did so, as did the response of the international community. This means that there is no reason to believe that in the future there couldn't be a case where similar principles are applied, a case where

30 UN SC Res. 361 (August 30, 1974).

31 As Ioan Lewis and James Mayall observe: "This was the first time that an unambiguously internal and humanitarian crisis had been designated as a threat to international peace and security" (1996, 94).

there was no significant overlap between the more conventional understandings of Article 51 and traditional notions of "peace and security." Both inside and outside the Security Council, there has been a precedent set that in cases of the gross violation of human rights the use of force (whether unilateral or multilateral) is legal.

This argument constitutes the "thin end of the wedge" that I discussed at the opening of this chapter. If both world society and the Security Council have been willing to consider these violations of human rights as relevant to the legal use of force (or as a threat to international peace and security), then there is no reason to believe that they could not and would not do so again. If, as numerous historians have argued, there had been no intervention with a rationale that was purely humanitarian in character, but they were nonetheless willing to consider human rights as relevant to the issues at hand, then there is no reason to believe that human rights could not likewise be relevant in the future. The primary purpose of the discussions of Haiti and Bangladesh was to show that in these mixed interventions, human rights were taken to be a valid part of the legal basis for intervention. The Security Council has recognized this relevance in its own declarations, and the international community has done likewise. Even in cases such as the Vietnamese intervention, international actors grudgingly accepted the claim that atrocities may at times justify intervention. With the next Cambodia, an intervening state may rely upon and further expand upon these assertions in a new, albeit similar context.

Clearly, this is not a decisive argument, and one should not overstate the human rights components of the UN Charter in relation to the authorized use of force. The Security Council still plays a role as the ultimate arbiter of the use of force within the UN system, although the grounds for such force are much broader than they are commonly understood to be. Additionally, the Council's Chapter VII powers to use force – as set out in Article 42 – limit the basis of their use to the goal of peace and security:

> Should the Security Council consider that measures provided for in Article 41 would be inadequate or have proved to be inadequate, it may take such action by air, sea, or land forces *as may be necessary to maintain or restore international peace and security*. Such action may include demonstrations, blockade, and other operations by air, sea, or land forces of Members of the United Nations.

By limiting the objectives of the use of force to the restoration of peace and security, the Charter has severely hampered the ability of the UN to justify the use of force in the name of defending human rights. This roadblock to a legal basis for humanitarian intervention, though imposing, is not an impassible one, as there are alternatives for the use of force within the framework of the UN Charter but beyond the authority of the Security Council.

Conclusion

At the opening of this chapter, I stated that the law of humanitarian intervention, as presented in this chapter, is much more controversial than the foregoing discussion of international legal personality. A large number of international lawyers are suspicious of a legal justification for humanitarian intervention and I doubt that this study has gone a long way to changing the minds of many. Sometimes, this wariness comes from the assumptions of the sovereignty thesis, other times it stems from a healthy skepticism towards international politics more generally. No doubt, this has developed from a sober view of the history of international relations. The US invasion of Iraq, conducted with dubious references to humanitarian concerns, has only strengthened their suspicions. This means that experts are usually unable or unwilling to accept the possibility of humanitarian intervention in the form I have set out here or in other forms.

Such controversy has certain consequences for my overall theory of international law. As I mentioned three chapters ago, there is no magic key to international law, such as the proponents of the various methodologies have asserted. There is no easy way to clearly determine what international law says on this or that topic. Rather, I asserted that it is ultimately up to the lawyers and others in the know to cobble together the various treaties, customs, and general principles in order to make their case – just as their opponents do. This means that a critic of the notion of humanitarian intervention, in order to reject my analysis, must engage in a project similar to mine, seeking to make coherent an overarching case in favor of sovereignty against forcible humanitarian action. The difference between the issue of legal personality and that of humanitarian intervention is that I am willing to concede that this critical project would be much easier here than in the former case. However, those of us who are cautiously bullish on the notion of humanitarian action in international law believe that things are changing and that certain forms of humanitarian intervention will become more acceptable in the future.

It is not the past cases that should concern the scholar, however. The legality of the use of force in 1978 Cambodia or 1971 Bangladesh are more a matter of scholarly debate than a necessary component of contemporary international law. Rather, the argument in this chapter is that there is no reason to believe that international law forbids armed intervention into the domestic affairs of other states in future cases. The point is to imagine future situations where such laws may be appropriate. The Security Council and the international community more generally *have considered these types of arguments relevant in past legal decisions*, even if those concerns were mixed with other, more conventional issues, such as self-defense. This means that in a future case, there is no reason to believe that concerns about human rights may not be used to justify intervention in light of some future atrocities. They may not only be relevant, but as I argued above, they may at times be sufficient justification for intervention.

I should hasten to add a distinction that is sometimes overlooked in the literature surrounding the international law of humanitarian intervention, trite though it may be: the distinction between what the law is, and what it ought to be. Frequently, criticisms of the law of humanitarian intervention have suggested that such laws are dangerous or undesirable, or that they will in the long haul be destructive to political security and human life. This may be the case (just as the opposite may turn out to be the case), but this does not entail that the law of humanitarian intervention is not a genuine part of international law – nor does it justify ignoring the law as it is. If the evaluation of the law in this chapter is correct, then those who wish to prevent future interventions should work towards changing those laws that make intervention possible, not denying their existence. A sober look at the law of humanitarian intervention can be equally useful to those who are skeptical about these interventions as well as those (like me) who support such interventions in certain contexts.

I suggested earlier that many of the conceptual objections to humanitarian intervention have been coupled with a concern about the consequences that such interventions have for international peace and stability. The argument – one that might be associated with what I had labeled the prudential diplomat in the first chapter – is that opening the door to legalized intervention could give powerful states cover for meddling in the affairs of weaker states. As one prominent international lawyer put it, the right to intervene is a right in which only strong states may partake. While I haven't directly engaged with this idea in this chapter until now (primarily because it is largely a question of whether a certain law is desirable and not about existing international law), I did not mean to sound dismissive with what is a very legitimate concern. The principle of non-intervention in international law has served a valuable function and no doubt prevented many conflicts that would otherwise have been disastrous. The argument that opening the door to legitimate interventions will be a permission slip for states to pick on others has a good deal of *prima facie* merit to it.

Of course, none of this means that the law of humanitarian intervention is not potentially open to abuse. Powerful states could seek to use theses laws in myriad ways to increase their influence among smaller states – finding excuses to butt into their domestic affairs or to replace unfavorable regimes. Stronger states are always bullying smaller ones, of course, by a number of means, some of which are legal others non-legal (does anybody believe that the Nazis would have abandoned their military designs were there no possible recourse to a legal principle of humanitarian intervention?). However, ambiguous notions of humanitarian intervention are more susceptible to abuse the more ambiguous they are allowed to remain. Were there a clear set of principles defining international humanitarian intervention, rules stipulating the circumstances in which one may invoke humanitarian principles to invade, these interventions would probably be less frequently abused by powerful states.

At the opening of this chapter I cited the view that humanitarian intervention represents an insoluble split between two competing conceptions of international law and the values that underlie them. To quote Bederman again:

> The riddle of humanitarian intervention lies at the center of international law discourse. It may reflect a handful of true value conflicts in the discipline, and while it would be easy to characterize the lines of division in expected ways… the reality is far more complex and unsettling. The lines of paradox in values of international law cut across expected frontiers. Some of the conflicts do exhibit tendencies of exacerbating debates between old and new objectives, but other feature battles between values within ostensibly common groupings (Bederman 2002, 137).

I hope that I have solved this paradox, at least in part. By suggesting that there is in most cases an overlap between the more traditional values of sovereignty and more humanitarian impulses, the approach outlined here need not rely on the radical split in values that Bederman makes. If one abandons the traditional notions of *raison d'état*, or the idea that states are creatures with intentions, than he need not cling strongly to the idea that states are things that are capable of making value judgments, much less things that are capable of having moral paradoxes. However, this line of reasoning will become clearer, I suspect, once the account of the agency of international legal actors has been more explicitly spelled out in the next chapter.

These last four chapters have been involved with understanding the nature of international law. Particularly, I have sought to explicate what I take to be the definition of what international law is, the proper way in which to conceptualize international law through the non-reductive definition outlined in Chapter 2 (and defended further in Chapter 3). Then, I have used this definition to explicate two central domains of international law: international legal personality and the international law of humanitarian intervention. Of course, this is not a comprehensive study of international law and a great deal of the legal doctrine must remain unconsidered for the sake of brevity. These two chapters have simply been an attempt to put the doctrine set out in Chapter 2 to use in two central areas.

These last two chapters have sought both to apply as well as to flesh out what international law looks like "from the inside" as it were. This is to say, I have sought to explain what it is that international lawyers (and others in the know – to revive a term from Chapter 2) take the law to be, or at least what they should take the law to be. This non-reductive approach to international law can be applied (and I would argue that it *is applied*) by practicing international lawyers in significantly more mundane matters than the one discussed here. In the next chapter, I will switch gears, so to speak, and address what I have referred to as the "reality" of international law. Rather than looking at international law in the abstract as a set of rules defined by a cadre of experts, in the next chapter I will look at what impact these rules have on the actual political behavior of various agents. In some sense then I will turn away from law and towards political science (and social science more broadly) in order to decide what makes a law "real" – thus targeting those realists who assert that international law is irrelevant.

Chapter 6

Empiricism and the Reality of International Law

When I discussed the skepticism of the realists in the opening chapter, I distinguished between *descriptive realism* on the one hand, and *prescriptive realism* on the other. The former, I argued, took the claim that international law has no empirical reality as one about the nature of international relations, while the latter maintained that even if international law were a valid lens through which to view the workings of international politics, it shouldn't be. It is the former, the descriptive realists, to whom I will turn in this chapter, leaving the prescriptive realists for the final chapter. Specifically, I will be explaining and evaluating the view that a correct understanding of international relations requires that one ignore the rules of international law or at least doesn't require recourse to international legal norms. Thus, when I use the term "realist" in this chapter, I will be referring to the descriptive crowd.

As I mentioned in Chapter 1, there are two possible means by which the realist can assert that international law is (to use their own term) *epiphenomenal.* There is the argument from moral psychology and the argument from the best explanation. The former approach asserts that, given the inherent nature of the states and their political activity, there is no way that international legal norms could influence political behavior. Whether or not individual people are capable of being moved by rules, norms, and laws in their everyday lives, surely states are incapable of being so moved. Interest, fear, and power, the stuff of conventional power politics, is what fuels political action, not principles and rules or other abstract ideals, however noble these values might be. Waltz, Posner, and Goldsmith among others, claim this view frequently appears as a theory of rationality embodied in game theoretical models: that is, the nature of rationality (or so the story goes) is to pursue one's self-interest at all times, and to subsume one's interests to law is not simply imprudent, but is fundamentally irrational.[1] Given such a conception of human (and political) nature, international law looks like a somewhat silly, if not downright dangerous approach to international relations.

But there are two good reasons for rejecting such arguments. First, such a set of assumptions are not immediately incompatible with asserting that international law is real in the relevant sense. One could accept the principle that states and other international political agents act out of their perceived self-interest, and still maintain that obeying the rules of international law can be (and often is) in the interest of these

1 As Waltz puts it (expounding on Rousseau): "If harmony is to exist in anarchy, not only must I be perfectly rational, but I must be able to assume that everyone else is too. Otherwise there is no basis for rational calculation" (Waltz 1959, 170).

agents. Following international laws can be advantageous for states for a number of reasons: giving them political leverage in particular situations, allowing them to avoid sanctions when they violate the law, or facilitating cooperation where states share mutual interests (and minimizing conflict when they don't). This view is common in modern international relations theory, frequently among theorists who work under the title "rational institutionalism." This school of IR-theory seeks to explain how international institutions such as international law and other political bodies develop as a result of interactions between a group of self-interested actors that have no common authority and in turn analyze how these institutions interact with the actors in their respective pursuit of their aims.[2] For institutionalism, "Institutions can modify anarchy sufficiently to allow states to cooperate over the long term to achieve their common goals" (Slaughter 2004, 27). Similarly in the realm of classic domestic political philosophy, Hobbes maintained that the rule of law was not only compatible with a group of self-interested agents but was even essential to it.[3] Thus, *pace* the descriptive realists, law can and often is justified by appealing to the self-interest of individual states.[4]

Second, moral-psychological arguments for rejecting international law are unsatisfactory because they are not fallible by their very nature, depriving them of any strong explanatory value (which does not mean that they are invaluable, of course). As I argued in Chapter 1, the fact that these theories cannot be disproved in an empirical fashion makes them unscientific in a very deep sense of the word. One of the strengths that the realists believed their position held was that they could offer a strong explanation of what happens in international politics, reducing the chaos on the front pages of newspapers to a set of clearly identifiable, quasi-scientific laws that can be applied to future circumstances. However, the realists who choose to base their views on this sort of moral psychology or rationality cannot truly offer a kind of scientific explanation simply because they cannot offer a counterfactual situation where a state would not be following its interests.[5] The primary assumption of moral-psychological realism is not falsifiable and thus does not stand as an adequate scientific explanation. To ask when would a state be construed as not following their own interests is to ask a question about the conditions for denying the realist thesis. Unfortunately, this question cannot be settled through the *a priori* categories of moral psychology alone (such as "interest"), but must refer to actual conditions of explanations for empirical events.[6] Realism begins to look more like a metaphysical principle based more on a particular conception of human nature.

---

2 For a critique of a rationalist-institutionalist foundation for international law see Arend (1999, 119–240).

3 Hobbes' views regarding the relationship between the international order and the pursuit of rational self-interest are more complicated than they are usually understood to be. For an interesting study of Hobbes' views on global politics see Tuck (1999).

4 I should note, however, that I am dramatically oversimplifying a long-standing debate in the theory of international relations here.

5 As an exasperated friend once put this point to me: "All states follow their own interests. Why did a state do something? Well, simply find some interest there."

6 "Every theory, to be worthwhile, must have implications about the observations we expect to find if the theory is correct" (King et al. 1994, 28).

Given this, it is perhaps better (and certainly more interesting) to understand descriptive realists as making a somewhat different claim: that the best explanation for all of the empirical data suggests that international legal rules ought to be ruled out of global politics. This approach, let's call it the *explanatory adequacy approach*, is a genuinely empirical claim and thus stands much closer to the methods of modern science insofar as the realist is understood to be engaged with the world and seeking to offer the best explanation of the events that have happened in the past and presumably will happen in the future. Similarly, the realist could have a much better chance of formulating predictions about future events, predictions that *could* be false, and thus meet epistemological criteria for a good explanation. Finally, a realism based in an explanatory adequacy approach seems to be better suited to critically and constructively engage with those theorists who are optimistic about the role that international law plays in international society. The two camps must compare their explanations for events, one using the law, and one refusing to do so, and see who "wins," that is, who has the best grasp of the relevant facts.

According to the realists, such optimists (I will refer to them in this chapter as "legalists") are viewed from an explanatory adequacy approach as offering explanations for political events that will ultimately fail on empirical, not theoretical grounds. Rather than being merely conceptually flawed, their failure stems from problems that arise when they use their ideas to understand actual events in the actual world. "When all is said and done," a realist would charge, "legalist approaches to international law cannot really be useful guides to understanding the world around us. While their philosophical foundations may be cogent, their utility in making sense of global politics, the world in which politicians, lawyers, and diplomats actually work, is nil. Anybody who cared to take international law as their guide to understanding global relations will quickly encounter roadblocks at every turn, whereas realists are much better able to explain global political events as they happen and predict how they will happen in the future." Here, the argument is not one about theoretical pedigree as much as one of value in understanding the world in which you and I exist, not to mention foreign ministers, diplomats, soldiers, and criminals. The explanatory adequacy approach then is a much better position from which the realist (and any other theoretical model of international relations) could assert the epiphenomenality of international legal rules than that of moral psychology. It has its "feet on the ground" as it were.

It is important to note that underlying such an approach is the equation of the reality of international law with its explanatory efficacy. This is to say that for international law to be considered "real" in a particular case, it must be part of an adequate explanation of the events that occur at a given time and place (and it should be noted, in the answer to a particular question about these events). In contrast, to say that a law is "not real" is thus to claim that it is useless *in this context*, in the particular events for which one seeks an explanation, to understand the events that occur.[7] We will see below that it would be imprudent and unwarranted to make vast generalizations regarding the reality of international law in its totality, abstracting

7 Following Risjord, I will ignore the distinction between "explanations" and "understanding" in social scientific analysis (Risjord 2000, 147–9).

from any particular context, case, or question. Given the arguments above, this approach is the most productive and philosophically grounded way to frame the long debated question of whether international law is "real" and not merely some chimera belonging to an elite society of naïve idealists.

However, putting the issue of the reality of international law in this way will impose some artificial language upon the analysis. The previous two chapters were dedicated to uncovering the rules of international law using the non-reductionist definition I spelled out in Chapter 2. To the extent that a rule of international law fits into this definition, we may say that the law is real. However, this determination has nothing to do with its explanatory adequacy, as the question of the "reality" of law is understood in this chapter. This entails that there will be a certain number of rules that meet the formal criteria of Chapter 2 (and are to that extent real), but fail to have any serious role to play in explaining events that occur within international society, and thus we must conclude that they are not real in the sense discussed in this chapter.[8] Perhaps with these rules we may say that they have a formal reality, but no material reality (or, as is sometimes said, there is a right without a remedy). However, for the purposes of this chapter, reality will be understood solely in terms of the previous paragraph, that is, in terms of its ability to explain events of global politics.[9]

The purpose of this chapter is three-fold: first, I will discuss the nature of explanations in general and argue that a particular form of explanation, rationalizing explanations, is the relevant sort for understanding debates surrounding the reality question in international law. Second, I will seek to understand what roles normative rules in general, and legal rules in particular, can play in these kinds of explanations. Here, I will seek to articulate a set of guides by which legal norms can be adequately understood to form part of a valid explanation of events, a set of criteria that indicate that a law is somehow in effect. That is, when is it appropriate to refer to the law (and to the notion of "following the law") when explaining a particular event or action? Finally, I will offer "counter-examples," evidence that could be used to refute the claim that law is not in effect in a particular case. These will serve as potential ammunition for the realists to respond to legalists in particular cases where they believe that international law is irrelevant.

Thus, my approach will take its guide from the social-scientific values of the realists but amplified with some philosophy of social science. In doing this, I hope to articulate a philosophical framework that is sophisticated enough to accommodate both realists and others (such as myself) who maintain that international law is real and is necessary to understand the unfolding of political events. Thus I will attempt to lay the groundwork for any empirical study of the roles that international law plays within global political society – the task of the next chapter. This chapter, then,

8 I am grateful to Michael Sullivan for pointing out this piece of linguistic trickery to me.

9 Another possible solution might have been to reject the term "reality" altogether and choose another term to explain the explanatory adequacy approach. However, given my preceding arguments regarding the futility of descriptive realism to adequately reject the reality of international law without resorting to an explanatory approach, I feel that changing terms in the middle of an argument would ultimately prove more confusing than illuminating.

will require a somewhat in-depth discussion of philosophy of social science and the role that explanations and rules play therein, as well as taxing some of our ordinary intuitions regarding the law and its relation to human behavior. Once this necessarily abstract work is done, we will then be ready to test our approach in the real world.

At the outset we can recognize that the claim made by some realists that international law is epiphenomenal cannot hold in any strong sense in an explanatory adequacy approach. The notion of epiphenomenality, taken from debates in the philosophy of mind, asserts that an epiphenomenal thing plays no essential role in the causal mechanisms of a given system, as if it were a gear on a machine that although it turned with the rest of the mechanism was attached to no other part (thus it is caused to move by the machine, but does not in turn cause something else to move). For example, philosophers of mind assert, "Only physical states have causal power, and that mental states are completely dependent on them. The mental realm… is nothing more than a series of conscious states which signify the occurrence of states of the nervous system, but which play no causal role" (Campbell and Smith 1998, 351). This assertion, if true, is not simply a brute metaphysical assertion of "the way things are," based on *a priori* conceptual analysis, as much as it is parasitic upon the explanatory power of modern cognitive science that is ultimately rooted in the explanatory power of biology and neuroscience. There is no social scientific theory that dismisses the causal power of rules with anything approximating the explanatory power of neuroscience, and thus attempts to rule out international law by fiat are unwarranted. This means that for the explanatory realist to make her skepticism towards international law compelling, she must go through the labor-intensive task of offering empirical accounts of international politics and showing that in no case are explanations that appeal to international law as having any explicit, causal role, the superior explanations. This, in turn, presupposes the work that this chapter sets out to accomplish.

In addition, I should further note that my argument as I will lay it out here is based on the fundamental assumption that it is possible to understand the behavior of political agents in international relations to a degree adequate to explain their actions. This may of course seem overly optimistic given the level of secrecy that surrounds modern diplomacy. The existence of covert, diplomatic communiqués, hidden agendas, and cloak-and-dagger intelligence activities always produce a certain degree of uncertainty in explaining international political events, even decades after the events to be explained have taken place.[10] But I should hasten to note that this is a problem for realists as well as for legalists alongside all other forms of empirical inquiry: new data may always arise, forcing researchers to reevaluate long-accepted beliefs about the world. Regardless, if this assumption is incorrect and international politics can't be explained in any meaningful way, then realists and legalists have nothing to argue over and political philosophy in general is dead in the water.

10 As I write this, the *New York Times* has reported on secret diplomatic cables between the US Embassy in Paraguay and Washington D.C. regarding US assistance in "Operation Condor," the attempt by numerous rightist governments in Latin America to crush leftist politicians and leftist governments in South and Central America in the early 1970s (Schemo 2001).

Explanations

Whenever a political event of any significance (X) happens, an army of scholars, news analysts, columnists, and other luminaries rush to television, radio, and print to *explain* what happened. In front of the cameras they tick off a series of causes and events all of which, when taken in their totality, point to how X inevitably must have occurred. The personalities, events, or circumstances (…T, U, V, W) that preceded X led to the set of choices that made X a necessary consequence. Some choose to point to events that took place years (and sometimes centuries) ago as lighting a fuse that slowly burned to the point where X took place. Others point to a few key decisions or a few basic mistakes made by important people that led to X. Finally others, such as Marxists, point to broad economic and social forces that in a more or less teleological fashion led to X. Regardless of their chosen method, these experts are all seeking to put X in a broader context wherein X is no longer a random event manifesting itself *ex nihilo*, but somehow "makes sense." To this extent, they are claiming to offer an explanation of why X must have happened.[11]

Of course, these expert accounts are frequently *ad hoc*, and are not taken particularly seriously by intelligent viewers, listeners, or readers *qua* explanations. Usually, they are set against others on a panel of speakers who may offer competing accounts of why things happened they way they did, from which the critical viewer may choose the one that seems best to her. However, other explanations seem to carry more weight, sometimes they carry the air of "scientificity," that is, they claim to be definitive and exclusive of any other valid explanation. In natural science, this is largely uncontroversial: the philosophy of science has a strong and fairly well articulated epistemology that allows the expert to distinguish valid science from pseudo-science. Despite the fact that there are some important areas of scientific explanations where there are profound differences among the experts, there is such a broad range of issues where scientists are in complete or nearly complete unanimity that we are usually willing to take their word as gospel when they speak on issues of genuine scientific merit (and not social policy). Thus scientific explanations seem, within the normal order of discourse, to be complete, exclusive, and decisive when they are presented in their field.

Social scientific explanations are, however, quite different. Such explanations do not claim to be mere opinions about an event, to be accepted or rejected at the listener's discretion. Nor are they tied into a broad "web" of other scientifically validated beliefs like those found in natural science. In fact, unlike most natural sciences, there is a wide array of views in social science and different social scientists will purport to be giving explanations that are exclusive, yet simultaneously incompatible with other plausible explanations of events. Unlike natural science, there is no broad base of accepted principles in social science and disagreements about the appropriate

11 "To explain the phenomena in the world of our experience, to ask the question 'why?' rather than only the question 'what?', is one of the foremost objectives of rational inquiry; and especially scientific research in its various branches strives to go beyond a mere description of its subject matter by providing an explanation of the phenomena it investigates" (Hempel and Oppenheim 1994, 135).

subject matter run much deeper than in natural science. For example, classical Marxists, structural anthropologists, and psychoanalytic approaches each contend that they are explaining a particular ritual of a lost, forgotten, and primitive tribe (call them "undergraduates"), but surely these explanations are, on the whole, mutually exclusive. Social scientific explanations are diversified among the different theoretical models and are not capable of unification (even in principle) into one seamless explanation. The undergraduate ritual of drinking large quantities of beer cannot be explained as both a manifestation of class struggle and an attempt to sublimate unconscious sexual urges (without appeal to some, larger explanatory theory that might unify these two approaches, which would only beg the question as another explanation would soon come along to compete with this one). Given this fact, how can we determine which explanation of a social-scientific phenomenon is the best, all things considered?

When we seek to explain human behavior, we usually want an answer to what philosophers refer to as a "why question," such as, "Why did my cat curl up on my chair?" or, "Why did the United States invade Grenada?"[12] Answers to these why questions may come in different forms, and thus philosophers have found it useful to distinguish between different kinds of questions (usually under the concept of erotetic logic) (Harrah 1984) as well as different kinds of explanations to such questions. We can say that different approaches develop different *explanatory strategies*. Mechanical, causal explanations, for example, are strategies that seek to explain behavior solely based upon the contents of the physical universe devoid of minds and other signs of sentience. To the banal question, "Why is John driving on the right side of the road?" a mechanistic explanation would simply state: "Because his steering wheel is oriented so that the car remains on one side of the street." The next step in this chain would be to state that the explanation for the steering wheel being so oriented is because his arm is in the position to keep it such a manner, and so on, and so on. In responding thusly we have offered a brief and quite unsatisfying analysis of why a person would drive on the right side of the road (unsatisfying, at least, from the standpoint of the normal questioner). In particular, such explanations tell us nothing that would be relevant for an analysis of human as well as political behavior unless we reduced this behavior to the model of a crude mechanistic psychology, denying any rational, intentional behavior on any agent's part. Whether these types of explanations cohere with the *weltanschauung* of modern physical science, they tell us nothing interesting or useful about political behavior.

Rationalizing explanations on the other hand are explanatory strategies that seek to understand an explanandum by looking at the reasons that compel a certain agent to act in a particular way. Here, we give explanations that may more properly be construed as "conscious" reasons for his behavior, and thus we can also refer to these explanations as "reason-giving explanations." When we give such explanations we assume a certain stance towards our subject matter: we see agents as, "rational purposive creatures, fitting our beliefs to the world as we perceive it and seeking to obtain what we desire in the light of them" (Hopkins 1982, Introduction).[13] Thus,

12 See and Risjord (1998) and Khalifa (2004).

13 See also Lennon (1994).

when we answer the question, "Why is John is driving his car on the right side of the road?" with, "Because he believes that it is appropriate," or "why is my cat curling up on my lap?" with, "Because she is sleepy and my lap is warm," we have given reasons to explain their behavior. Thus, the formal property of all rationalizing explanations is that they explain an act or event by appealing to beliefs and reasons (rather than mechanical causes), and if the reasons ascribed are satisfactory, we say that the event has been explained. An exploration of the principles governing rationalizing explanations will show why they present the most compelling avenue by which to explore the role that international rules play (or don't play) in global politics.

To be effective, rationalizing explanations make several assumptions about the events, actions, or agents that they seek to explain (which philosophers call the explanandum). First, the explanandum must be the doing of a being that possesses beliefs and desires that influenced the event that took place and effectively eliminated the other possibilities (Wallace 1990, 355) (rationalizing explanations do not explain why a cell divides into two or why earthquakes happen). This intentional element is of course imperfect, that is, we do not always do what is in our best interests when we act in a particular way and the agent may appear intentional, but not in fact be so. Additionally, our choices and acts may be subject to a rational explanation. The act may turn out to be mistaken, imprudent, or downright stupid, but this does not make the activity any less rational. Third, the act must have been intentional, that is, the agent must have knowledge of what he, she, or it, was doing at the time of the deed and the act must be willful. Accidentally spilling a cup of coffee does not warrant a rationalizing explanation. Finally, rationalizing explanations invoke the idea that we are not mere parts or a larger whole but that human interactions involve individual agents that are responsible for our own actions and are capable of acting *qua* individuals. These assumptions are necessary for a rationalizing explanation to be valid and, equally important, to be believable.

It is clear from this discussion that international political behavior (legal or otherwise) can be productively understood through the explanatory strategy of rationalizing explanations. And given what we have already said about explanations and the ontology of law, it follows that whether one chooses to accept the idea that international law is "real" will depend upon whether one can fit law into a rational explanation of a particular event. The tools used by the realists in order to explain political behavior, such as the notion of national interest, appeal to reasons why a state or other international political agent would act in the way they do, and thereby offer rationalizing explanations:

> "Why did state X do act Y?"
> "Because X believed that it was in its interest."

This sort of explanation offers reasons for an action that are neither the product of blind mechanisms of cause and effect, nor are they the best understood as simply a cog in a mechanism that produces broader results. Such explanations preserve agency – in fact, they rely upon it. Alongside the realists, I will argue in the next section of this chapter that the best way to understand legal behavior is according to the behavior underlying rationalizing explanations. Thus, when scholars seek to offer the best explanation of any agent's behavior (be it Kenya, the Foreign Minister of the United Kingdom, or my cat) in a form that preserves the essence of his, her, or its agency, they will always be offering rationalizing sorts of explanations.

Having determined which category of explanations is most suited to the social-scientific understanding of international relations, the next step is to clarify the relationship holding between such rationalizing explanations and the notion of law. This is to say, we must inquire into exactly what forms of rationalizing explanations cohere with our considered intuitions about "following the law," and which reasons for behavior undermine this notion. I propose to do this by first explaining how legal norms may be appropriately used in rationalizing explanations (that is, when we may properly say that a person is "following the law" as an explanation for their behavior) and then to show when such explanations would fail to explain behavior. Thus, I will start with the assumption that laws are possible candidates for explaining political behavior when certain criteria are met and that they are not good candidates, when explanations cannot meet these criteria.[14] This is to say, I am shifting the burden of proof away from legalism and onto realism. Rationalizing explanations begin with the assumption that most political activity is law abiding unless it can be proven to be otherwise.

A further note must be offered regarding *what* is to be explained. Any event of any kind is a valid candidate for explanation and one can tailor one's inquiry to suit one's own aims and interests. This is to say that what one considers to be important or worth explaining is up to the needs and interests of the individual researcher and any event can lead to virtually an infinite number of why questions that may be asked in a number of different ways. Going back to the example of the individual driving down the road one may ask: "Why is John driving on the right side of the road?", "Why is the car on the right side of the road?", "Why is the steering wheel oriented in the way that it is?", "Why isn't John slamming into the oncoming car in the same lane?", and so on. To ask for an explanation requires a somewhat arbitrary determination of the scope of what is to be explained, to seek to understand a single, isolated event in the vast, interconnected flotsam and jetsam of the universe. This is, of course, not problematic, so long as we keep the pragmatic purpose of inquiry clearly in view: we are seeking explanations for things because we either find something interesting in them or we find something useful for the future. These issues should guide any concerned researcher who looks at international relations and asks, "Why?"

The significance of this point is that both realists and legalists must be careful when offering competing explanations of an event. They must be on guard that

---

14 This means that international law may be considered effective in a particular context *unless* one of these failure criteria can be offered in an explanation. This explanatory prejudice puts the burden of proof squarely on the realists who must show that the law is not in effect rather than on legalists. This prejudice seems to be warranted, given the relatively low amount of conflict which actually happens in global politics as well as the overall complicity of states and other agents with international legal norms. However, the real case for shifting the burden of proof onto the realists will only become apparent in the next section of this chapter, where the notion of "following the law" will be explicated in greater detail.

they do not seek explanations for two different, but closely related events, thereby characterizing a broader phenomenon from different angles. An international political event taken as a candidate for a rationalizing explanation can have a virtually infinite number of why questions nested within it. While, "Why did state X do act Y?" is one of the most abstract questions one can ask about an event in international relations, one can ask a number of valuable and important subsidiary questions such as, "Why did diplomat D of State X hand a communiqué to a diplomat from State Z?" or, "Why did the soldiers from State X seize the ship which was flagged to State Z?" All of these are valid questions, and all are possible subjects for a rationalizing explanation, but they will not all be of interest to a particular researcher, with her individual concerns and goals for studying a particular case. Thus, when explaining some event of international politics, it is important to keep in mind which questions one is seeking to answer and only from there seek to determine whether international law is relevant to the explanation (it goes without saying that the larger the question one asks, the bigger the event one seeks to explain, the more likely there is to be a plethora of subsidiary events, some of which will require international law to explain them, some of which will not). A "case," be it a conflict, a negotiation, or a cooperative effort, is really a multifaceted, multilayered affair which can be seen from a macro-level (an interaction between states or coalitions), a micro-level (commanders in the field, diplomats in embassies), or innumerable levels in between. There is no natural way to carve up a complex political affair and no necessary questions to ask about it.

Explanations and the Efficacy of Legal Norms

There is a strange paradox that develops when we talk about rules in explaining someone's behavior. When human beings act intentionally, we generally require appeal to some kind of motive or desire in order to explain their action: the reason why Henry is writing his dissertation is because he wishes to earn his Ph.D. and (hopefully) a rewarding teaching career at a college somewhere (and he believes that obtaining this degree will help him to achieve this goal). Similarly, the reason why a child does not steal candy that lies tantalizingly close to her grasp (and her mother's back is momentarily turned) is because her fear of what might come to pass should she be discovered by her mother. Psychoanalysts even claim to find hidden, subconscious motives for elements in our behavior that seem to have no purpose or aim, and no apparent reason for them to happen. When we cannot find an intention or motive behind an act, we are usually unsure about how to categorize the act, and even struggle to say that the person really performed the act (when we learn of a person who slips with a knife in his hand, cutting his hand, we do not really believe that he cut his hand, as much as he acted unintentionally – and thus it is not a candidate for a rationalizing explanation).[15] With each candidate for a rationalizing

15 As Wittgenstein pointed out, "Let us not forget this: when 'I raise my arm', my arm goes up. And the problem arises: what is left over if I subtract the fact that my arm goes up from the fact that I raise my arm? (Are the kinaesthetic sensations my willing?)" (Wittgenstein 1963, paragraph 261).

explanation, there must be some psychological impetus or motive that moves the person to do or refrain from doing an act.[16] Thus, when we ask, "Why did person X do act Y?" we appeal to some motive, desire, or interest (coupled with a related belief) that, we commonly say, explains the act.

Whatever normative rules such as laws might be, they are not motivations in this sense. Extraneous factors, related to the existence of a rule might be part of the person's motivation for an act, but these are certainly different from the norm itself. That a person does not wish to go to jail may be his motivation for not stealing a large sum of money from his job at a bank, but this fear of possible punishment is different from the rule that one should not rob banks. Kant argued that behavior is not truly moral unless the exclusive motivation for action was respect for the rule itself (and thus from a Kantian perspective, we might say that the only moral explanation for an act would be, "because the act was moral") (Kant 1996, 397–9). In order for normative rules to have any traction in human behavior, we must somehow fit the norms into the belief-desire systems that are necessary elements of rationalizing explanations. A norm must be explicable in terms of the agent's own beliefs and desires in order to fit into a rationalizing explanation.

The plot thickens, so to speak, when we think specifically about the law in terms of human motivations to follow rules. While our initial reaction to understanding legal rules in explanations is to see the fear of punishment as the real motivation for an act, such as Austin did, it quickly becomes apparent that law-governed behavior is significantly more complex than this. Take the common case of law-governed behavior mentioned above: driving on the right side of the road in the United States.[17] It is a law that all drivers on two-way streets must drive on the right side of the road at all times, and its violation would merit (somewhat) severe legal punishment. But would this be the reason why, when I get in my car I drive on the right side of the road? In fact, I behave in this way for a variety of reasons, any of which (or none of which) may be in my head at a given moment. I may drive on the right because I don't want to die in a horrible car wreck, I may drive this way because I don't wish to get a ticket, or (as is probably most often the case) I drive on the right simply out of habit, an unreflective act that I've performed thousands of times before. Regardless of what is going through my mind as I pull out of a parking lot and hug the right curb with my car, it would not in any way be incorrect to assert that I am "following the law" here. In fact, it is not a stretch to argue that no matter what may be going on in my head as I drive down the road, the fact that the law dictates that drivers stay on the right explains why I am so driving[18] (however, we will discuss an important counter example to this scenario shortly).

---

16 This view was first articulated in modern philosophy by David Hume who held a very strict separation between reason and motive (Hume 1978, 413), but has found new life with David Henderson (Risjord 2000, ix).

17 Again, I owe this example to Mark Risjord.

18 Immanuel Kant recognized this feature of legal behavior in his *Metaphysics of Morals*, and in response made a sharp distinction between the moral imperative of acting from duty and the legal imperative of following a rule. When we determine that a person's behavior is legal, we may factor out the individual's own interests, but when we determine that a person is behaving morally for Kant, we require that the person's motive be pure.

This example points out nicely that there are a number of reasons why a person's behavior may be described as following the law, but the agent herself may nonetheless have reasons that are quite distinct from a pure regard for the validity of the legal norm. A vast number of motivations for a rational action, motivations that would presumably fit into a rationalizing explanation of why a particular agent did a particular act, can be legitimately considered to be "following the law." Fear of a sanction is one motivation for following the law, a belief in the legitimacy of the law another, simple habit is a third, and fear of other sorts of harm (such as negative publicity) a fourth. All of these possible explanations of events cohere with the notion that an agent is following the law but none assume that somehow we are following the law for its own sake or out of respect for the law itself, much less out of a fear of sanctions. Thus, explanations of political behavior that appeal to legal norms are not incompatible with complex psychological motivations or notions of self-interest but in fact are simply a part of a legalist explanation that may vindicate the role of law in a particular case.

A good political system will use a wide array of tools to get people to follow new laws: appealing not only to individual self-interest, but also to patriotism, to reason, and to a sense of justice – anything that is likely to make the legislation more effective. A legislator who simply passes laws without a sophisticated plan to encourage and ensure compliance, or who relies solely on enforcement mechanisms would surely fail in winning acceptance for her law. At times domestic governments pass regulatory laws rewarding compliance, such as environmental laws that reward individuals for using alternative forms of transportation, rather than simply punishing violators. At other times, new laws are accompanied with elaborate public relations campaigns to get citizens to accept them, either by giving these laws an aura of moral rectitude that they never previously possessed (one thinks of anti-drug laws in the United States as a reasonably successful attempt to moralize the use of recreational drugs or anti-music downloading campaigns) or making the citizens aware of the undesirable sanctions (criminal, civil, or otherwise) that would befall the violator of the new law. These strategies frequently overlap in the ongoing attempt to strengthen the rule of law in the domestic sphere and few governments could survive that did not combine these strategies with a large degree of success. No legal system would survive on an enforcement model of law alone.

It is important to note that there are plenty of cases where an agent may be following a law without knowing that their behavior is in fact being determined by it. An example may help clarify my point: a soldier who is ordered to treat prisoners of war with a certain degree of care such as is dictated by international humanitarian law may possess no knowledge of the Geneva Conventions or other treaties that outline the care of such prisoners, but nonetheless his behavior may be explained, genetically at least, by referring to the law. An adequate story as to why the soldier is treating her prisoners in a particular way (say, not shooting her enemy after he has dropped his weapon and surrendered) must ultimately appeal to the existence of the laws of war and the treatment of prisoners of war. An individual who is ignorant of the law but is still following the law for other reasons *that can be traced back to the law* are nonetheless following the law. In these cases, the chain of explanation must reach beyond the beliefs of the agent herself (in this case, the soldier) to find the legal element of her behavior, but we still may say that she is following the law. These may be considered special cases of "following the law," and they are most likely rare ones for our concerns here (at worst, we might say that this is a "gray area" in our common intuitions about following the law – and it causes no harm to suggest that in such cases an agent is following the law).

Failure of Law

Having explained what kinds of rationalizing explanations are compatible with the claim that an agent is "following the law," we need to consider cases where the law fails as an explanation for behavior. This next step is important for two reasons: first, to allay fears that the conception of "following the law" I am advocating here is so loose that it is impossible to find an act that would not be considered following the law. Such an objection, if legitimate, would make this approach no less falsifiable than the realists whom I attacked at the opening of this chapter. Second, there are surely many cases where the law does not play any role in political events, and thus we want to say that the law had no reality in these contexts. Given that this entire discussion is framed in terms of possible explanations for an agent's behavior, we should try to understand when an event cannot be legitimately explained by an appeal to law. Thus, the short list below could best be understood as a series of counterexamples to the analysis of the notion of following the law in rationalizing explanations that I have set out so far.

I will discuss four primary cases where the law fails as an explanation of an agent's behavior: (1) Parroting the law, (2) Deliberate violation, (3) Corruption, and then I will discuss a gray case, that of (4) Inconsistency.

A key place where explanations that appeal to international law rub against those that would seek to eliminate these laws in an explanation are cases where action *is according to the law* or parroting the law but the relevant agent is not *following the law*.[19] This distinction is no mere semantics, and a brief discussion of it will reveal just how tricky explanations that appeal to law can be. Take the example of a small child who somehow gets her hands on a set of car keys.[20] She herself has no knowledge of traffic laws and presumably has no idea that drivers traditionally stick to the right side of the road in the United States. However, it happens that she prefers the view which is on this side of the road as it is lined with pretty flowers and thus sticks to it as she drives around the neighborhood in a mad search for candy. To the extent that she remains on the proper side of the road (and only to this extent), her acts are in accordance with the law, but it would ultimately violate principles of language and common understanding to suggest that she is following the law. In essence, she had a desire to be on the right side of the road, but had no beliefs that relate to the law in any way. Here we might say that the behavior that seems law-governed (her driving on the right side of the road) is in fact not, and an explanation

19 This borrows from Kant's distinction between acts which accord with duty and those which follow from duty (see 1993, Ak. 397–9).

20 I owe this example to Mark Risjord.

of her behavior that appealed to the law would be false (while one that appealed to her love of flowers would be a better explanation).

This case bears some superficial resemblance to that of the soldier's treatment of prisoners of war discussed in the previous section of this chapter, and the two might be easily confused. However, if we look closer, these two examples differ in several important ways that tell us something valuable about the roles that laws play in rationalizing explanations: first, while neither of these agents has explicit knowledge of the law, in the case of the soldier there is a direct line of explanation that traces back to the beliefs of other individuals who do in fact know the law and have influenced the soldier's behavior (specifically, her commanding officers). The child driving on the right side of the road does not have such beliefs. Similarly, the desires of the respective agents differ in their relation to the law. The desire of the soldier to avoid court martial for not carrying out her orders is quite different from the desire of the child to see the pretty flowers off to the side of the road. The soldier's desires can be traced back to the existence of the laws of war while the child's desires do not similarly trace back to traffic laws. The reason why the soldier wants to treat her prisoner in a particular way is because of the law (or her fear of punishment for violating the law), while the reason that the child wants to drive on the right is simply because of her desire to see something pretty.[21] While we may agree that in these cases, both agents share a common ignorance of the rules of law, in the case of the soldier the law plays a real role in explaining the behavior of the agent (and thus to some degree explains her behavior) and in the case of the child it doesn't.

This extremely contrived counterexample is intended both to get to the outer limits of the use of law in explanations, and to illustrate just how flexible the concept of law can be in understanding empirical events: it need not be the essential reason for an agent's behavior in a particular case, but it must be *a* reason for the agent's actions. That is to say, the existence of a rule of law need not be in the mind of the particular agent at the moment of its action, nor need it be the primary motive for the act for the action to be explained with reference to law. Insofar as the rule explains the behavior of the agent in the myriad of ways discussed above, there is no reason to require anything further in order to say that the law is functioning in a particular case. This distinction between a case where the agent is merely parroting the law, but is not following the law serves to show one of the few situations in which seemingly lawful behavior does not require an appeal to explanation.

A second and significantly more common case where appeals to law fail as explanations of political behavior is where an agent knows that a particular law exists and nonetheless chooses to behave contrary to the law; an act of *deliberate violation*. A criminal or a rogue state both understands the law on a particular issue, say, the development and testing of biological weapons, and chooses to ignore this law in pursuit of its own interests. These are the cases where realists can make their case most clearly, and this is what most of them have in mind when they suggest that international law is not real, or is not really law. Realists might even go so far as to say

21 Had the child been driving on the right side of the road because she noticed that her mother always did, she would (to this extent, at least) be following the law by so doing.

that the fact that all international laws are potentially subject to deliberate violation with few consequences invalidates the fact that there is in fact international law, pointing to the vast number of situations where a state refuses to heed international law in the pursuit of its own interests and fears few consequences for exposure. In cases of deliberate violation, an agent has a desire, and feels that the fulfillment of this desire contradicts international legal norms, but chooses to ignore this law and acts to fulfill its desire.[22]

Of course, many of these violations of international law are coupled with legal sounding justifications. Large states employ a vast network of expert lawyers who are able to stretch and twist the rules of international law in order to rationalize the behavior of their home state. There are numerous ways that an agent may do this: sometimes a state's lawyers will appeal to the principle of *rebus sic stantibus*, that circumstances have changed, to annul a treaty or modify it in scandalous ways. Other times, states will appeal to their "unique circumstances" that they argue justify the claim that their behavior is in fact legal despite the condemnation of the world polity. States will resort to highly tendentious interpretations of legal terminology and legal concepts to assert that they are within the law.[23] When these fail to garner the support of the international community (as they frequently do), these states will simply assert that they are following the law and refuse to justify themselves any further.[24] The fear that results from this is that if international legal norms are so malleable that anything can be justified as following the law (and thus, there are not violations of law) then the notion of following the law again becomes so broad as to be meaningless.

Fortunately, however, the method laid out in Chapter 2 for determining a rule of international law gives us some leverage to respond to these concerns. In that chapter I argued that international laws are determined by the beliefs of international

---

22 This claim is also coupled with the observation that these deliberate violations frequently do not meet with any serious response beyond choreographed expressions of outrage from the violating state's enemies.

23 For an example of this, see the letter submitted by the Minister for Foreign Affairs of the Islamic Republic of Iran in *United States Diplomatic and Consular Staff in Tehran (United States v. Iran)* which argued that the (blatantly illegal) seizing of 63 US Embassy personnel "results from an overall situation containing much more fundamental and complex elements. Consequently, the Court cannot examine the American Application divorced from its proper context, namely the whole political dossier of relations between Iran and the United States over the last 25 years." Reprinted from *Judgment of 24 May, 1980*, paragraph 10.

24 In the legal maneuverings leading up to the *Nicaragua* proceedings, there was an effort on the part of the American legal team to avoid the jurisdiction of the ICJ by appealing to the "Connally Reservation," barring the Court from deciding on matters under the domestic jurisdiction of the United States as determined by the United States itself. This is clearly a specious argument and was quickly dropped from the official US legal position. As Thomas Franck observes, "The failure of the United States to use its Connally shield is a form of tribute to the determinacy of the term 'domestic.' What lawyer would want to stand before the fifteen judges of the ICJ and argue that US bombing of Nicaraguan harbors was a domestic matter? When a rule is so inelastic that certain legal arguments purported to be based on it become laughable, the rule may be said to have determinacy" (Franck 1995, 32).

lawyers, but also allowed for disagreements among lawyers to be settled by a process of reflective equilibrium. Such a method was designed to allow us to distinguish between proper and improper invocations of the law. Thus a small minority (even if they may be affiliated with a very powerful country) cannot argue for gross violations of international law without strong objections from other lawyers. There is a limit in this model to exactly how far the law is able to stretch. Thus, the ability for a state's lawyers to claim that an act is not in violation of international law is limited by the credulity of the international legal community and the decisions of legal tribunals (both domestically and internationally). If the community of international lawyers, those "in the know," finds a legal rationalization for an act to be unjustified, then we can properly say that the agent violated international law when it decided to fulfill its desire.[25]

We should not confuse these cases however with situations where a law is contentious or ambiguous and an agent chooses to interpret the law in a fashion most favorable to its interests. There will always be gray areas in understanding a particular issue and good lawyers, sincere lawyers, will commonly disagree on important matters of legal doctrine. This fact is neither shocking nor particularly upsetting from a theoretical standpoint. International lawyers (and many other lawyers, for that matter) get paid a great deal of money to make what were once seemingly clear rules of law fuzzy, and to make what was once a gray area clear in pursuit of the interests of their clients (any theory of law that didn't accept and somehow deal with this phenomenon would have a very puzzling shortcoming). In actual adjudication, it is often precisely the correct interpretation of law that is at issue between the two competing parties and we should expect nothing different when we move beyond domestic legal systems. International lawyers and international legal experts disagree on particular rules of law. These unsettled areas of legal doctrine ebb and flow with the development of law. Sometimes a settled part of law is thrown into chaos, sometimes a confused portion of law falls neatly into a set of clearly understood principles.

A third case where we might suggest that the law failed is the case of *corruption*. An agent who bribes a judge to make a bad decision is a case where the law on paper looks as though it were formally in accordance with international law, but in fact is simply covering up for violations. As corruption this blatant is a rarity in international law, and the ramifications are more-or-less obvious for the notion of the rule of law, it need not trouble us deeply. Suffice it to say that if a legal decision were to be a product of corruption, and this fit, the agent would not be following the law.[26]

---

25 The further claim, that is, that the violation of international law was deliberate, may be difficult to determine in some cases (given the secrecy of the decision-making processes in many foreign-policy-making bodies). However, the sincerity of the agent's claims that it was unaware of the illegality of its act prior to committing it has limits, too.

26 The strange possibility of a judge being bribed to make the right decision (which is an interesting hypothetical possibility, if only that) would presumably be similar to behavior which is in accordance with the law but is not following the law.

A fourth case is somewhat blurry and will require some explanation: *inconsistency* in legal behavior. A state that engages in an act of humanitarian intervention in a situation where it is politically advantageous (say, by increasing its influence in the region), but ignores a similar humanitarian disaster in a region where there is less at stake for the intervening state may be able to make a legal case for its intervention in the latter case, but for it to do so somehow seems disingenuous.[27] Such cases, where a state acts according to law in one circumstance, but fails to do so in another justifiably raises suspicions about whether the law is simply functioning as rhetorical cover, justifying actions in one case but ignored when the costs are too high for action in another. When the law is being followed inconsistently it is difficult to claim that the law is somehow working and that other influences on political behavior, national interest, public relations, or political posturing, are the determining factor for the agent.

Before one can make a legitimate charge of inconsistency, however, the accuser must first show that the two cases that are being compared are legally similar and that the inconsistent agent is really the same agent in both cases.[28] Or put somewhat more cynically, can a state give a good reason why its failure to act in one case, while acting in another, is based upon legal difference between the two? Here, we must again contend with slippery lawyers who can justify any action or inaction of her home state with a battery of sophistries. Similarly, assuming that these inconsistent acts happen at different times (which, admittedly, is not necessarily the case with charges of inconsistency),[29] the accuser must show that the inconsistent agent is in fact the same in both cases. A state's behavior cannot be expected to be consistent over a period of 20 years, given the dramatic shifts of domestic and international power, as well as shifts in policy that influence its foreign relations. Nor can an elaborate and complex, but well-intentioned foreign ministry always be expected to have consistent policies towards disparate parts of the world despite its desire to do so (frequently, the logistics are too complex to coordinate such policies). These elements, necessary for an accusation of inconsistency to be effective, will be both contentious and hard to prove, making the charge of inconsistency a little more difficult to make effective than is commonly thought, but nonetheless they are important criteria for determining inconsistency and to prevent what is usually an easy charge to make from being carelessly leveled.

When somebody charges a state with inconsistency as in the case of humanitarian intervention discussed above, what act is being deemed illegal? Is it the earlier failure to intervene that is wrong, or is it the later intervention that is a violation

27 The case I have in mind is similar to some of the objections that were brought against the NATO bombings of Yugoslavia in 1999 in relation to the inaction of the United States and the other great powers to the horrors which took place in Rwanda five years earlier.

28 The fundamental dictum, "Treat like cases alike," which underlies the charge of inconsistency (that similar cases are not being treated similarly), is only valid if the cases are really alike.

29 One can imagine a situation where a state holds sanctions against one state for policies it deems criminal while refusing to impose sanctions against another state for similar policies. This charge is made frequently against the inconsistent sanctions policies the United States holds towards China and Cuba at present.

of international law? Most likely, the critic is claiming that the failure to intervene was illegal, and this makes the later intervention suspect. But this later act, suspect though it may be, cannot be illegal and (importantly) cannot merit sanctions of any kind. Acts that follow the law, such as is done in the later case, can never (by definition) be grounds for legal punishment whatever the motivation of the agent's involved.[30] An agent's actions may be considered suspect (as well they should be) when they engage in inconsistent behavior, but those acts that follow the rule of law are not illegal and do not merit sanctions. This means that a charge of inconsistency in many cases is actually a charge of deliberate violation, the claim that a state failed to follow international law in one case, but lived up to its obligations in another. It is the failure that is wrong, the failure to intervene in the earlier situation, not the later act that, despite prior behavior, was legal.

However, the charge of inconsistency does have some validity, aside from morphing into a form of deliberate violation. Inconsistency, if it can be shown to fit into a broader pattern of behavior, connecting both legal and illegal behavior, definitely merits some skepticism towards international law. Ten or fifteen years of foreign policy of a particular state can be explained by such a macro-level inconsistency fits one issue into a significantly larger context than the one that interests me here. In this form of inconsistency, however, we have moved far beyond the explanation of particular cases and into a much larger view of broad patterns of global relations.

These four different failure criteria, which are probably not exhaustive, when applied to a particular case, make the best arguments for skepticism towards international law. In any particular circumstance where they are found it is most likely legitimate to assert either that international law is not there (in the idiom of this chapter, it is not real) or that it has failed to do its job. If every single international political event could somehow be explained via one of these criteria, the realist would have won her case and international law would be rejected *en totum*: that is to say, it is epiphenomenal, as was discussed at the opening of this chapter. Were the vast majority of international events, a vast number of questions for which we might search for explanations, subject to these failure criteria, the skeptic would similarly make a compelling case for ignoring international law in understanding global politics. The descriptive realist case, when taken as a problem of explanatory adequacy hinges upon the applicability of parroting, deliberate violations, corruption, and inconsistency to the actual events of international relations. However, I believe and will later argue, that such skepticism is unwarranted and that international law plays a definite role in the explanation of global politics.

30 I leave aside the issue of moral sanctions, which seem perfectly relevant in a case of inconsistency. However, I should be quick to note that inconsistency in relation to international law is a very different thing from inconsistency in terms of a moral foreign policy. There are many cases one can imagine where a state would be legally consistent but nonetheless immoral.

Is There the "Rule of Law" in International Relations?

The notion of the "rule of law" in a particular sphere of human life is, of course, an important one for understanding the structure of international politics and its law. Unfortunately, despite this fact, the "rule of law" is not a very well understood or well-defined concept in contemporary legal theory. The *Routledge Encyclopedia of Philosophy*, for example, defines it as "the idea that everyone is subject to the law, and should therefore obey it" (Allan 1998, 388). This definition, unfortunately, is a normative claim about what every agent *ought* to do and is unsuitable for the empiricist approach that I have followed here. However, we could agree with this definition in regards to international law, while accepting that it is routinely violated (in the final chapter I will seek to address normative issues in international law somewhat more directly). Similarly, *Black's Law Dictionary* (Second Edition) defines it as "the supremacy of regular as opposed to arbitrary power" and "the doctrine that every person is subject to the ordinary law within the jurisdiction." What it means to be "subject to law" is a vague notion given the empirical difficulties in understanding law (and understanding law-governed behavior) that I have described in this chapter.

The issue may perhaps be productively understood empirically in terms of whether a set of legal rules is generally effective in human life. Does a set of laws constrain a set of agents in the ways that laws are meant to? As an explanatory strategy, is law effective in understanding political life? This notion of the rule of law must then be dependent upon the legal system in question, and whether its laws are followed in the manner prescribed by it. This further entails that the rule of law in an international context must be understood in terms of the structures of international law itself, and not in relation to domestic civil or criminal law. The rules must be international rules, the sanctions must be international sanctions, and the actors analyzed must be international ones. I have already argued that international laws function in a fashion that is quite different from domestic legal systems and should not be judged on the latter's terms. It doesn't work primarily through enforcement mechanisms, and it gives most legal actors wider latitude than one would find in a domestic legal system. This does not impugn the rule of law in these contexts, it simply means that one must temper one's conception of the international rule of law given the structure of the international legal system.

I have already suggested that international law is sometimes violated, and at times it is violated flagrantly. At times agents have knowingly and openly violated a recognized rule of law. One might also observe that all domestic political societies have criminals who knowingly and openly violate laws with impunity. This means that at times the general rule of law has been violated. However, one should not conflate isolated phenomena (and they are more isolated than most critics realize) with the overwhelming trend that international legal rules almost always structure the nature of international politics through both coercive and non-coercive means almost all of the time. To use Henkin's famous formulation "Almost all nations observe almost all principles of international law and almost all of their obligations almost all of the time" (Henkin 1979, 47). The point of this chapter is to suggest that a broad, overarching view of "the" structure of international society "as such" (and whether an international law rules this society) is too empirically crude to be a useful starting point for a scientific study of international affairs.

Thus, the existence of the rule of law is not an empirical claim about actual states of affairs, a claim about whether or not agents obey the law, rather, it is a claim about whether people *believe* that the law is obeyed and ought to be obeyed. That is, do people feel that the law deserves respect? In regards to international law, much of the argument about whether or not it is "really law" is a self-fulfilling prophecy of sorts: it is argued that international law is not really law and because of these arguments, it is believed that there is no rule of law in international affairs. This, in turn, affects agents' future behavior, leading them to ignore the law when it crosses their path. Whether or not international law really makes a difference in the everyday affairs of diplomats, foreign ministers, customs officials, or any number of anonymous operatives who must confront it is irrelevant in these sorts of calculations.

Conclusion

The point of this chapter has been three-fold: first, to suggest that the best way to determine whether international laws are "real" is empirical, and not through mere theory; this means that for a law to be considered to some degree real is to say that it is relevant and at times essential to explaining a political event; second, to outline a series of criteria that would allow us to claim that the law is relevant in an explanation of an event, understanding what kinds of rationalizing explanations are compatible with the claim that an agent is following the law; and finally to offer some criteria for counter examples, cases where we might justifiably say that the law is being violated or is ineffective. For this analysis, such a claim means that law fails as an explanatory strategy for the selected "case." These failure criteria serve to limit the cases where an agent's behavior may be explained through the use of law. Thus, the ground rules for the question of the "reality" of international law have been laid out in this chapter as guidelines for explaining real-world political events.

The approach that I have put forward here has a few noticeable conclusions, some of which will be developed further at the end of the following chapter. First, international law is not as radically distinct from international politics as some theories have led us to believe. The approach outlined here understands international law as a force (among many) that influences the outcome of events on the global political landscape. International law is "down and dirty," so to speak, a part of real-world politics and not simply a pristine set of rules standing haughtily above the fray. This does not subordinate international law to politics or make it a servant of power as both the realists and the "New Stream" approaches discussed in the opening chapter would maintain, but it is in competition with politics, it is a part of politics, and stands in relation with other forces exerting themselves on the global stage. The separation between law and politics as it is traditionally understood is a false dichotomy: law is an element of politics.

Similarly, international law is not a zero-sum game. This is to say, international law may indeed fail in a number of circumstances and for a vast number of reasons but this fact alone does not entail that international law as such is a myth or a noble lie, nor does it remove its obligations from the table of global politics. Skeptics who tend to focus solely on the dramatic failures of international law miss the broader context where international legal norms work as laws on a daily basis. A stamp placed on an envelope and successfully mailed from Paris to Hong Kong arrives safely in its intended recipient's hands because of international law. A foreign diplomat expelled from a country instead of facing charges for criminal behavior is allowed to leave because of international law. While international law certainly fails to determine the outcome of events in some disappointing ways, this most definitely does not eliminate all meaningful talk of international law. International laws are not epiphenomenal in cases where they are explanatory, and I would argue that such cases, when stacked against these failures, indicate that international laws are real and function in most cases quite nicely. But ultimately this is an empirical question, and one that is subject to the messy uncertainties of empirical inquiry.

Finally, this approach to the reality of international law tells us something very different about the implementation of international law than less empiricist approaches. By avoiding thinking in too abstract and theoretical a fashion when we study the role of international law in global politics we can learn things that are significantly more useful about these politics. By making the reality of international legal norms something that we determine on a case-by-case basis, these determinations can serve as guides for those who wish to strengthen international law (and also those who seek to influence the future trajectory of this legal regime). In essence, by explaining a particular event in terms of international law, we can gain insight into the motivations of the relevant agents that led to the legal behavior that is explained. These insights can in turn provide a useful guide to getting other agents to follow the rules of international law in the future, strategies for ensuring the future success of the international legal order. If states can follow laws for a vast number of different reasons (and in a vast number of different fashions), then it is certainly useful to know what these reasons are in a particular case and whether they might be extended to future situations with similar features. An empiricist approach to the reality of international law as outlined in this chapter can be useful as a practical guide to understanding global politics (thus responding to one significant realist objection expressed in the beginning of this chapter) whereas a purely theoretical approach to why states follow the law in general, such as is often found in traditional international relations theory, is not so clearly useful.

In the next chapter, we will use this approach to understanding the roles of international law in two case studies. This will involve asking "why questions" about the actions of various real-world agents and using law as part of the answer to these questions. From this, we will better be able to understand some of the ways that law visibly and invisibly structures human interactions, even where enforcement seems to be missing. This, in turn, will lead to a final discussion of the normative dimension of international law, personified by the prescriptive realists.

Chapter 7

Pinochet and Nicaragua

In the last chapter, I suggested that the question of the "reality" of international law should not be settled in a purely or even heavily theoretical fashion. Our theoretical understanding of law cannot be separated from the actual events in the real world. This means that legal scholars should strive to understand the diverse ways that law serves to structure our political and social life. To ask if international law is "real" is not to search for some theoretical model that somehow shows that law matters, nor is it to find some normative argument that "proves" that one ought to follow the law. Rather, to ask about the reality of international law is to ask whether or not an analysis of its rules can be made to fit within an overall explanation of a set of events that one wants to understand, to fit international law into the answer to a question about why something has happened. This means that in order to understand the reality of international law, we must delve into the messy details of actual events and inevitably disputable accounts of both historical and current international affairs.

In this chapter, I will take this point somewhat further by developing two brief case studies and evaluating the role played by law in them. Here we will look at the attempted extradition of Augusto Pinochet, the former dictator of Chile, in 2000 from the United Kingdom by a Spanish investigating judge and the dispute that went before the International Court of Justice in 1986 regarding clandestine American intervention in Nicaragua. In each case I will seek to show where international law played a role in the relevant events and where it failed to play such a role.

These analyses will provide us with a few rules of thumb about understanding the diverse roles and functions that international law can play in the course of a series of events. I have previously argued that law does not play one single role in world politics, so it follows that the generalizations to be drawn may only be rough ones – empirical theories developed out of events, not deduced *a priori*. They may turn out to be entirely inappropriate to the analysis of other events – there is no single approach that will make law effective or ineffective in all circumstances. There is little space for pretensions of scientific certainty in the understanding of law in political events. A rough series of principles may be drawn from these studies, but no systematic, deductive laws of international affairs can be drawn that would work in all places and at all times.

There are a number of reasons why I have chosen to discuss these cases in particular. One of the compelling things about these cases is that both in some sense relate to interests that are usually considered to be crucial for the functioning of the modern international system of sovereign states. Additionally, each is an important, even canonical case of modern international law. *Nicaragua* is often cited in numerous international law contexts (but command responsibility, self-defense, and the jurisdiction of the ICJ are the most common), and much enthusiasm has developed about the possible impact of the *Pinochet Case* on notions of individual accountability for human rights violations before international law (Human Rights Watch, 2002). This means that these cases have had a hand in shaping current perceptions of international law both inside and outside of the academy. Finally, both cases are controversial: each side of the disputes finds adherents and the legal decisions of all the courts involved in each case invite controversy and criticism. Along with the intrinsically interesting features of these cases (and their dramatic quality), their controversial status within the international legal regime makes them ideal tools for discussing the roles of international law in international affairs.

Where law fits into an account of a political event depends a great deal on the approach that one takes to the topic at hand, the level of analysis (states, organizations, individuals, and so on), and the delineation of the explanandum. In turn, the appropriate explanation will depend upon the kinds of questions one asks. If we ask, "Why did the President of the United States do such-and-such?" our answer will be very different than if we ask "Why did the US do such-and-such?" (even if "such-and-such" is the same action in both cases). Like all empirical research, the study of political events is researcher-driven. The inquirer in part predetermines what types of answers are expected by the types of questions that she asks and the way that she frames the questions. These questions are determined, in turn, by what the inquirer is interested in – why she cares about the subject she is researching, and what she hopes to get out of the results.

Sometimes our understanding of the effectiveness or function of law reflects a philosophical naiveté about the nature of law. For example, were we to ask, "Did the law work in this case?" or, "Did the relevant actors obey the law?" we will be making some important but ultimately misleading assumptions about the functions law plays in social life. The first question assumes that law represents a zero-sum game: law either "works" or it absolutely fails to determine the outcome of events. The question of whether or not the law "works" begs the question, "works for whom?" Moreover, it raises further teleological questions about what it ultimately means for the law to "work." Often, the inquirer imports strong normative assumptions into this analysis – the law "works" when it protects human rights, promotes peace, protects the sovereignty of nations, and so on. This question similarly assumes that obedience is the framework through which one should understand law-governed behavior, that is, the law is only relevant when an agent obeys the law and behaves in a way that they otherwise would not. As I argued in the previous chapter, such an approach depends on certain misleading psychological assumptions about the interconnection between law and human behavior.

Rather than putting the matter in such a fashion, we can rephrase the "work" question to make it a little more complex: *How* did the law affect the outcome of events? Did it produce an outcome satisfactory to those involved? These questions depend upon a different set of assumptions about the nature of law and its role in shaping international politics than does the aforementioned "works" approach. This latter pair of questions implies that law can do many different things, some predicted by those involved in the case and some not, some in keeping with traditional notions of law and some diverging from them. It could turn out that the law worked through processes of enforcement, but it could just as likely be that it will work in other ways such as are suggested by terms like compliance. Other circumstances, however, may look nothing like either obedience or compliance. Moreover, this approach avoids the pitfall of assuming that law must either succeed or it must fail. Of course, as we will see, this approach does allow for the law to "fail" in a meaningful sense (by answering the question with, "It didn't work in any ways that really matter for us"), but the failure is different. It is a failure because it is not important for us to understand what happened in a particular instance.

Such questions, in some form or another, have been raised by numerous historically-oriented international law scholars. Those scholars of international legal history who understand international law in relation to historical events (as opposed to historians of legal doctrine and scholars of the history of international relations), have gone about the project of understanding international law's role in international politics in a number of different ways, each framing their analyses in a different fashion. For example, Louis Henkin has broken down his analysis of international relationships into the categories of "success" and "failure" and evaluating the cases in terms of their respective ability to control world order, although he grants that the law can also be viewed in terms of "influences" in regards to the Cuban Missile Crisis (Henkin 1979, 280). Thus, for Henkin, the Suez crisis of the mid-1950s represents a mixed result ("The law works, then fails but is vindicated"), the kidnapping and trial of Adolph Eichmann by Israel a failure ("The law fails"). Michael Byers has chosen a somewhat different tack, producing a narrative of the extradition of Augusto Pinochet that makes no final judgments about the success or failure of the law (Byers 2000, 416). How we frame the analysis, what criteria we use to determine the legal quality of the events (success, failure, effectiveness, works, vindication), will inevitably impact on the outcome of an analysis, funneling the data towards a single conclusion.

While Henkin's and Byers' approaches can be helpful, probably the most useful way to pose questions about the role of international law in international society was set out in the series published by Oxford University Press in the mid-1970s under the title *International Crises and the Role of Law*. Here, the legal and diplomatic scholars (some of which were participants in the crises they analyzed) emphasized a number of interrelated aspects of political decision-making in order to properly determine the role played by international law. In particular, the series asked:

> What part international law, norms, or agencies played in the decisions and actions of the major protagonists? How did such rules, norms, or agencies influence what was done or how it was done? How were they used for legitimating political actions, for rallying support, or for imposing restraints? What role did they play in resolving the crisis? (Bowie 1974, ix).

The appealing aspect of such an approach is that it is not based on any artificial state-construction that would ask whether or not "Cuba," "Egypt," "France," or "the United States" followed the law, or whether or not the law "works" (as in Henkin), but recognizes that individuals and groups make a series of concrete decisions in each of these crises and it is here where law interacts with politics. Further, this approach acknowledges that the law can impact on these agents in a diverse number of ways, authorizing them to act, disempowering them, leading them to choose a particular means to achieve their desired goals, and so on. Finally, this approach recognizes that law can play diverse roles in the life of international relations and doesn't simply serve to constrain political activities. For these reasons, my approach will be modeled upon this series, although there will be some modifications to it.

I should also acknowledge at the outset that the two case studies presented in this chapter could have been written in such a fashion that law could have been written completely out of each one. A plausible account of the events I will describe could make little or no reference to the law. A Marxist could reduce everything to a struggle between competing classes, a realist to power relations, or a postmodernist to the relation of texts. Whether or not a realist, Marxist, postmodern, or legalist approach to these events is the correct one is a complex issue and cannot be settled at the level of the explanations themselves, but must rely instead on theoretical debates between the different approaches. A Marxist approach might point to deeper economic forces that determine the course of events and thereby dismiss the legal dimension discussed here as "superstructure," but the extent to which one finds such explanations compelling will depend largely on independent arguments regarding the intellectual credibility of Marxism (or realism, or psychoanalysis, for that matter). Facts are not simply "there" to be explained: one's theoretical commitments will in many ways influence what facts one considers important or relevant to understanding an event (Quine 1961; Kuhn 1962). To prove the Marxist wrong requires a different form of critique. Although these debates are in some sense "factual," they are usually more than this. This discussion, however, requires a more abstract debate and is best reserved for a different context.

One final note – as in previous chapters, I will have to walk a fine line between a number of different disciplines, not all of which may be equally familiar either with the facts of these cases or the legal questions they involve. I will try to make my analyses as clear and straightforward as possible, but discussing issues that may strike scholars in a particular field as obvious is nonetheless required.

The Pinochet Affair

On October 16, 1998, Balthazar Garzón, a Judge-Magistrate in the Central Investigating Court in Madrid sent a request to the Government of Great Britain requesting, "The pre-Trial detention of AUGUSTO PINOCHET UGARTE for the crimes of genocide and terrorism." Pinochet, the former Chilean strongman (who peacefully left office in 1990 with his status as "senator for life" serving as a guarantee of legal immunity) had been in England, as he had been many times before, visiting old friends, shopping, and for health care.[1] In his warrant, Justice Garzón asserted that, in the period 1976–1983, during "Operation Condor" (a coordinated effort on the part of the various rightist military juntas in South America to fight leftists on the continent), the dictator imposed, "Orders for the physical elimination of persons,

1 For an account of Pinochet's relations with the UK and its government prior to and through the General's indictment see Beckett (2003).

the torture, kidnapping, and disappearance of others from Chile and of diverse nationalities from different countries though the operations of the Secret Service (DINA)" (Spanish Request to Arrest Augusto Pinochet, 16 October 1998).[2] These, he maintained were crimes that could be punished under Spanish law and thus merited extradition. A second warrant (issued on 22 October 1998) relied on the British laws against torture, specifically the Criminal Justice Act of 1988, which outlaws, "Intentionally inflict[ing] severe pain or suffering on another in the performance ... of his official duties," by, "a public official or person acting in an official capacity, whatever his nationality ... in the United Kingdom or elsewhere (Criminal Justice Act 1988, Sect. 134 (1))." In both communiqués Garzón respectfully requested that Pinochet be extradited to Spain by the British government to be put on trial for his alleged misdeeds.

Spain's case for extradition was rooted in three different principles of international criminal law: one substantive and the other two procedural. Substantively, Garzón relied on the international legal prohibition against torture and its description as an international crime. Of primary importance for establishing this was the 1987 Convention Against Torture and Other Cruel, Inhuman or Degrading Treatment or Punishment (the "Torture Convention"), which requires that, "Each State Party shall ensure that all acts of torture are offences under its criminal law."[3] Procedurally, the extradition request was rooted in the notion of "universal jurisdiction," the principle of Spanish law (and British law) that certain crimes may be prosecuted regardless of where they occur and regardless of the nationality of the victim. A second procedural issue revolved around issues of UK extradition law and the doctrine of "double criminality" – the principle that an individual can only be extradited for a crime that is prosecutable in both the requesting and the requested states (Gilbert 1991, 46). The argument, then, is that the treaty treated the crime of torture as a crime for both Spain and England (thus giving Pinochet's offense double criminality), with universal jurisdiction, making it irrelevant *where* the alleged crimes were committed.

The General's attorneys appealed to a number of principles of English and international law in an effort to refute Spain's right to obtain and try Pinochet and, more pressingly, to quash the provisional warrant issued by the British government. Most forcefully, they appealed to the principle of head of state immunity – the idea that government leaders like Pinochet are immune from prosecution for criminal activities that took place while they were in office, "In exercise of his functions as head of state" (Napley 2000). Here, they relied on the Vienna Convention on Diplomatic Relations and Britain's State Immunity Act 1978, both of which provide some form of immunity to heads of state. Similarly, they refuted Spain's jurisdiction over crimes that had taken place entirely within Chilean territory and claimed that there was no principle of universal jurisdiction in English law, particularly in relation to the crime of murder.[4] Here, they cited the British Extradition Act of 1989 and the Offenses

2 For two good English language accounts of the Pinochet Regime see Spooner (1994), and Valenzuela (1991).

3 Article 4.

4 Letter to the Home Secretary from Pinochet's Lawyers seeking cancellation of the First Provisional Warrant October 21, 1998. See also Bianchi (1999, 237–77).

Against the Person Act of 1861. As the crimes alleged by Garzón were not crimes under British law, they argued that Spain's extradition request was null and void.

Garzón's warrants were initially quashed by the British magistrate on two slightly different grounds, but both concluded that the crimes alleged by Garzón lacked double criminality. However, in relation to each warrant the grounds for quashing the extradition request were slightly different: in regards to the first warrant (for murder, kidnapping, and so on), the court ruled that there was no jurisdiction over the crimes under UK law because they had not been committed on British territory. Despite the fact that some of the victims mentioned in the first extradition request were British citizens, "The murder of a British citizen by a non-British citizen outside the United Kingdom would not constitute an offense in respect of which the United Kingdom could claim extra-territorial jurisdiction... The United Kingdom courts only have jurisdiction to try a defendant where he has committed a murder outside of the United Kingdom if he is a British citizen."[5] The second grounds for quashing the warrant was the immunity that international law traditionally applies to heads of state and former heads of state. Here, the court evaluated the different international texts on the issue, along with the ways that they were incorporated into UK law, foreign rulings from the US and elsewhere, and scholarly treatises in international law, ultimately concluding, "The applicant is entitled to immunity as a former sovereign from the criminal and civil process of the English courts."[6] Because, under UK law, Pinochet had not committed any crime that could be prosecuted there, there was no double criminality and hence no grounds for extradition.

The Crown Prosecution Service appealed the case and the ensuing legal dispute rendered three major legal decisions by the British Law Lords. The first ruling (*Pinochet I*) was the broadest of the three, giving the UK, and thus Spain, jurisdiction over a wide range of international crimes.[7] However, following the revelation that one of the Judges who issued this ruling, Lord Hoffman, was affiliated with Amnesty International (a party to the case) the House of Lords made a second ruling (*Pinochet II*) that was largely without precedent in British legal history, determining that Lord Hoffman's affiliation left an appearance of bias and ordering a rehearing.[8] In its third and most significant ruling on the affair, the court made a determination that was more limited than *Pinochet I*, but nonetheless gave Spain jurisdiction over the General.

The ruling in *Pinochet III*, the decisive opinion in the affair, revolved around the connection between the legal concept of torture as set out in the Torture Convention and the notion of head of state immunity. According to the Convention, "torture" is, "Any act by which severe pain or suffering is intentionally inflicted on a person ... when [it] is inflicted by or at the instigation of or with the consent or acquiescence of a

5 Decision of the High Court of Justice for England and Wales, 28 October 1998, paragraph 33.

6 Ibid., p. 88 (paragraph 74).

7 Decision by the Appellate Committee of the House of Lords, 25 November 1998, see also Fox (1999, 207–16).

8 Decision by the Appellate Committee of the House of Lords, 15 January 1999 (lead opinion of Lord Browne-Wilkinson).

public official or other person acting in an official capacity." Because the convention restricts "torture" to public officials acting in their official capacity, Lord Brown-Wilkinson observed, "All defendants in torture cases will be state officials." This means that, if Pinochet is considered to be immune for acts of torture committed under his orders, *every official but the head of state* will be criminally liable for this act of torture – which would be both illogical and unacceptable. "[I]f the former head of state has immunity, the man most responsible will escape liability while his inferiors (the chiefs of police, junior army officers) who carried out his orders will be liable. I find it impossible to accept this." Thus, he argued, "The implementation of torture as defined by the Torture Convention cannot be a state function." And because the legal immunity provided to former heads of state is not immunity *tout court*, but rather foreign leaders are only immune for official acts or "state functions," Pinochet cannot use this immunity to escape criminal liability – at least for crimes that were committed after the Torture Convention went into effect. This reduced the scope of crimes for which Pincohet was liable, but nonetheless authorized transferring the General to Spanish custody.

However, despite the ruling of the Law Lords in *Pinochet III* that he could be extradited to Spain to face charges, the British government did not surrender the General to Spanish custody for transfer. After British specialists ruled that the General was medically unfit to stand trial,[9] Jack Straw ordered that extradition procedures be stopped on humanitarian grounds. Pinochet was released from custody on 2 March 2000 and a Chilean military jet flew him back home (Hoge 2000). Straw's decision was controversial in Chile, the UK, and in Spain (along with the three other countries who had requested his extradition). Adding to the controversy was the fact that Straw did not publicly disclose the contents of the medical exam until after Pinochet had left the country, preventing their conclusions and Straw's actions from being questioned in the UK courts and by the public at large. Nonetheless, Pinochet returned to Chile where human rights activists there began developing a case for prosecuting their former leader in a domestic court.

The prevailing law justifying Straw's decision was the UK Extradition Act 1989. Specifically, Section 12 of the Act provides the Foreign Secretary with a good deal of leeway in determining when extradition is appropriate, particularly at the end of the legal process when all efforts to quash a warrant have failed.[10] As Straw interpreted

9 See the British Medical Report of 15 February 2000.

10 The relevant passages of the Act are as follows:

> 12.—(1) Where a person is committed under section 9 above and is not discharged by order of the High Court or the High Court of Justiciary, the Secretary of State may by warrant order him to be returned unless his return is prohibited, or prohibited for the time being, by this Act, or the Secretary of State decides under this section to make no such order in his case.
>
> (2) Without prejudice to his general discretion as to the making of an order for the return of a person to a foreign state, Commonwealth country or colony—
>
> (a) the Secretary of State shall not make an order in the case of any person if it appears to the Secretary of State in relation to the offence, or each of the offences, in respect of which his return is sought, that—

the Act in his letter to the Spanish Ambassador justifying his refusal to extradite Pinochet:

> The Secretary of State is the only authority on whom a general discretion is conferred whether to order extradition. He has had regard in exercising it to the principles expressed by the courts on a number of occasions that the proper exercise of that discretion by the Secretary of State is the principal safeguard for the accused against oppression.[11]

Here is a case where a certain amount of prudent discretion is provided to governments within the law and the Secretary is free to act in his role as a political figure rather than as a magistrate. The Home Secretary may refuse to extradite under certain circumstances if it is not in the interests of prudence or justice.[12]

Analyses of politics and law

The brief account of the Pinochet affair that I have given here relies heavily on a legal reconstruction of the relevant events: That is, I have made reference to the legal aspects of the case and have minimized its "extralegal" aspects (on my reading of the case, everything was "by the book" and in an otherwise unorthodox set of events, the law was largely followed). However, this is not the only way to understand the events surrounding the arrest and attempted extradition. There are a number of different possible lenses through which one can view them, and again, the lens one chooses and one's conclusions regarding the qualities of the case depend on what one is looking for in it. Here I will examine the case from a political standpoint, examining how putatively extra-legal factors that influenced the case's outcome.

Michael Byers, in "The Law and Politics of the Pinochet Case," argued that politics and law are bound together in *Pinochet* and that it represents a political as well as legal milestone. More significantly, however, he argues that a legal account (such as the one that I have presented above) is insufficient to grasp all of the relevant events in *Pinochet*, although, "The existence of legal rules and institutions shaped the options available to judges and politicians involved in this case, and ultimately constrained their behavior." This is to say that the construction that I have just set out is insufficient in some meaningful sense. As Byers phrases it:

> The case cannot be fully understood solely from a legal perspective. A variety of non-legal factors shaped both the proceedings and the outcome: domestic politics; international diplomacy; the arms trade; the individual personalities, backgrounds, and self-perceived roles of judges and politicians; the activities of non-governmental organizations, transnational

---

(i) by reason of its trivial nature; or

(ii) by reason of the passage of time since he is alleged to have committed it or to have become unlawfully at large, as the case may be; or

(iii) because the accusation against him is not made in good faith in the interests of justice, it would, having regard to all the circumstances, be unjust or oppressive to return him.

11 Letter from the Home Office to the Spanish Ambassador of 2 March 2000.

12 For a more detailed account of the Home Secretary's decision, see Blakesley (2000, 1–98).

corporations, and the growth of transnational networks between judicial authorities from different countries; and the media and international public opinion (Byers 2000, 416).

Thus, according to Byers, one must go beyond the law to understand how the events occurred the way they did. He does not deny the relevance of law as a realist might, rather, he denies the sufficiency of law as an explanation for *Pinochet*.

Byers' insight merits unpacking because it provides some guidance for understanding the functions of the law/politics distinction in relation to *Pinochet*. But his piece raises a number of important subsidiary questions that can help us unpack this case: first, what does Byers mean by "fully understanding" a case? That is, how does Byers delineate the explanandum? Second, what distinguishes legal from non-legal factors in his view? Moreover, is he assuming that these two are in conflict, that is, when a non-legal fact explains an action, then the law is not working?

As I argued in the previous chapter, an approach that seeks to understand law as an explanatory strategy in a pluralistic context can provide some insight on Byers' analysis as well as the *Pinochet* case as a whole. While it is clear that a "complete understanding" of a complex event like *Pinochet* is an unachievable ideal, the law is nonetheless a part of any reasonable account of this case. Likewise, politics, economics, psychology, and virtually any other field that one finds useful can be helpful in developing as complete an understanding of the case as possible. The psychology of General Pinochet, Judge Garzón, British Prime Minister Tony Blair and others are helpful. Likewise, the lucrative trade between the two countries had an impact on the case as we will see. Similarly, the legal and the extra-legal need not be in conflict, as legalistic understandings of human behavior (particularly when we put them in terms of "why questions") do not exclude other types of explanations but may be completely compatible with them. One type of explanation for the actions of Pinochet, the UK government, or Spanish authorities does not necessarily eliminate others, but rather each provides a different framework to understand the case, a fuller understanding of what happened. The validity of different approaches depends as much on pragmatic considerations as it does epistemological ones. As I said in the previous chapter, what matters, and what does not depends as much on the interests of the questioner as it does on the answers that one might provide. Here I will briefly set out some of the political issues underlying the case. Once I have done this, I will place it in terms of the "why questions" that I described in the previous chapter.

Many political analyses of *Pinochet* have focused on the decisions facing Secretary Straw and the Blair Government or the reasoning of the Law Lords themselves. It is clear that Straw was in a difficult political position throughout the course of the case. Prior to joining the government, he had spoken out against the Pinochet regime and the Labour Government had vociferously advocated the international prosecution of torture and opposed legal immunity for heads of state. A refusal to help Spain pursue the General, a *cause célèbre* for human rights organizations, would have put Straw in an awkward political position with his Labour party's supporters who had widely applauded Pinochet's arrest and supported his extradition. Members of Blair's party had also loudly supported the Spanish move and were closely monitoring the government's actions in the case (Davis 2003, 130).

On the other hand, there would be clear repercussions from allowing the General to be extradited: trade was threatened – Chile was a long-time customer for the UK arms industry and Pinochet himself had helped Chile acquire British arms (Davis 2003, 130). Moreover, a number of prominent conservative British politicians had expressed outrage over Pinochet's arrest, including former Home Secretary Michael Howard as well as Former Prime Minister Margaret Thatcher. Thatcher went so far as to pen a letter to *The Times* objecting to the arrest of a "good friend" of England who, she asserted, had helped save British lives during the Falklands-Malvinas conflict (Davis 2003, 132).[13]

This dilemma helps explain why the Foreign Ministry neither endorsed nor objected to the initial extradition efforts during the trial proceeding but portrayed the government's approach as one of applying the law strictly. Clearly an endorsement of the extradition effort would have further damaged Chilean-British relations and increased the outrage in the Tory opposition. On the other hand, any open effort to subvert the extradition effort would have been perceived domestically as an effort to undermine international human rights and to subvert the course of justice. This dilemma helps explain Straw's declaration of 9 December 1998, that he would leave the decisions to the court – it allowed the British government to avoid making a difficult decision without appearing cowardly.

The Spanish political issues are no less complex and multifaceted than the British ones. Not only did Spain have its own checkered human rights history (particularly in regards to the Franco regime [Riding 1998], but also in relation to its handling of Basque separatists), but Judge Garzón, a former politician, had a reputation for grandstanding. Since the Pinochet case, Garzón has targeted Henry Kissinger, prosecuted members of the former Argentinian *junta*, called for the closing of the US prison at Guantánamo Bay, Cuba (Sciolino 2006), and prosecuted a number of terrorist organizations like ETA and Al Qaeda operatives in Spain (BBC News 2005). Many critics suggest that the Judge's pursuit of Pinochet was motivated less by the pure pursuit of justice than by naked self-promotion (Lamont 1999). Finally, Spain wished to promote itself as a defender of human rights and international justice, bringing to justice torturers and dictators from around the world, and towards that end the prosecution of the General would have been a feather in the Spanish Government's cap.

David Robertson, in "The House of Lords as a Political and Constitutional Court" (2000, 17–40) takes a somewhat different approach to the law/politics distinction in the *Pinochet* case. Unlike Byers, who focuses largely on the political influence of actors *outside* of the courtroom, Robertson examines the politics of the Law Lords themselves. In a manner akin to classical American legal realists, Robertson sees the Pinochet rulings as a reflection of the legal ideology of different judges as well as a reflection of the political role of the Law Lords in British government. A different combination of judges with different biases would have led to very different conclusions (particularly when a case is decided by only a small number of judges as in the *Pinochet* rulings). Thus, he argues that a larger pool of judges would have rendered a different result. "Above all, deciding cases by a partial empanelling

13 Lady Thatcher's letter was published in *The Times* on 22 October 1998.

creates the problem that far too often it is quite easy to see that a major decision might very well have gone the other way but for the happenstance of who heard it" (Robertson 2000, p. 37). Thus, for Robertson, the "politics" of *Pinochet III* is not to be found in the manipulation of events by the various governments, but rather in the beliefs about law expressed by the judges in a case.[14] If the judges were changed, then *Pinochet III* would have turned out differently.

While there is much to be gained from such a perspective on *Pinochet*, as a critique of the case it only goes part way (to be fair to Robertson, he himself never conceives of his project as a critique of the substance of the Law Lords' ruling. Rather the target of the criticism is the organizational structure of the English court system). Clearly, the Law Lords' ruling on this case was not beyond the pale of legal reasoning, moreover, the explanation of the ruling as fundamentally a consequence of the ideologies of the Law Lords overlooks the significance of *Pinochet II*. There, the court rejected one of the judges and re-heard the case primarily because of, "An appearance of bias not actual bias."[15] There may be room to debate whether or not the court's reasoning was the correct one, but there seems to be little ground to assert that it was decided in bad faith or as a manifestly "political" (rather than legal) framework.

Why questions

Now that we have given different "legal" and "political" accounts of *Pinochet*, we can examine the relations between them as well as points of potential conflict, that is, significant places where the legal explanations fail to make sense of what happened, while other explanations are more helpful. When we frame the Pinochet affair in terms of various "why questions," we can see a number of different answers that historians, lawyers, and political scientists might offer as well as the divergences in their respective analyses. The questions that I will focus on here are: (1) Why did Spain ask the British government to extradite General Pinochet?; (2) Why did the court rule that Pinochet deserved a retrial?; (3) Why did the court in *Pinochet III* allow for Pinochet's extradition?; and (4)Why did Jack Straw allow Pinochet to return to Chile? I will give both legally and politically slanted answers to each question and then discuss their compatibilities as well as their tensions.

Why did Judge Garzón ask the British Government to extradite General Pinochet?

This question is a complex one that can result in several different possible answers. In particular, this question can provoke different responses when juxtaposed with different *foils* or alternative possibilities. For example, the question, "Why did

---

14 As he phrases the matter himself: "I shall use [the word] 'political' throughout [the article] as a shorthand, but it must be understood that this does not imply that judges are acting other than as judges, and does not suggest any conventional partisan role or linkage" (Robertson 2000, 18).

15 Decision by the Appellate Committee of the House of Lords, 15 January 1999. Reprinted in Brody and Ratner (2000), pp. 189–202, 197.

Spain ask Britain to extradite the General instead of letting him go?" is going to result in a set of different answers than, "Why did Spain attempt to have the General extradited rather than someone else?" or, "Why did Spain attempt to have the General extradited from England rather than from Chile?" (Or somewhat absurdly, "Why did Spain attempt to have the General extradited from England rather than sending him roses and a get well card?") These are all very different questions and entail varying responses, invoking different interpretations of England's domestic and international legal obligations as well as different descriptions of the political situation in Spain and the UK at the time.

The simplest, but probably the least satisfactory answer to this question is purely legal in character: "Spain sought to have Pinochet extradited because the General had committed acts of torture in violation of international law." There are several obvious problems with such a simplistic response. As discussed in the previous chapter, this answer stands open to the objection of inconsistency. Clearly there's more to the choice of prosecutorial targets and the means of obtaining these targets than such a simple answer lets on. There was more to this case than a mere violation of a law. After all, other torturers were ignored by Spain, and Garzón had waited until the General was in England (and had been waylaid by back surgery) before he sought his detention and transfer.[16] Moreover, such an answer naively ignores the notion of discretion in law, that legal actors may (within limits) selectively apply the law in cases that they find appropriate.[17] Therefore such a purely legalist answer is clearly not specific enough to be satisfying to all but the most simplistic analyst.

One could likewise look beyond the law and use different "political explanations" to answer this question, and undoubtedly a satisfactory or complete answer to it would have to offer a lot more than pointing out that the General had been suspected of international crimes. A fuller explanation would examine the domestic politics in Spain or the interests of Spain as a European power with an interest in being a leading light in the field of international human rights. Other, individualistic answers would look at the ambitions of Judge Garzón or the efforts of human rights activists in Spain and the UK. Clearly, each of these explanations will refer to a number of factors, some putatively legal, such as the existence of an extradition treaty between the two countries, while others will not appeal to such factors.

Nonetheless, recourse to law is clearly a useful tool for answering this question. While there are obviously "non legal" elements to the targeting of Pinochet by Garzón during October, 1998, none of these clearly amounts to a rejection of the relevance of law for explaining the choice. The judge had grounds to believe that Pinochet had violated the law and felt that he had reasonable grounds for asserting jurisdiction over the General. Of course, his decision was influenced by other political events, and other torturers were ignored. Nonetheless, one need not reject the importance of the law for understanding this decision. Answers such as, "The legal case was

---

16 In terms of the erotetic model of questions, such an answer would only work with a few foils. That is to say, such an answer might be appropriate if this "why question" were something like, "Why did Spain ask the British government to extradite General Pinochet rather than ignore him?" However, even here it is an intuitively weak answer.

17 For an interesting analysis of the role of legal discretion, see Davis (1980).

stronger against Pinochet than against others," or, "Judge Garzón wished to set a precedent for future dictators and concluded that Pinochet was a good candidate for this," are both plausible answers to this question, neither of which deny the role of law in *Pinochet*. Again, such a brief synopsis of the case cannot fully explore these questions, much less arrive at a determinate conclusion regarding the matter.

Why did the British Government allow the extradition process to go forward?

As Woodhouse points out in her analysis of the *Pinochet* extradition process, law and politics both played a part in the Blair government's decision-making process. "Although these [extradition] issues were located in the political arena, they were tempered by considerations laid down by the Extradition Act and susceptible to challenge in the courts... Hence the decisions of the courts were crucial to the progress of the senator through the extradition procedure" (Woodhouse 2000, 87). While we have already discussed some of the significant features of this political context above, we can see that there are numerous answers to this question. Legally speaking, under UK extradition law, there was little room for the Home Secretary to act to prevent the extradition process, particularly at its early stages. The type of warrant that was used to detain the General is known as an emergency or provisional warrant which does not go through traditional, diplomatic channels, nor does it require the authorization of the Home Secretary (Davis 2003, 129; Bedi 2001, 276–8). As Davis points out, "Whatever contacts took place in the immediate run-up to the arrest between officials, lawyers and ministers, well-established procedures were being followed and any political interference by the Home Secretary would have been both legally improper and politically risky. By the time Straw had the opportunity to have any hand in the proceedings it was already clear that no political 'quick-fix' would be possible" (Davis 2003, 129). Clearly, in response to this question at least, law played a clear role in determining the actions of the political actors involved, forcing them to act in ways that they would not have otherwise acted.[18]

Why did the court rule that Pinochet deserved a retrial?

Another question that we can pose regarding the case refers to the actions of the court in *Pinochet II*. Clearly, the decision to vacate the first *Pinochet* ruling and reconsider the case represented an unorthodox move on the part of the court, and thus merits some form of explanation. Evadne Grant answers this question in a largely legalistic fashion, referring to the basic procedures in the House of Lords, while nonetheless acknowledging that *Pinochet II*, "laid down some new [legal] principles," and was an application, "without precedent" (Grant 2000, 43). The legal argument was premised largely on the legal principle that, "A man may not be a judge in his own cause" and, given Lord Hoffman's relationship to Amnesty International, there was a question about his objectivity and, further, the image of the court as an impartial body was

18 According to Davis, one of the central reasons why the warrant was not quashed was Straw's pledge to allow the case to go "by the book." See also (Davis 2003, 134–6) and *The Independent* (1999).

threatened. This opinion was novel in that the Law Lords had never been asked to set aside a complete ruling and hear a case anew. Grant herself argues, "The decision in *Pinochet II* is generally regarded as being satisfactory in the sense that justice had been done and had been seen to be done," but simultaneously recognizes that it, "May prove to have limited impact, since the circumstances in which automatic disqualification may arise… appear to be limited to facts which are very close to those surrounding the *Pinochet* litigation" (Grant 2000, 58).

A purely legal analysis, based on the assumption that Hoffman's presence created the appearance of bias requires further explanation. The law might be enough to explain why the case was set aside, but it doesn't explain why the issue was raised in such a novel context. There are several possible answers to this question that are primarily *political* in orientation, each of which has a different relation to a legal explanation of the ruling. To start with, the allegations of bias presented to the Law Lords were an embarrassment to the institution (Mason 1998; Tweedie 2006) and the ruling, "Suggested that the final court was naïve and unprofessional" (Woodhouse 2000, 98). Moreover, in such an important case, under such intense scrutiny, and with potentially harmful or beneficial consequences for the British government as well as for the international community as a whole, it is easy to imagine that the court wanted to appear beyond reproach. Finally, it is possible that the court wished to revisit and temper the findings of *Pinochet I*, curtailing its scope and possible international repercussions, fearing that these could prove dangerous.

Again, only some of these arguments impugn the claim that law mattered in this case and that it is relevant to understanding *Pinochet II*. It does not impugn the role of the law to carefully scrutinize a case for the appearance of bias. Even if the amount of scrutiny given to *Pinochet I* was unusual, in and of itself, it was no violation of law and it does not make the case "political" in the sense that the descriptive realists use the term. Had Lord Hoffman's ruling been allowed to stand as it was written, it could just as easily have satisfied those who wish to read *Pinochet I* as a wholly political ruling. The principle of an unbiased judiciary is one of the bedrock principles of modern law.

Why did the court in Pinochet III *allow for Pinochet's extradition?*

This question, referred to by Robertson and Davis, is one about the various influences upon the legal actors themselves: as Davis asserts, the ruling in *Pinochet III*, and in particular the strict limitations to extradition given by the court, "raises the question of the extent to which, in making their decision, the Lords were sensitive to the legal and political pressures upon them." For him, this ruling does not merit a legal analysis *per se*, but rather gives the impression, "That the lords were inclined (though in a way that avoided damaging the reputation of the court further) to find a way out of a case that had become both a legal embarrassment and a political liability"[19] (Davis

19 As evidence of her claim, Davis asserts that "Some lawyers in the case (on both sides) to whom I spoke in the course of research where privately willing to vouchsafe their conviction that the aggregate decision was the result of behind-the-scenes horsetrading amongst the lords in a bid to find an acceptable way out of the case" (Davis 2003, 139).

2003, 139). Robertson similarly argues that the unique personalities of the judges involved in the cases, and not the law itself, played an important role in determining the outcome of the case.

Davis and Robertson's approach to the case, and the lens they use to evaluate the politics/law distinction therein, is difficult to respond to clearly. Whether or not it amounts to a refutation or rejection of the role of law in favor of politics in examining *Pinochet III* (or the halfway point that Byers takes), it requires speculation about the intentions of the Law Lords and their attitude towards the *Pinochet* case in general. The important point, however, is that the limitation imposed by Hoffman in his opinion in *Pinochet III* still allowed for the extradition of the General to Spain. The case may have proven an embarrassment to the legal process and to the British government, but were it a serious embarrassment, it could have been remedied by simply giving the General immunity and allowing him to return to Chile. Because the Law Lords did *not* decide this, their embarrassment was not so extreme as to halt extradition. This in itself is enough to cast doubt on the argument that the motivation for *Pinochet III* was to leave the entire affair behind.

Why did Jack Straw allow Pinochet to return to Chile?

This question requires slightly different responses than the previous one. In this case, unlike in the preceding one, the law *authorizes* behavior, it does not mandate or expect certain behavior from actors (however, given the discretion provided by the majority of the world's criminal justice systems, it is probably inaccurate to say that criminal justice systems *require* the enforcement of criminal law). Thus, the answers to this question will be different to the others. Clearly, political concerns influenced the creation of UK extradition law and the granting of a wide degree of discretion to the Foreign Secretary, and the decision to send the General home were influenced by politics. Thus while the answer to this question may be non-legal ("he was responding to the diplomatic fiasco that the *Pinochet* case had generated"), the answer can also have a legal quality ("UK extradition law allows humanitarian exceptions to the requirement that suspected criminals be extradited"). Most useful answers to this question will not use this second answer as it seems less insightful than the first, but it nonetheless does provide some useful information that can explain the income of the case (as I have said, what matters in understanding a particular case and what doesn't is a more-or-less arbitrary issue depending on the aims and interests of the inquirer).

However, were we to ask a different question, not a why question about what caused the relevant agents to act, but rather a simple question about the law that was applied: "Were Straw's actions in *Pinochet* legal?" (or perhaps "Did Straw violate the law by allowing Pinochet to return to Chile?"), we would obtain a much clearer answer. It is clear that in this case nobody knowingly broke any clearly articulated laws, however unhappy the results might be for Pinochet's and Blair's critics. Regardless of whether it was an act of political cowardice or humanitarianism to allow Pinochet to leave, it is clear that Straw was well within his powers as Home Secretary to release the General. His political cowardice was abetted by the law, he did not need to violate it in order to achieve the results that he desired.

Human rights activists have maintained that the Blair government betrayed their principles by allowing the General to return to Spain. Burbach, for example, argues that Home Secretary Jack Straw sold out the humans rights values that he had once supported

> While Straw had at one time been an activist in the solidarity movement against Pinochet's reign of terror, he now acted as the consummate politician, intent on ending a legal and human rights drama that was no longer of interest to the Labour government. On January 11 he declared that he was 'minded' to halt the extradition process and send the General back to Chile (Burbach 2003, 121).

Of course, examining the role of law in *Pinochet* is *not* to judge Secretary Straw's fidelity to his own declared values nor can it be to judge the human rights standards of Tony Blair or his government. Rather, the question of law in this case must be examined by asking whether or not obligatory legal principles were violated by any of the agents involved. The moral fiber of Blair and Straw is certainly an important issue, but beyond the scope of legal analysis.

Consequences of Pinochet: legal and political

The influence of the *Pinochet* rulings (particularly, *Pinochet III*) have been significant, regardless of the lens through which one examines them. According to the interpretation of many of its fans, the ruling effectively ended the concept of head of state immunity for international crimes in many different contexts and provided a legal basis for extraterritorial jurisdiction for numerous crimes that were previously considered beyond the reach of prosecution.[20] It likewise prompted prosecutions for human rights violations committed by former members of Latin American regimes both in their home countries and in Europe.[21]

The *legal* consequences of *Pinochet* must not be overstated, however. While it is no doubt true that the ruling marks a milestone in international accountability for certain categories of crimes, it does not establish a principle of universal jurisdiction *stricta sensu.* The ruling was dependent upon the existence of a number of treaties

---

20 Although these implications are debated. See "Arrest warrant of 11 April 2000" (*Democratic Republic of the Congo v. Belgium*) Judgment of 14 February, 2002. For a critique of this case in relation to the *Pinochet* case see Wirth (2002), and Sands (2003).

21 In her study of the effects of the *Pinochet* case, Naomi Roht-Arriaza (2003) points to numerous cases that "either followed from or were inspired by the Pinochet case." These include prosecutions in Argentina, Mexico, and Guatemala, as well as efforts to extradite and prosecute former rightists in Europe. However, she argues that in many cases, this has not been an effect of the *Pinochet* case as a legal precedent, but rather it has served as a catalyst for these efforts. As she puts it, "Most importantly, the Pinochet case has played a catalytic role in stimulating and accelerating judicial investigations in the target countries. There have been some places where the jurisprudence of the Spanish courts has been taken up by other magistrates but the effects of the case are less a question of advances in legal theory than in the realm of the imagination. It is true that the Spanish court's finding that the amnesty laws of Chile and Argentina... violated international law has helped domestic trial judges in these countries bolster the legal argument" (Roht-Arriaza 2003, 210).

between England and Spain which limited the General's legal accountability and was conducted within the confines of the UK legal system. Moreover, Pinochet was a former head of state and was not in power at the time of his detention, which similarly limits its relevance for currently operating heads of state and other diplomatic figures.

The British *Pinochet* case is not the end of the legal events surrounding the General and the political and legal implications of the Law Lords' ruling on Chile itself were tremendous. Shortly after returning to Chile, the General was stripped of his immunity and hounded by Chilean prosecutors for different offenses until his death in December 2006. While these changes in Chilean attitudes towards the government did not result from the enforcement of international law, they nonetheless resulted directly from the *Pinochet* ruling. Were we to ask further why questions about the ramifications of the *Pinochet* case for the General *beyond* the events in the UK (such as "Why was General Pinochet stripped of his immunity?"), we would find many different direct and indirect consequences for the decision. His status at his death would probably have been very different were it not for the international norms that authorized the Spanish extradition request as well as the legal reflections of the British Law Lords.

The results of the *Pinochet* ruling left much for both sides to be unhappy about and those who examine the law through a policy-oriented perspective are likely to describe the case as a "failure," to use Henkin's way of framing the roles of law in international politics. On one hand, the human rights community lost an opportunity to prosecute the former dictator and, theoretically at least, deter future dictators from committing misdeeds. On the other hand, Pinochet's supporters had to endure a humiliating series of interrogations and saw the former leader stripped of his immunity by a foreign court, leaving him a much weaker person. Politically, speaking, however, despite these facts, there is no reason to believe that the law was openly violated by anybody involved in the proceedings. Complaints about the procedures of the trial amount to no more than complaints about the prudence of the Spanish court and the ideological commitments of the Blair government.

Nicaragua

In 1979, the pro-US, anti-communist Somoza regime collapsed in the small Central American state of Nicaragua. Somoza himself fled the country and the leftist Sandinista government, headed by Daniel Ortega, promptly assumed power. The new regime was avowedly socialist, sharing an ambiguous relationship with both Cuba and the Soviet Union. Upon assuming power in early 1981, the Reagan administration quickly concluded the Sandinistas were a serious threat to US interests and security and accused the Nicaraguan government of supporting leftist militias seeking to undermine the neighboring states of Honduras and El Salvador. In 1981, the US government ended all economic aid to the Nicaraguan government after charging that the Sandinistas were allowing the Soviet Union to ferry weapons to the communist rebels (State Department, 24 February 1981). Further, the CIA began supporting ant-Sandinista rebel forces (or *contras*) and conducting its own clandestine operations against the Nicaraguan government, including mining the harbors of Managua and coordinating attacks against Nicaraguan ports and oil refineries. Some of these actions were carried out by both Nicaraguan and US forces, others were carried out solely by the CIA with instructions issued that the rebel forces would take credit for them when they became public. Ortega and his Sandinista government became public enemy No. 1 in the western hemisphere for the Reagan administration.

These US-sponsored attacks caused a good deal of havoc in Nicaragua, undermining its authority and damaging its economy. The inability of the government to completely stop the insurgents or prevent the American government from funding them ultimately prompted the Sandinista government to begin proceedings against the US at the International Court of Justice (ICJ) in April 1984. In its filing, the Nicaragua government charged that, "The United States of America is using military force against Nicaragua and intervening in Nicaragua's internal affairs in violation of Nicaragua's sovereignty, territorial integrity and political independence and of the most fundamental and universally accepted principles of international law." The Nicaraguan government charged that the US had sponsored some 10,000 mercenaries encamped just outside Nicaraguan territory who were acting against the Nicaraguan government. These groups, they charged, had attacked targets within Nicaragua in an effort to destabilize its leftist government.

The case, entitled, "Case Concerning the Military and Paramilitary Activities in and against Nicaragua (*Nicaragua v. United States of America*)" resulted in two significant decisions and three ancillary decisions from the ICJ. The first significant judgment concerned the jurisdiction of the Court over the matter and the second was a ruling on the merits of the case. The other two orders related to Nicaragua's request for interim measures, attempting to stop US activities against Nicaragua, and a 1991 decision on Nicaragua's request to discontinue the case and disavow reparations.[22] Each is in some ways significant for understanding the effect (or *lack* of effect) of international law on this case and later international conflicts, so each will be briefly discussed.

While *Pinochet* can perhaps be characterized as a qualified success for international law in Henkin's terms, the *Nicaragua* case is, at least on the surface, an unmitigated failure.[23] *Pinochet* dealt with the alleged crimes of one individual and the appropriate legal categories which apply to him, and the forum where the case was handed was a set of domestic courts. On the other hand, the *Nicaragua*

22 For purposes of brevity I will pass over the attempt by El Salvador to intervene on the side of the US.

23 As with *Pinochet*, there are several different proceedings that constitute "the *Nicaragua* case" as I will describe it here. In total, there are five orders and two judgments. We can say that there are at least four major aspects of the proceedings: *Nicaragua I*, an order of 10 May 1984 regarding provisional measures (stopping US-sponsored attacks on Nicaragua), *Nicaragua II*, a judgment of 26 November 1984 on the jurisdiction of the ICJ over the conflict, *Nicaragua III*, the judgment of 27 June 1986 on the merits of the case, and *Nicaragua IV*, the attempt to obtain reparations from the US (along with the military conflict before April 1984 and the consequences after the rulings) will constitute "the *Nicaragua* case" for the purposes of this study.

decision is a complex, explicitly inter-national affair relating to numerous aspects of international security and the role of international courts *vis-à-vis* sovereign states. Moreover, *Pinochet* mixed features of international law with those of domestic law. It was as much a case about UK extradition law as it was about the authority of international criminal law. *Nicaragua* was more purely "international" in the sense that it involved interstate litigation as well as some of the most basic principles of the sovereign political order – the right of states to protect themselves against other states and limitations on the use of force. This means that the overall effects of the *Nicaragua* case upon international law and international relations are broader and more difficult to gauge than in *Pinochet*.

One of the compelling aspects of this case is that, while the ICJ did render two separate decisions on the affair – one on the question of admissibility as well as one on the substance of the case – one of the parties to the case was absent during the latter portion of the case. Having failed in its efforts to prevent the Court from asserting jurisdiction over the matter, the US withdrew from the proceedings and severed virtually all of its legal ties with the Court. With the party with an unquestioned military and economic superiority refusing to acknowledge the ruling, the opinion, whatever its formal, legal merits, was effectively dead on arrival. However, as we will see, this does not mean that the law was *completely* meaningless to US–Nicaragua relations or to US policy in Central America. It simply means that the law did much less than legalists would have liked it to do in affecting US policy in Nicaragua.

Attorneys for the US government set several roadblocks before Nicaragua's lawyers and sought to exploit several loopholes in order to prevent the Court's asserting jurisdiction over the matter. They made several different arguments during the two preliminary phases of the case (one on the effort to prevent the Court from offering provisional measures and the other on a much longer hearing on the jurisdiction of the ICJ): appealing to the priority the Security Council in matters of the use of force, similarly arguing that the Nicaraguan appeal to the Council preempted action by the Court. Most intriguing, however, was the US effort to withdraw from the court's compulsory jurisdiction *vis-à-vis any Central American state* effective immediately and continuing for two years shortly before Nicaragua submitted its application to the Court.[24] This attempt was rejected because the US had not given the requisite six months notice before withdrawing. A second effort on the part of American lawyers argued that Nicaragua had not accepted the compulsory jurisdiction of the Court because it had never received the ratified document.[25] This, too, was rejected by the Court on the grounds that Nicaragua had accepted the jurisdiction of the Permanent Court of International Justice (the ICJ's predecessor)

24 Notification of 26 August 1984 (signed by US Secretary of State and submitted to the UN Secretary General).

25 The issue here is somewhat technical. The compulsory jurisdiction of the ICJ is limited to cases where all parties have accepted such a commitment (Article 36(2) of the ICJ statute). However, the Nicaraguan government had not accepted the compulsory jurisdiction of the ICJ, but rather had accepted the Court's predecessor institution: The PCIJ which is "grandfathered" into the ICJ by the same article of the ICJ statute.

and thus had accepted the Court's jurisdiction over the matter (Greig 1991; Chimni 1986; Leigh 1985).[26]

The US lost the case in both the procedural phase of the trial as well as on the merits. The merits ruling in particular is a stinging rejection of the American position and a forceful interpretation of the laws regarding the use of force and the rights of sovereign states. Here the Court ruled that, "the United States of America, by training, arming, equipping, financing and supplying the *contra* forces or otherwise encouraging, supporting and aiding military and paramilitary activities in and against Nicaragua, has acted against the Republic of Nicaragua in breach of its obligation under customary international law not to intervene in the affairs of another State"[27] (one can plausibly argue that the failure on the merits was so pronounced because the US had not participated in this part of the case, effectively meaning that Nicaragua's claims went largely unscrutinized by the judges, save for the occasional interjection by Judge Schwebel). Further, the Court decided that, "the United States is under a duty immediately to cease and to refrain from all such acts as may constitute breaches of the foregoing legal obligations" (§5), and ordered that hearings be conducted for determining the appropriate reparations due Nicaragua from the United States.

Despite the fact that the ICJ had dismissed the argument that the US was beyond the jurisdiction of the Court in this case, the US nonetheless refused to cooperate with it and virtually ignored all further proceedings. In October 1985 the US withdrew from the Court's compulsory jurisdiction, stating that it had, "concluded that continuation of our acceptance of the Court's compulsory jurisdiction would be contrary to our commitment to the principle of the equal application of the law and would endanger our vital national interests" (Weinraub 1985). Moreover, having lost in its efforts to deny the ICJ jurisdiction on *Nicaragua* proceedings, the US government ceased all cooperation in the case and announced that it would not participate in any further proceedings involving Latin America in the ICJ (Taylor 1985). This meant that in many senses the *Nicaragua* judgments were dead on arrival.

The Court left the issue of reparations to later hearings and the Nicaraguan government submitted a claim for $17 billion. While there was some pressure on the US to pay, they never did ('Europeans say the US should pay Nicaragua,' *The Guardian*, 1990). Rather, a change in government in Nicaragua and the departure of Ortega's Sandinista government led to a different attitude from the US and, under heavy economic pressure from the US government (and in spite of a good deal of resistance from many Nicaraguans) (Uhlig 1990), Nicaragua withdrew its claim from the world court in exchange for trade and foreign aid packages (Janis and Noyes 1997, 445; O'Connell 1990). Thus, as in *Pinochet*, although the legal judgment was

26 It is also worth noting that the US had one further avenue by which to dispute the ICJ's jurisdiction: the assertion that the conflict between the US and Nicaragua was a "domestic matter" and that the US did not consent to the Court's acceptance of the case. The so-called "Connally Amendment" to the US's accession to the ICJ allowed the US to make such a determination. The US opted not to do this out of a concern that such a move would dramatically undermine the Court in future cases (Collier and Lowe 2000, 7; Briggs 1959, 301–18). For its specific application in the *Nicaragua* case see Reichler (2001, 36).

27 Military and Paramitlitary Activities in and against Nicaragua (*Nicaragua v. US*), Merits, 1986, ICJ Rep. 14 (Judgment of 7 June) at 146.

in some sense thwarted by ensuing political events, a formal legal ruling from a court acted as a catalyst for a number of different political actors.

Law and politics in Nicaragua

In many ways the *Nicaragua* case is an abject failure of law, to use Henkin's terminology. The US dismissed the ruling, refused to attend the proceedings on the merits, ignored the Court's final decision, and continued its policies in the area as though the ruling had never taken place. The White House denounced the appropriateness of the Court's ruling as well as the substance of its findings, with the State Department's spokesman asserting, "The court is simply not equipped to deal with a case of this nature involving complex facts and intelligence information" (Shipler 1986). Moreover, the Court's deliberations had little effect on the development of US policy in Latin America (in either Congress or the White House): two days before the ruling was issued, the US House of Representatives endorsed the Reagan administration's plan to give $70 million in military aid to the Contras (Lewis, 1986). The US further vetoed a proposed UN Security Council resolution on the *Nicaragua* opinion that affirmed the importance of compliance with the Court's judgments (Stiles 2000, 401–25). In short, the ruling seemed to have little relevance to US foreign policy: There was no enforcement, compliance, or any other term that is used to describe law-governed political behavior.

As with *Pinochet* we can ask a series of "why questions" about the events surrounding the *Nicaragua* case. However, it is here that the relative weakness of the case in relation to international politics reveals itself in some dramatic ways, without making any generalized statement about the role of law in international politics. When one looks at the case, there are significantly fewer interesting "why questions" that we can ask in regards to US policy in Nicaragua that require a reference to the World Court's ruling. Were we to ask questions such as "Why did the US do X?", few would be significant for somebody wanting to understand US policy towards Nicaragua or El Salvador where this case is involved. Trivial questions, such as why did the US veto Security Council Draft Resolution S/18250 (1986), which reaffirmed "The role of the International Court of Justice as the principal judicial organ of the United Nations and a means for the peaceful solution of disputes," and called for, "Full compliance with the [*Nicaragua*] judgment"[28] (UN Doc. S/18250) can be explained by reference to the case. This might be an interesting question in some contexts, but it is probably of limited general interest.

Unlike *Pinochet*, the influence of *Nicaragua* on the ensuing events in Central America was minimal and it has only played a small role in later accounts of the US–Nicaragua conflict. Robert Kagan's over 800 page history of US–Nicaragua relations during the Cold War mentions the ICJ only three times, and there only briefly (Kagan 1996). To this extent claims of international law's epiphenomenality and irrelevance seem more compelling in *Nicaragua* than in *Pinochet* – the law doesn't seem to do

28 See also UN Chronicle (Nov, 1986).

much explanatory work in this context.[29] As one scholar concluded, "The opinion of the International Court of Justice in the *Nicaragua* case will be of interest primarily because of its general pronouncements on questions of international law. Its impact on the immediate controversy appears slight" (Morrison 1987, 160).

However, when one shifts away from an analysis of enforcement or compliance (away from whether or not the ruling changed US behavior) and instead looks at the case in terms of the expectations of the various actors involved in it, the outcome of the ruling looks somewhat different. For example, it is naïve to suppose that the Nicaraguan government believed that the Court's ruling would, in and of itself, affect US policy in any significant way. Clearly, by the time they had initiated proceedings against the US, the Sandinista government was aware of the limitations of such an approach to directly constraining US foreign policy when it was being made by a president as militantly anti-Communist as Ronald Reagan. By this time, many of the clandestine operations against Nicaragua had been uncovered and attempts to arrive at a negotiated settlement had largely failed. Clearly, there were good reasons for Nicaragua to be skeptical about the power of an unenforceable ICJ ruling to affect American policy.

Nonetheless, there were good reasons for the Sandinista government to take its complaint to the Court, and from their perspective, the case was at least partially successful. Clearly, the ruling had the potential to be a public relations coup for the Nicaraguan government and to embolden international and domestic critics of American policy towards Nicaragua.[30] Heavy-handed US actions against the Court (the same court that they had used so effectively to sanction the Iranian government after they took US embassy staff hostage in 1979)[31] hurt the United States' status around the world, making the US appear hypocritical in its demands that Iran obey the Court while refusing to do so itself.

Beyond these efforts to claim the moral high ground and acquire global sympathy for its situation, the Nicaraguan government had some very specific goals in mind when they initiated proceedings against the US. Rather than placing the American congressional debate on American policy towards Nicaragua in Cold War terms (viewing in terms of a democratic and capitalist United States opposed to the Soviet-aligned Marxist Sandinista government), supporters of the proceedings hoped that the suit would force the American people and their government to confront the legitimacy of their Nicaragua policy framing it in terms of US ideals regarding the rule of law. As one attorney representing Nicaragua said:

29 For a thoughtful attempt to balance realist readings of the *Nicaragua* case with those who are naively optimistic about the significance of law in US–Nicaragua relations see D'Amato (1985, 657–64).

30 Critics as famous as Noam Chomsky have made reference to the *Nicaragua* ruling as proof that that United States is a "rogue regime", see Chomsky (1989, 66).

31 As Meyer points out, the American denunciation of the ICJ judges in the *Nicaragua* case was particularly ironic given that the US itself had given such credence to the Court in the *Hostages* case and, "There were not many changes in personnel on the Court between the time that the United States went there and got in 1980 what it wanted regarding the *Tehran Hostages* case and the filing of the Nicaragua case in 1984" (Meyer 2002, 135).

> It was clear that to win the debate in Congress we had to change the question.
>
> That was the reason for proposing that Nicaragua sue the United States in the World Court: to change the focus of the debate in Congress in order to win forthcoming votes on Contra aid. The question would no longer be the simplistic one asked (and answered) by the Reagan Administration: whether the Sandinistas were Communists whose very existence threatened US interests. With the United States in the defendant's dock in The Hague, members of Congress would have to ask themselves whether US national interests were truly served when America wantonly disregarded, and thereby undermined, the most fundamental principles of international law (Reichler 2001, 23).

According to this view, the point was not to reach a judicial ruling that would be enforced against an uncooperative US, but rather to expose and embarrass the US, shaming congressional leaders into action and thereby shift US policy. As one participant in the proceedings asserted: "It was not necessary to change everyone's thinking on US policy toward Nicaragua. All that was required to defeat Contra aid was to change the votes of about fifteen or twenty members of Congress, most of them House Democrats."[32]

However, here, too the ruling failed to significantly change the direction of US policy towards the Sandinistas. While there was some congressional resistance to the thought of funding the Contras given the ruling, Congress nonetheless voted on the matter two days before the ICJ handed down its opinion on the merits of the case.[33] As a result of personal lobbying from President Reagan, the House of Representatives approved $100 million in aid ($70 million of which was planned for military use) for the Contras by a vote of 221–209 (Greenhouse 1986) (the President had accused those who opposed Contra aid of being deceived by Communist subterfuge and ultimately supporting a Soviet beachhead in Latin America [Boyd 1986]). Thus, beyond the moral outrage that the ruling generated in US editorials,[34] the ruling had few effects on Congress's attitude towards the Reagan Administration's foreign policy.

Why did the Court assert jurisdiction over the Nicaragua–US conflict?

One of the central points of contention in *Nicaragua* is the legitimacy of the Court's role in adjudicating the US–Nicaragua conflict and the extent to which the Court's rulings, particularly in regards to jurisdiction, were unduly influenced by political factors. In order to address this, however, we must abstract the *Nicaragua* decision from broader issues of US policy in Central America and look at the possible political influence on the legal reasoning of the ICJ itself. Here we can see that there is some debate about whether or not the Court's reasoning in *Nicaragua* was unduly influenced by extra-legal concerns and it is inevitable that a court that must inevitably handle politically controversial cases like *Nicaragua* will be suspected of political partisanship. For example, Leigh charges, "the Court's line of reasoning in reaching

---

32 Reichler (2001, 23–4).

33 See Lewis's article in the *New York Times* along with Sen. Moynihan's address to a law school mentioned in Chomsky's *Manufacturing Consent*, Chomsky (2002).

34 For examples see Scheffer (1986, 5), and Gardner (1986).

the conclusion that Nicaragua has accepted the compulsory jurisdiction of the Court is so preposterous that the State Department has been given strong provocation for its unprecedented action" (Leigh 1985, 446).[35] On the other side, Franck argues, "No part of that decision… appears to this American international lawyer to be insupportable in law and thus, evidently a manifestation of 'politicization.' It is a decision as to which reasonable men and versed in the law can and will differ" (Franck 1985, 384).

Assuming, for the sake of argument, that the reasoning was "preposterous," then what else explains the Court's actions in accepting jurisdiction over the matter?

Critics of the *Nicaragua* ruling have charged that the ICJ was being unacceptably "activist" in the sense that it was undertaking a role that was beyond it – attempting to uphold the rule of law in situations of violent conflict. Under this interpretation, the Court was idealistically and perhaps naively seeking to insert itself in cold war politics. Thus Moore (a counsel to the US in the case), in a blistering critique of the Court, charged that the case was a "judicial tragedy." Behind this error, however, he sees a noble, if naïve legalist ideology and a little sympathy for the David of Nicaragua against the Goliath of the US:

> The motivation of the majority of the Court in the *Nicaragua* case was almost certainly good. The dedicated judges believed they saw an opportunity to curtail some of the increasing violence sweeping the world and to uphold the rule of law. Possibly, they also wished to strengthen the role of the Court in dealing with world order disputes. And some may have internalized early hopeful assumptions about the Sandinista revolution against Somoza (Moore 1987, 152).

Thus, the political explanation for the Court's acceptance of the *Nicaragua* case is either the naïve idealism of the Court's justices or a hidden sympathy for Nicaragua's communist government (of course, this argument assumes that the Court was naïve enough to harm its standing based on a purportedly unsupportable reading of the law). Such views were not only represented by defenders of US policy in Nicaragua, but also by those who believed in the principles of the complaint, but feared damage to the Court (Janis 1987).

On the other hand, some participants in the case on the side of Nicaragua were worried that political concerns would lead the Court to pass on the case, using legal technicalities as an excuse to avoid rendering a judgment that had very little chance of influencing American behavior. Such an outcome could humiliate the Court and underscore its limited power to directly influence world affairs when other actors refused to cooperate. Nicaragua's lawyers feared that, "The Court – especially if it were reluctant to confront the United States – might seize upon the technical imperfection in Nicaragua's acceptance of compulsory jurisdiction as a convenient vehicle for disposing of the case" (Reichler 2001, 29). This argument assumes that the Court had legal grounds for adjudicating the matter and any decision otherwise would have been a political one.

As in *Pinochet*, there were a number of possible outcomes to the ICJ's decision, each of which had a political side to it. Thus, as is often the case, "political" analyses

35 For another criticism of the Court's decision on admissibility see Reisman (1986).

can cut both ways: a legal decision can be viewed as a product of political calculation regardless of what conclusions the legal actors arrive at. An acceptance of jurisdiction would have been activist and a refusal to take the case would have been an effort to avoid irrelevance. If it had refused it would have been cowardly, seeking to escape from a trap that would undermine its professional standing. The point here is not to answer these questions, rather the point is to show that politics and law can both be used as explanatory strategies, both can explain the case. However, if Franck's (1985) analysis is correct, the law clearly mattered in the Court's ruling.

Consequences of Nicaragua

However, despite the fact that the impact of the *Nicaragua* ruling on US policy was minimal, the public relations consequences of the ruling were significant, at least if they were seen as a part of the broader war in Central America. A number of different countries condemned the US attitude to the Court and it became an embarrassment for the Reagan administration. Kagan places the ruling within the broader context of international opposition to US policy in Central America, seeing it as a part of a host of reasons for disliking the US. "The cost to the United States… was more than financial. In international forums the conflict was an embarrassment for the United States, the cause of an adverse ruling at the International Court of Justice and of repeated denunciations in the United Nations" (Kagan 1996, 571).

Reichler argues that the *Nicaragua* proceedings are more significant than bad publicity for the US. He argues that the interim decision of the Court requiring the US to cease all military activities against Nicaragua contributed to the US Congress's ultimate decision to cut off military funding to the Contras.

> While a number of factors contributed to the House's defeat of Contra aid, Nicaragua's suit and its focus on international law, the Reagan Administration's ham-handed attempts to escape judgment, and the Court's rulings in Nicaragua's favor on interim measures and (later) jurisdiction indisputably played their part (Reichler 2001, 35).

This, in turn, resulted in efforts by Reagan administration officials to circumnavigate the Boland amendment and illegally support the rightist paramilitaries.

> The World Court delivered what turned out to be a devastating blow to the Reagan Administration's war on Nicaragua. It set off a chain reaction that helped convince Congress to cut off funding for the Contras, gave Nicaragua the respite it needed to turn the tide of battle, and forced the White House into egregious tactical errors that ultimately undid its entire policy (Reichler 2001, 35).

While Reichler agrees that the US failed to follow the law in this case, according to his analysis, international law nonetheless had a profound impact on US policy in Nicaragua, and ultimately changed the realities of the Cold War in Latin America. Whether or not Reichler's analysis is correct, it shows how, even though the ICJ decision was ignored and could not be enforced, the law can have a profound impact on ensuing events.

Conclusion

The purpose of this chapter has been to frame the question of the "reality" of international law in an empirical, rather than a purely theoretical light, and to put this approach to work in understanding two significant cases. As was argued in the previous chapter, legal rules stand or fall based upon their relevance for understanding a series of events, not their position in a theoretical model. This requires that one look at cases and examine their processes and their consequences, subjects that are always open to numerous contradictory analyses and conflicting interpretations. Furthermore, the law may matter in innumerable ways beyond the means that terms like "obedience" or "enforcement" would suggest. Finally, the questions that one asks about a case determine the significance or insignificance of law.

The conclusions that may be drawn from these analyses do not have the status of a set of necessary laws of international affairs. Rather, any broad conclusions that can be reached are inductive generalizations that are often messy and fallible. Human affairs are a complicated subject and international relations like all parts of human life cannot be *definitively* explained. International law exists as part of the discourse of international relations and insofar as the subjects of this discourse are inevitably controversial and indeterminate, so must be our conclusions about law. There is no doubt that historians and scholars will find fault with my analysis of *Pinochet* and *Nicaragua*, and many descriptive realists will find its claims about the role of law dubious. A plurality of explanations for an historical event or series of events is not a problem, but is rather a sign of robust scholarly debate.

Some of the effects of international law result from something like obedience or enforcement, others are "political" in the sense that treaties and judicial opinions can change the dynamics of situations even if the law is not "enforced" in a recognizable sense. Despite the fact that Pinochet "got away with it" in the sense that he avoided extradition to Spain, he most likely would not have faced later charges in Chile had his aura of invincibility been punctured by the actions of a Spanish judge and the rulings of the British Law Lords. Moreover, there were numerous political and public relations consequences for the US that resulted from *Nicaragua* and, if Reichler (2001, 35) is correct, it ultimately played a role in undoing the Reagan administration. Finally, *further* consequences of these cases resulted from their lingering effects as precedents picked up and used by jurists in other contexts and given new life and new meaning. These cases can be used to understand other events that happened later, even if they had limited effects on those directly involved in them.

Of course, this approach is a much weaker form of analysis than general theories of international politics which generalized covering laws may offer. The generalized insights that professional scholars of international law in international relations can provide in the approach attempted here are of about the same quality and possess the same certainty as the insights of an historian who seeks to come to some larger principles from the mass of data that she has available. The truth is, human events are governed by so many different forces, both at the micro level (the personality of individual leaders and diplomats along with their ability to relate and understand each other) and the macro levels (economic forces, concerns about geopolitical security, or stratagems for obtaining and maintaining political power) that any serious effort to construct general models will have limited applicability. The analysis that has been offered here can only offer vague principles not hard laws – under different circumstances they could easily prove irrelevant.

Finally, one thing that we can see is that the distinction between law and politics is not a clear one when one uses them to understand actual cases. Accusations that a legal actor is being "political" is as much a rhetorical tactic that is used by all sides of a contentious case as it is a tool of scholarly analysis. Parties that were supportive of Judge Garzón's attempt to extradite Pinochet, as well as his critics, accused the Court of "playing politics." Similarly, opponents of Nicaragua's Sandinista regime believed that the Court was being political in accepting jurisdiction over the case and supporters of Nicaragua felt that the Court would be political if it did not rule in their favor. One's opinion of whether or not the Court is being "political" is more a function of where one stands *vis-à-vis* a particular ruling, not whether the ruling is political *per se*. In such cases, "politics" is in the eye of the beholder.'

This chapter and the preceding one have been primarily involved with a critical discussion of descriptive realism. In the next, final chapter, I will turn to the *prescriptive* realists described in the first chapter. While these two chapters have been concerned with issues of the philosophy of empirical social science ("when does a law *matter*?"), the next chapter will be more concerned with normative theories of law. That is, we will not be asking whether or not the law matters for international relations, but rather *should* it matter, whether politicians, diplomats, and other international actors should follow international legal norms? Even if law does shape global events as I have argued there, for prescriptive realists, this may not be a good thing, all things considered.

Chapter 8

The Prescriptive Realists

In the opening chapter, I entertained numerous arguments against the possibility of a truly international law, the majority of which I have already confronted. However, one genre of skepticism so far untouched is that belonging to the skeptics that I labeled "prescriptive realists" in Chapter 1. These are the thinkers who reject international law on specifically normative grounds. While I portrayed the *descriptive* realists as morally neutral, unconcerned with the utility or legitimacy of international law (preferring instead to reject them on social-scientific grounds as useless for understanding the machinations of global politics), the prescriptive realists are an entirely different animal. These thinkers assert their views in distinctly moral or normative language and do not rely on the realist politics of the descriptive realists. We may say that what separates the descriptive and prescriptive realists is that the latter employ values in their arguments against international law. This is simply to say that they believe that serious minds *ought* to reject international law. It is to this camp of international legal skeptics that I now turn in this final chapter.

To briefly recap the discussion of Chapter 1, I broke down the prescriptive realists into three rough categories: The *prudential diplomat*, the *moral relativist*, and the *republican*. The former, probably the most common among this camp, argues that the stakes involved in international politics, with thousands (if not millions) of lives in the balance in any major decision, requires that political leaders be given as much freedom as possible to pursue international peace and stability by any available means. This effort, they claim, would only be hamstrung by unnecessary concerns about the legality or illegality of political behavior, diplomatic niceties that only interest well-behaved nations anyway. The relativists, on the other hand, assert that the substance and processes of international law, along with the conceptions of law that come with them, are biased towards powerful (usually Western) interests and Western standards and therefore lacks any true international or cross-cultural legitimacy. Finally, the republicans assert that the leaders of states receive their legitimacy from their domestic constituencies and would be acting illegitimately if they subordinated these interests to those of the international community. Insofar as international law undermines the interests of their own people they ought to be ignored by these leaders. These three different views will be the subject of critical analysis in this chapter.

This section of the work will differ from its predecessors in some important ways. My central goal here is to suggest that the prescriptive realists have in fact misunderstood or mischaracterized the nature of international law. This in turn, has led them to oversimplify the various roles that law plays in international politics. I hope to show here that international law, as it has been characterized in the preceding chapters, is a legal regime that is both subtle enough and sophisticated enough to effectively respond to most of these concerns. Thus, rather than further detailing my conception of law, in this chapter I will be highlighting some of its strengths as a rebuttal to the prescriptive realists. This chapter could not but have come at the end of this work; it is only after adequately laying out the analysis of international law that one can actually defend it against certain possible criticisms. Given the conception of international law that I have set out, the concerns of the prescriptive realists are in fact misapplied. Rather than being complete rejections of international law, the prescriptive realists are best seen as offering a series of warnings regarding the wise formulation of law, programs for legal reform, and principles of just application, or so I shall argue.

This chapter could have been written quite differently, however. Rather than completely placating the fears and concerns of the prescriptive realists by revealing that their understandings of the law are misguided, I *could* have attacked their arguments on purely normative grounds. For example, I could have argued against the relativists by showing how, by their very nature, international legal norms are not relative, that certain values (such as those embodied in the Universal Declaration of Human Rights) are in fact rooted in the way things really are and thus are universal in a deeper sense than by the simple fact that every state has signed onto this document. Similarly, I could have argued that the values embodied in law are of a higher order than those valorized by the prudential diplomat and therefore, law *ought* to play a strong role in international politics, independent of whether it really does. Finally, I could have shown that there are good philosophical reasons for thinking that legal obligations can exist beyond the state, against the claims of the republicans. These arguments would be expressly normative, in many ways, credible, and would have taken this chapter in a very different, but no doubt equally interesting direction.

I will not take this tack in seeking to grapple with the prescriptive realists for several reasons. First, a normative, value-laden approach to this question would be at odds with the fundamentally empiricist method I have used so far. I have sought, wherever possible to avoid making any overt metaphysical or metaethical claims about the nature of reality as such (be it political, legal, or moral reality) and have chosen to stick with what is at hand in the actual practice of international lawyers, diplomats, and statesmen. This approach has a number of advantages, it seems to me: first, it appears most appropriate to the significant and deep moral and political divisions in international society, divisions that make general, normative discussions intensely problematic. Thus it is more amenable to pluralism. Second, it seems to me that before such normative discussions can take hold, before we can discuss what we *ought* to do, it is first necessary to prove empirically that these kinds of values *actually do* play a role in international relations. Without any empirical understanding of what international law is, it becomes pointless to speculate about what it ought to be or ought not to be. Finally, I am generally somewhat skeptical about the meta-ethical projects, projects that try to deductively prove that morality has, and requires, a metaphysical foundation. Such discussions are interesting reading, of course, but generally of limited utility for confronting the complex moral dilemmas that those involved with international law and international relations more generally are faced with.

I should warn the reader that what will follow might seem to be a dizzying compilation of categories and sub-categories under the single heading of prescriptive realism. This taxonomy, my attempt to understand these positions in as sophisticated a fashion as one could reasonably hope for, required that I distinguish subtly different positions in a fashion that might seem arbitrary to some readers. Some of these positions have been extrapolated from the views of real people, be they philosophers, politicians, or lawyers, while others have been created out of whole cloth, as it were. At times, I admit, the prescriptive realists I cite could have been placed in other camps than the ones I have chosen for them (Hegel, for example, has views obscure and complex enough to occupy virtually any position on the theoretical map). The latter, novel positions are in essence my effort to anticipate some future objections that might be offered in defense of prescriptive realism or to explore some ideas that I have yet to find in the available literature. They are creations of my own although they may be rooted in some other views. I hope that the reader will bear with me and recognize that Occam's razor has remained sharp and that entities have not been multiplied needlessly.

The Prudential Diplomat

In the opening chapter, I attributed to the prudential diplomat a distinct moral objection to the rigidity of legal thought: the stakes are very high in international politics and a great deal hangs in the balance when individual states or the international community as a whole must make a decision. The large amount of resources necessary for the development of poor nations and the continued prosperity of the wealthy depend upon the wisdom of their choices. Further, the neighborhood in which diplomats must operate is a particularly rough one, filled with shady and dishonest characters of all stripes. Those with the power over life and death can be thoroughly unpleasant individuals, and often show contempt for the agreements they make, legal or otherwise. For these reasons, those involved in making important decisions need to keep their hands as free as possible in order to make the right choices. Necessary diplomatic choices may involve using the complete arsenal of Machiavellian weapons in order to keep global peace, including compromise, guile, and hypocrisy.

International society is a nasty and brutish place and even those with the best of intentions at times must dirty their hands in order to achieve noble goals. This may require violating international laws (not to mention the codes of conventional ethics) in order to avoid consequences that would be disastrous for all. A legally binding promise made to placate an angry dictator may later turn out to have regrettable, even disastrous consequences if it is not broken. An extradition treaty made in good faith between states may require that an accused terrorist be extradited despite the threat of hostilities erupting with a third state. A dictator under siege may only peacefully surrender her power if she is offered a putatively illegal amnesty for crimes against humanity. These violations, regrettable though they may be, are nonetheless justified by the aforementioned realities and complexities of global politics. The amount at stake in the global diplomatic game requires that good countries sometimes tolerate bad ones (and even criminal ones) in order to assure that everybody is better off.

Dictators and other tyrants are a constant reality of international relations. These leaders prefer force to law in achieving their ambitions, and diplomats, regardless of their personal moral rectitude or overall respect for the rule of law, must deal with them. When confronting these leaders diplomats and heads of state ought to be given as much latitude as possible. They could not make the deals necessary to maintain international order and peace were these diplomats concerned about the legality of their acts, or their own legal liability for their compromises. Similarly, leaders must break their obligations in tricky situations where fulfilling them would be onerous. A notion of law, when applied to places such as the Middle East, would only undermine any attempt to seek a just and lasting peace and those who seek to use law in this arena do nobody's cause any good. Most leaders of the various states and factions in Israel and Palestine have committed some kind of international crime in their careers, but to impose criminal sanctions upon them (for example, arresting the leaders of the Palestinian *intifada*) would be to nobody's advantage and would only result in setting back the cause of peace years. Effective responses to such situations require a capacity for compromise and a moral flexibility that is prohibited under most legal regimes.

Recalling Kennan's argument from the opening chapter, the prudential diplomat maintains that a legalist mentality forces a uniform doctrine upon what is in fact a vast plurality of complex and shifting political situations. The naiveté of the legalist mentality undermines the goals that the legal system itself was created to provide. This uniform becomes a straitjacket when peace-loving states must confront novel and complex political situations and make unpleasant choices. Those who hope for the rule of law to provide a road map to lasting international peace wind up making the violence more prevalent and more brutal by underestimating the complexities of international politics and the ability of law to solve it. Thus, despite their undeniably good intentions, Kennan asserts, international law only "makes violence more enduring, more terrible, and more destructive to stability than did the older motives of national interest." Prudence and compromise, not the harsh imperatives of law, are what is required to maintain peace and stability in a complex world. Both the lawyer and the diplomat agree about the ends of their work, the need for peace and the avoidance of war, but not the means by which to achieve them.

The prudential diplomat need not reject international law in its entirety, of course. She need only assert that the authority of this law is limited in complex and precarious situations. Treaties, customs, and other sources of international law can be beneficial when applied to mundane contexts. However, as we move to the level of so-called "high politics," involving issues of national security where the stakes are more dramatic and the overlapping interests, power, and commitments become progressively more elaborate, the returns provided by international law rapidly diminish. In such cases, legal concerns should take a back seat to other, more immediate goals. Trade agreements, travel agreements, and other international laws are largely innocuous, but legal commitments to engage in armed conflict or to arrest powerful persons, however laudable in principle, do not merit serious concern in the conduct of good foreign policy. International law is most likely not to be regarded as nothing for the prudential diplomat, but as a normative system it remains subordinate to other ends pursued in international diplomacy, ends that must be pursued in a non-legal fashion.

The prudential diplomat's critique is usually not a critique of international law in general, but is most often restricted to a few of its more moralistic spheres such as the laws of armed conflict, international criminal law, or the international law of human rights. These domains, it is argued, represent the biggest threat to international peace and stability and most often hamper the diplomat's efforts to maintain such peace. It is hard to make a case that international trade law or the law of international organizations for example, would have generally onerous consequences (which is not to say that this couldn't happen or doesn't happen). A trade agreement may have consequences that do not benefit a particular state in the long run, but this is a more base kind of diplomacy, rooted more in the realism of the republican than that of the prudential diplomat. The diplomat's critique is rooted in morality, not in a chauvinistic nationalism and is therefore concerned with the health of the international community as a whole (including states, organizations, and individuals). The diplomat is concerned about what is beneficial for *all*, not with the benefits that will accrue to her particular state. It is only when international law threatens to undermine the political compromises quietly cobbled together in back rooms that the diplomat deems it threatening, and thus normatively invalid.

A famous (or perhaps infamous) proponent of the prudential diplomat's view is the former American National Security Advisor and Secretary of State Henry Kissinger. Kissinger has continually argued that a great deal of the behavior that characterized US foreign policy during the Cold War, the same policies that have been roundly condemned by the international community, were warranted by the realities of the conflict. State acts such as Indonesia's invasion of East Timor in 1972 (with tacit American consent) are necessary given the strategic balance of power (especially given the position of Indonesia in relation to China and the Soviet Union). Kissinger himself laments the incursion of law into foreign policy asserting that legalism merely makes diplomacy more difficult:

> Whatever the merit of the individual legislative actions, their cumulative effect drives American foreign policy toward unilateral and occasionally bullying conduct. For unlike diplomatic communications, which are generally an invitation to dialogue, legislation translates into a take-it-or-leave-it prescription (2001, 27).[1]

Whereas diplomacy gives flexibility in confronting problems, law works through a series of ultimatums that ultimately serve to preclude peaceful and productive dialog between conflicting states. At times, circumstances may require that a good state, a state that would prefer to follow international law, must violate it for the sake of the common good.

Dean Acheson, another seminal figure in twentieth-century US foreign policy similarly holds a prudential diplomat's views on international law, although in a slightly different context. In an oft-cited address before the American Society of

1 Note also Kissinger's critical discussion of universal jurisdiction (2001, 273–82).

International Law, discussing the legality of the US blockade of Cuba in 1962, Acheson bluntly points to the limited utility of law in the international sphere.

> I must conclude that the propriety of the Cuban quarantine is not a legal issue. The power, position and prestige of the United States had been challenged by another state; and law simply does not deal with such questions of ultimate power – power that comes close to the sources of sovereignty. I cannot believe that there are principles of law that say we must accept destruction of our way of life (1963, 108).

It should be noted that Acheson is not being a mere nationalist, simply asserting that the United States had no legal obligations in relation to Cuba, but rather that *no state* in similar circumstances need consider legal justifications for its acts. His arguments are universal: the consequences of a legal approach to the weaponization of Cuba would have been patently unacceptable to anybody (presumably, Acheson would have asserted that the Soviet Union had no legal obligations during the crisis, either). "Wisdom for the decision [of policy towards Cuba] was not to be found in law but in judgment" (Acheson 1963, 108). Acheson and Kissinger, unsurprisingly both professional diplomats, engaged with the tensions and complexities of foreign affairs in a particularly tense and complex time, assert that law would hamper global peace and human flourishing, not provide it.

As mentioned above, I could criticize the prudential diplomat by attacking the meta-ethical philosophy standing behind act utilitarianism and prudential ethics more generally, arguing that we would all be better off if international law were followed. This would be a somewhat sterile, academic critique, far removed from the world in which these diplomats move. Thus, rather than asking whether this brand of skepticism stands on a solid philosophical foundation, and in keeping with the overall spirit of my approach, I will ask a different question: does the prudential diplomat, so characterized, have an adequate grasp of the substance of modern international law? Or to put the question somewhat differently, what flexibility does the contemporary international legal system offer for the ethical diplomat to deal with tricky situations, and is it enough? One of the key insights of this work is that international law is not what it is commonly taken to be (especially by its critics) and any critique that relies heavily on a particular conception of this legal regime ought to have an adequate grasp of what it criticizes. Since we have fleshed out the major contours of international law in the foregoing chapters, we are now in a good position to compare the prudential diplomat's characterization of international law with its actual nature and functions.

A sober look at the international legal system in its present form shows that the prudential diplomat's skepticism is overstated. A great number of international legal texts and principles, as well as the major players on the international legal scene, are keenly aware of the stakes involved in their deliberations and do not take lightly the consequences of their decisions (particularly those consequences that are unforeseen). The international system has the prudence the diplomat demands *built into* the legal system in a number of different ways. The fact that diplomats play a significant role in the creation of these legal norms is testament to their roots in a doctrine of prudence (that they were created by prudent individuals is a good sign that they are prudent in character). Naïve idealists, oblivious to the consequences of their work, do not formulate international law. Structurally speaking, international law is a very flexible legal system and does not provide the "one size fits all" or the "take it or leave it" approach described by Kissinger and Acheson.

Here, I will point to three features of the modern international legal system that are indicators of its flexible character: *escape mechanisms*, *margins of appreciation*, and *equity*. These are not primarily jurisprudential principles to be cited in briefs, treaties, or opinions (although this is sometimes the case) as much as themes that can be found running throughout the international legal system. Each in its own way helps to make this legal system better able to confront the types of situations that concern the diplomat, giving it a sufficient degree of latitude. They serve to "soften" the mechanical application of a rule, providing it with sensitivity towards political context and history. However, they are not "extra-legal" factors that somehow delegitimize the role of law in these cases, but rather are an intrinsic part of the international legal system as such. Further, such aspects of this legal system provide good reasons for understanding international law not as a pure abstraction but rather as engaged with many of the concerns that trouble prudential diplomats. "Let justice be done, should the heavens fall," may be a maxim of moral philosophy, but it is certainly not a guiding principle of modern international law.

Escape mechanisms

Those who fashion and interpret treaties – one of the fundamental sources of international law – are not stupid, nor are they robots who mechanistically spit out rules that they anticipate will be blindly applied and obeyed. Most intelligently written treaties and similar international legal apparatuses give states and other legal agents a certain degree of flexibility in confronting tricky political situations that were unanticipated by the treaty's authors. "[T]he majority of modern treaties are expressed to be of short duration, or are entered into for recurrent terms of years with a right to denounce the treaty at the end of each term, or are expressly or implicitly terminable upon notice."[2] These escape mechanisms can appear in a number of forms, allowing for states to withdraw from the treaty's obligations by performing a set of diplomatic acts within a certain period of time (Helfer 2004). Usually, this involves an official pronouncement from the state that it no longer regards itself as bound by the treaty and a certain passage of time. Arms control treaties have provisions allowing for unilateral withdrawal when the state no longer wishes to remain bound by its conventions – presumably because of the changing nature of threats to the state's security. As Oliver Lissitzyn puts it:

> A treaty is made because two or more states have a common or mutual interest in establishing a new relationship or modifying an existing one. The natural penalty for the violation of a treaty establishing or regulating a mutually desired relationship is the disruption or impairment of the latter. When national policies change, clauses permitting

2 International Law Commission Report p. 257. Cited in Henkin (1993, 517). For an IR-theory perspective on treaty durations and flexibility see Koremenos (2001).

termination or withdrawal by a unilaterally given notice often serve as safety valves which prevent pressures for treaty provisions from building up (1966, xv).

Such structures, found in almost all treaties, prevent states from abandoning obligations on a whim while simultaneously keeping a state's commitments from becoming too onerous. Treaties and other legal obligations are not binding to the point of destruction.

In addition to the escape mechanisms found within the text of the treaties themselves, a number of general principles of treaty interpretation further provide lawyers and diplomats with the flexibility necessary to avoid potential disasters. The Vienna Convention on the Law of Treaties, codifying customary principles, cites several grounds for a state to withdraw from onerous treaty obligations. Article 31 requires that "A treaty shall be interpreted in good faith," and Article 32 rules out any interpretation that "leads to a result which is manifestly absurd or unreasonable." No treaty is absolutely binding to the point of a state's destruction or war. International agreements are not suicide pacts between states, but rather contain clauses and are interpreted with principles that allow for a certain degree of flexibility.

For example, peremptory norms of international law provide an escape mechanism for international legal rules by nullifying any treaty (or interpretation of a treaty) that would lead to terrible consequences were they followed strictly. These norms trump a treaty's *prima facie* claim to validity. In this situation, the treaty is not violated (nor is it violated without consequence), but rather, the treaty itself is rendered null and void by its violation of *jus cogens*.[3] Specifically, Article 53 asserts:

> A treaty is void if, at the time of its conclusion, it conflicts with a peremptory norm of general international law. For the purposes of the present Convention, a peremptory norm of general international law is a norm accepted and recognized by the international community of States as a whole as a norm from which no derogation is permitted and which can be modified only by a subsequent norm of general international law having the same character.

Similarly, Article 64 states:

> If a new peremptory norm of general international law emerges, any existing treaty which is in conflict with that norm becomes void and terminates.

While the precise content of these preemptory norms is notoriously fuzzy, the few that could usually be cited, such as the *jus cogens* norm against the commission of genocide could probably be justifiably considered to be prudent.[4] Similarly, Article 51 of the UN Charter (allowing an inherent right of states to defend themselves) is

3 For a brief history of the creation of Article 53 see Rozakis (1976, 97–149).

4 Article 53 asserts:

For the purposes of the present Convention, a peremptory norm of general international law is a norm accepted and recognized by the international community of States as a whole as a norm from which no derogation is permitted and which can be modified only by a subsequent norm of general international law having the same character.

likewise a *jus cogens* norm.[5] No treaty can force a state to dramatically undermine its own political life or the stability of international society.

Further, the determination of a violation of international legal obligation is influenced by a number of circumstantial issues, some of which preclude a violation of the law. Chapter V of the International Law Commission's Draft Articles on State Responsibility provide several grounds for states to violate *prima facie* legal obligations without accruing any liability (Cassese 2001, 194–6). Among these are self-defense (Article 29), *necessity* (Article 33), *distress* (Article 32), and *force majeure* (Article 31 – "that is the occurrence of an irresistible force or of an unforeseen event, beyond the control of the State, making it materially impossible in the circumstances to perform the obligation"). These principles certainly do not provide a *carte blanche* for states to absolve themselves of responsibility for any violation of law, and each of these grounds comes with a list of limitations, but they are nonetheless legitimate means by which a state may avoid obligations when their consequences become too onerous. Each principle tempers the rigidity of legalism with a healthy dose of prudence.

Although it is rarely invoked, the principle of *rebus sic stantibus* (Oppenheim 1947, 843–50) can be invoked when treaty obligations are too onerous.[6] Needless to say, this is a very contentious part of law. As Bederman describes it, *rebus sic stantibus*

5 Among the candidates for *jus cogens* norms suggested by the International Law Commission when they formulated the Vienna Convention were the norms on human rights, the rules concerning the equality of states, the principles of *pacta sunt servanda*, and *rebus sic stantibus*, along with self-determination, and the freedom of the seas, see Rozakis (1976, 47) See also the ruling of the ICJ on the *North Sea Continental Shelf Case* (paragraph 72).

6 Specifically, Article 62 says:

> 1. A fundamental change of circumstances which has occurred with regard to those existing at the time of the conclusion of a treaty, and which was not foreseen by the parties, may not be invoked as a ground for terminating or withdrawing from the treaty unless:
>
> (a) the existence of those circumstances constituted an essential basis of the consent of the parties to be bound by the treaty; and
>
> (b) the effect of the change is radically to transform the extent of obligations still to be performed under the treaty.
>
> 2. A fundamental change of circumstances may not be invoked as a ground for terminating or withdrawing from a treaty:
>
> (a) if the treaty establishes a boundary; or
>
> (b) if the fundamental change is the result of a breach by the party invoking it either of an obligation under the treaty or of any other international obligation owed to any other party to the treaty.
>
> 3. If, under the foregoing paragraphs, a party may invoke a fundamental change of circumstances as a ground for terminating or withdrawing from a treaty it may also invoke the change as a ground for suspending the operation of the treaty.

See the *Free Zones of Upper Savoy and the District of Gex* (*France v. Switzerland*), PCIJ, 1932, Ser. A/B No. 46, p. 158, and the *Fisheries Jurisdiction Case* (*United Kingdom v. Iceland*), ICJ Rep (1973), p. 3.

> has the potential of being utterly destructive of good faith and predictable observance of treaty obligations. It has nonetheless persisted in treaty law because of the need for a mechanism of peaceful alteration of treaty obligations that are no longer considered desirable. The League of Nations Covenant even embraced the idea that the international community could reconsider "treaties which have become inapplicable, and [those] conditions whose continuance might endanger the peace of the world" (2002, 172).[7]

While *rebus sic stantibus* remains a little used weapon in the diplomat's arsenal, it clearly can be used to modify, nullify, or disregard existing legal obligations when their fulfillment would produce disastrous consequences. "[D]espite the strong reservations expressed with regard to it, the evidence of the acceptance of the doctrine in international law is so considerable that it seems to indicate a recognition of a need for this safety valve in the law of treaties."[8] Thus, *rebus sic stantibus* provides diplomats with further flexibility in confronting novel, dangerous circumstances without having to step outside of the law.

Equity

Similarly, general principles of law as set out in Article 38 of the ICJ statute – such as the general principle of equity – can be used in the interpretation of international legal obligations in order to prevent too onerous a result.[9] As Brownlie (2003, 25) puts it, equity is "often necessary for the sensible application of the more settled rules of law." Like the peremptory norms previously mentioned, equity suffers from a certain ambiguity, but is generally considered a principle of consistency and fairness in international legal decision-making (incorporating sub-principles such as estoppel and acquiescence).[10] Such rules, internal to the law of treaties itself, play a prudential role in the function of law, regulating its interpretation and softening its sharp edges, ends valued by the prudential diplomat and serving as her motivation for rejecting international law. As Christopher Rossi puts it, "One interpretation [of equity], which reduces to the volitional elements of judicial decisionmaking, considers equity a corrective used by judges to mitigate unnecessary hardship caused by the application of general principles, or, specific rules ... " (Rossi 1993, 21). Thus equity stands as a buffer between the strict formulation of a rule on the one hand and the human context where this rule is applied on the other, requiring judges "to look at the substance and not stick in the bark of legal form."[11]

---

7 Internal citation is to Article 19 of the League Covenant.

8 International Law Commission Report, 1966. Cited in Henkin (1993, 517).

9 Here I am distinguishing between equity as a general principle of international law and Article 38(2), which allows the court "to decide a case *ex aequo et bono*, if the parties agree thereto." For a discussion of this distinction see Higgins (1994, 219–237).

10 See the *Gulf of Maine* case (ICJ Rep. 1984, p. 246 at 306), cited in Harris (1998, 51). See also, *The Diversion of Water from the Meuse Case*, *Netherlands v. Belgium* (1937), pp. 76–7.

11 *The Cayuga Indians Case*, American and British Claims Arbitration, *Nielson Reports* 203, 307, 1926. Cited in Janis (1997, 123).

Such principles of equity can function either *infra legem* (interpreting the law in softer fashion than a strict interpretation would normally entail), *praetor legem* (filling in a gap in the law), or *contra legem* (ameliorating a particularly harsh law or nullifying an otherwise binding legal obligation).[12] Each function, however, produces the same general effect: they provide legal rules with the flexibility required to confront the inherent complexity and precariousness of human political life. They achieve this result as a principle of interpretation either by tempering the consequences of *prima facie* obligations or by removing legal obligations that would produce inequitable results. For example, Dr. Shafeiei, a judge on the Iran-US Claims Tribunal rejected a decision of the majority of the Tribunal on the following grounds:

> Enforcement of this totally materialistic and unmerciful formula leads to results which a judge cannot easily accept. In reality, the nonperformance of the contract was occasioned by external events and occurrences. The contractual relations of the Parties were severed, and now their account should be settled equitably.[13]

Under certain circumstances, by citing the principle of equity a state could violate a treaty or other legal obligation simply on the grounds that fulfilling this *prima facie* obligation would produce onerous results without violating international law.

Margins of appreciation

In many important decisions of the European Court of Human Rights, the notion of a "margin of appreciation" afforded to member states has arisen and subsequently received a good deal of support from the international legal community. Generally speaking, this concept has arisen in order to handle two separate, but related problems: differences between the values found in different European states on the one hand and the unique political difficulties confronted by each of them on the other. I will reserve discussion of the former issue for confronting the relativists later in this chapter, but the latter use is directly related to the flexibility and prudence underlying modern international law and thus warrants some discussion. This idea of a margin of appreciation is one feature of the law that has provided diplomats and lawyers with strategies for confronting complex political issues while nonetheless remaining within the bounds of the law.

Each state has its own unique problems within its borders and needs a good deal of flexibility in order to deal with them appropriately. Whether it is England's problems with the Republican terrorists in Northern Ireland,[14] Italy's struggle with

---

12 For particularly interesting discussions of equity see Lowe (1992), and Franck (1995, 47–80).

13 Opinion of Dr Shafei Shafeiei in *Gould Marking Inc. v. Ministry of Defense* (1984) 6 Iran-US Claims Tribunal R 272 at 293–4. Cited in Lowe (1992, 65).

14 *Brogan v. United Kingdom*, European Court of Human Rights, Ser. A, No. 145-B, 11 EHRR 117. Cited in Steiner and Alston (1996, 601–610).

the mafia,[15] or the unique cultural values of Austrian Catholics,[16] the court has recognized that European Human Rights standards are not a "one size fits all" set of rules. In fact, the court has recognized that local and municipal authorities are often those best capable of dealing with local problems and should be given a good deal of leeway when doing so. The court has asserted that states should be provided with a "margin of appreciation" that gives states a free hand to deal with certain problems that are indigenous to their region.

> The Court recalls that it falls to each Contracting State, with its responsibility for the life of its nations to determine whether that life is threatened by a "public emergency" and, if so, how far it is necessary to go in attempting to overcome the emergency. By reason of their direct and continuous contact with the pressing needs of the moment, the national authorities are in principle in a better position than the international judge to decide both on the presence of such an emergency and the scope of derogations necessary to avert it. Accordingly, in that matter a wide margin of appreciation should be left to the national authorities.[17]

Judges in Strasbourg are not adequately equipped with the skills or information necessary to gauge the appropriate response to any and all threats that occur on the continent. Although the court is clear that this margin has its limits and that domestic concerns may not be used as a *carte blanche* by states to violate the civil rights of its citizens whenever it wishes, the court has nonetheless made it clear that in certain cases, international norms should defer to local efforts to combat difficult problems.

This principle of European human rights jurisprudence can be understood more generally to refer to a broader principle of public international law, a consistent prejudice in favor of local or domestic remedies for solving disputes that are largely domestic in character. As Shany (2005, 939) asserts, there is a "a growing acceptance on the part of many international courts and tribunals of the margin of appreciation doctrine." A number of international legal systems and principles of general international law recognize the complexities of domestic politics and policies and are structured to give them a certain degree of deference. Many international legal regimes stretching from environmental law[18] to human rights law, to criminal jurisdiction (see below) provide states with a certain measure of flexibility in complying with their regulations. While domestic laws cannot justify violating international law, the accommodation that frequently takes place between the two favors the priority of domestic jurisdiction. However, as Shany (2005, 931–6) has

15 *Labita v. Italy*, Eur. Ct. of H.RA.

16 *Otto-Preminger*, 295 Eur. Ct. H.RA.

17 *Brannigan and McBride v. United Kingdom*, Judgment of May 1993, Series A, No. 258-B; 1994, 17EHRR 539 para. 43 of judgment. Cited in Jacobs and White (1996, 323). See also, the *Lawless* case. It is important to note that in this respect the margin of appreciation is explicitly tied with Article 15 of the European Convention of Human Rights which allows member states to derogate certain rights, "In times of war or other emergency threatening the life of the nation."

18 For a study of one state's application of the margin of appreciation in environmental law, see Cullet (1999).

pointed out, the doctrine has an uncertain status at the ICJ, particularly in its recent jurisprudence. Thus, when international courts or other bodies insert themselves into domestic situations the fact is that they are frequently aware of the compromises that have gone into it. Whenever international rules give domestic political and cultural circumstances a certain amount of leeway, they are granting international agents a margin of appreciation in the sense that I mean here.

International criminal laws usually allow domestic criminal courts and domestic political bodies a certain amount of leeway to pursue domestic remedies for tricky situations. The International Criminal Court, for example, works on a principle of "complementary jurisdiction," providing states with the right to assert jurisdiction over their own nationals when necessary. This exists for numerous reasons, some of which are a political compromise with the state powers, but also because there is a recognition that domestic remedies are preferable to international ones. The two *ad hoc* tribunals established by the UN Security Council worked on a different principle, where the Tribunal's prosecutor may assert jurisdiction against the wishes of the sovereign states. Regardless, prosecutors at the *ad hoc* tribunals have allowed several criminals to be charged and tried before domestic courts and the overarching trend is that found in the permanent court, a tilt in favor of domestic jurisdictions.

International law at present may be more adequately accused of having too *much* flexibility, not too little, arguably making it too easy for states to evade their obligations. The descriptive realists, although overstating their case at points, certainly can provide good evidence that international law can fail in its appointed tasks in many circumstance and at times serves little or no actual function in international relations. Its built-in flexibility can easily lead international law to seem an exercise in *ex post facto* justification. The fears of people like Acheson are the fears of what international law might become, certainly not what it is at this moment. If the history and present trajectory of international law is any evidence, this fear is misplaced.

Of course adherents to a philosophy of prudence can always claim that things *could* be done better in a universe without law. Had the law been ignored, things could have been resolved more beneficially for everybody, a counterfactual game where hypothetical choices lead to more appealing results than the ones that actually happened. One of the most appealing points about the concept of prudence as a strategy of argumentation is that it always leaves open the question of whether there was a better way that should have been pursued. Even when the relative costs of international law are low, they *could* perhaps be ignored for the sake of some small benefit in the short term. However, without a God's eye view of all of the potential consequences over months, years, and centuries for our decisions, it is perfectly reasonable to claim that a flexible and reasonably constructed set of international laws may be the best guide to the peace, stability, and prosperity around which the prudential diplomat bases her entire moral perspective. At least, this view is no less reasonable than a rejection of international law in general.

The response to the prudential diplomat in a nutshell is to point out that international law is not a machine, but a human system with rules that are made, interpreted, and enforced by human beings, and it is acutely aware of this human dimension. The system itself has *built-in* mechanisms to address the concerns of the diplomat and is not so rigid in its structure that it cannot cope with the political quandaries that frequently confront the international community. The concerns of the prudential diplomat, where they are sincere, are the same concerns that guide many of the rules underlying the international legal system. Those who craft treaties are perfectly clear about the commitments that these treaties create and are keenly aware that they may prove onerous in the future. Of course there will be a trade-off: at times following the law will not lead to the most desirable result. However, the prudential diplomat must concede that the latitude that actors have in international law to respond creatively to politically complex and morally difficult situations is much broader than it initially seemed. For the most part, the demands of prudence and the demands of rule-based social structures are compatible in the international legal system.

Relativism

The second prevalent form of prescriptive realism bases its arguments upon the simple fact that cultures differ. Each human community on the planet has a unique set of values, a unique conception of justice, and its own distinct legal traditions designed to confront the problems that have arisen in its history. Zambian law differs dramatically from English common law as well as from Chinese law. Each was created in a particular cultural, political, and even spiritual context that has, in turn, shaped its processes and principles. This indigenous heritage provides it with legitimacy in its political, cultural, and geographic domain, and those who remain subject to it immediately provide it with an intuitive legitimacy. All real norms are ultimately of local origin.

This view of the normative foundations of law, of course, puts international law's claim to bind all peoples in a seemingly untenable position. As there is no legal system handed down from the heavens, existing independently of particular states, cultures, communities, and traditions that formulate particular sets of laws, there cannot be a single, universal legal order. Nor can the international community *as such* be considered a community with an indigenous political system for such a conception of community would be so broad that it could not produce a sufficiently deep notion of law or justice. If this conception of culture (and the resulting conception of norms) is the case, then international law is one of two things: either international law is the arbitrary imposition of one group's standards on others, or it is entirely a fabrication – a pointless and meaningless institution lacking any normative foundation. In neither case, however, is it truly binding on those for whom its dictates are alien.

International law is unique among all legal systems since by its very nature its dictates must transcend cultural and political boundaries to constrain and control diverse groups, communities, and political entities. This means that a set of rules that were valid in one political and cultural system with its own values must somehow extend beyond this system and possess a similar validity elsewhere. A decision rendered by a group of people in The Hague who have a shared set of values, training, and legal concepts is supposed to bind people in China or Brazil who either do not share the values of the people in The Hague or find legal traditions of the judges to be entirely foreign to their own history. This, of course, flies in the face of some common intuitions regarding the provincial genesis of norms, a suspicion that all valid norms must originate and find their legitimacy within a particular community. The relativist asserts that it is illegitimate to impose legal concepts and categories, not to mention the substantive legal rules, from one tradition upon others. Legal standards and other normative claims cannot extend beyond particular cultural and political borders and retain their validity.

This theoretical problem about the foundations of normative structures becomes even more acute when one reflects upon the pedigree of modern international law. This legal system was not created through any global consensus or through some actual social contract among different peoples in a global original position. Rather, the vast majority of its rules and principles developed in one specific region (Western Europe) with a set of shared moral and cultural values (Christianity) and common political problems which was ultimately extended to cover the globe. As Verzijl asserts:

> The law of nations, as it stands today is in all its vital aspects mainly the outcome of Western European practice and theory; *theory* to which the legal thinkers and philosophers of many nations have each made their specific individual contributions thus enriching and diversifying it, and *practice* which has grown up largely by a process of trial and error in the application of general principles of law to the ever shifting complex of relationships among the political entities constituting the disintegrated medieval society which gradually became consolidated as the Sovereign States of the modern world. To this development no extra-European nation made any essential contribution and such resemblances as may be found between our institutions and those of the ancient world are fortuitous rather than the outcome of any form of historical continuity however tenuous (Verzijl 1955, 146).

Any serious history of the law of nations clearly shows that the development of its modern form came about through the universalization of Western legal culture and its related standards to other groups on the "outside" (Nussbaum 1954). Usually this historical process was intimately connected with colonialism, enslavement, and the destruction of ancient ways of life that effectively forced these other societies to adopt the values that made possible the European legal system that became modern international law.

Even the notion of the state itself has its origins within the Western political discourse of the seventeenth century (Mazrui 1998, 3–4). While other political systems of independent sovereign entities have existed in history, most of the world has developed in a vast array of tribal, imperial, or nomadic arrangements, which related to each other quite differently than the modern states system. The present international arrangement was an expansion of the post-Westphalian European political system, much of which was imposed upon societies where they did not properly belong. The process of decolonization after the Second World War, laudable though it may have been, created political systems that were alien to the cultures and practices of these colonies, creating a legacy of war that persists to this day. This, coupled with the arbitrary boundaries of many of these colonies (crossing tribal boundaries and frequently cutting peoples off from their traditional sources of income or sustenance) undermines any organic relation between the colonized people and their newly founded political systems. Thus, according to this argument, the political arrangements that underlie the present international legal system are as illegitimate as the rules that occupy this system as such.

What the ultimate implications of these different value systems are for international law is a complex matter to untangle, however. Relativism is not a single, clearly defined view, but instead has a number of different variants depending upon the cultural, philosophical, and political origins of a criticism as well as the target of the relativist critique. To simplify things, we can break down the different relativist views into three major sorts of claims. The first, and most common claim is that the content of international law is presently biased towards the interests of the dominant world powers. I will label this view *soft relativism* – "soft" only in comparison to some of the more extreme versions of relativism. Second is the claim that concepts of law vary from culture to culture to such a degree that a conception of "law" that claimed to transcend these particular understandings is not only doomed to failure, but is by its very nature unjust. This I will call *hard relativism* – and its consequences differ significantly from those that result from soft relativism. Finally, *extreme relativism* is the view that cross-cultural value judgments (whether legal, moral or political) are impossible and that all trans-cultural norms are simply the unjust imposition of the values of one tradition upon another. Each view has its own basis and its own consequences for an international legal regime that we will now briefly explore.

Soft relativism

The soft relativists do not claim that there is something intrinsically wrong with the notion of an international legal system as such but rather that the international legal system that presently exists is biased towards wealthy and powerful states, particularly the United States and in Europe, and disproportionately reflects their indigenous values. This is explained by the dominant role that these regions have played in developing coherent international legal doctrine on all fronts. The power given to the permanent members of the Security Council of the United Nations is just one example of the ways in which international law and its affiliated institutions are skewed in favor of the wealthy and powerful North Atlantic states. In addition, these powerful states kept minor states in a subordinate position and developed legal principles that both support and provide a veneer of legitimacy to their colonial hegemony.

The soft relativists critique can be leveled at virtually any significant domain of public international law. Following much of the traditional debates in international relations theory, we can break down the major debates along two axes: North–South, and East–West. While this familiar distinction is an oversimplification, we can nonetheless use these two variants of soft relativism as foci for discussion. The former, representing primarily the views of the Latin American states during the Cold War argues that certain laws that were created during the colonial era are biased against their interests. The latter asserts that the liberal, Western origins of human rights are hostile to the communal, tradition-bound ways of life that have been a part of their culture of millennia. Both have various adherents but share the common thesis that international law is hostile to their particular interests, values, and concerns.

The so-called North–South schism in modern international law stems from the economic and social conditions confronting the present leaders of the Third World, and their roots in centuries of European colonialism. Mass disparities in wealth and military force between the former colonizers and the recently liberated have left their mark on the international legal regime in ways that are dramatically unfair towards the former colonies. As Rajni Kothari says:

> [C]entral to the struggle for living standards as a basis for the achievement of human rights and fundamental freedoms is the issue of equity. It is an issue that permeates the relationship between the North and the South, stratification within the South and stratification within the North…
>
> Given this overall framework, it is clear that basic changes in the North are critical for overall structural change in the international order (Kothari 1989, 138).

This shared predicament has given these underdeveloped states a certain collection of common grievances against the international legal regime. As Henkin puts it:

> The Third World has been united and determined on matters on which a substantial group of them felt strongly. Many of them being recently independent, they united to have the principle of "self-determination" enshrined in high status in international law… The particular animus against colonialism has made the Third World intolerant also of general law which they think stands in the way of ending the remnants of white colonialism (Namibia, Rhodesia), even the law against the use of force.
>
> The Third World has been united… in regard to law that would further their common qualities, needs, and attitudes. They are "have-nots," inevitably questioning laws which seem to favor the "haves" and seeking new laws that will accelerate change, bring them to industrial development and technological sophistication, afford them status and prestige, give them a greater share of the world's goods and a greater say in the world's affairs (Henkin 1979, 126).

This distinction plays out in numerous fora: state succession, environmental law (Obdrzalek 1992; Sand 1993), and human rights, to name a few. In each case this conflict is not simply an attempt to reach a common agreement, "but a project from which one side looks to gain materially at the expense of another" (Vincent 1986, 76).

For proponents of "Asian Values," the primary human rights doctrines are biased towards the ideals of the Western, colonial powers, undermining their claim of universality and their applicability in Asian and other non-Western cultures. The emphasis on individual rights as opposed to the rights of a family and a community, as well as the lack of any discussions of individual responsibilities towards the larger social unit do not represent a truly universal notion of justice, but only Western, liberal biases. Errol Mendes describes the Asian value system as set out by its major adherents:

> respect for hierarchy and authority including a deference to such authority, centrality and cohesion of the family, social consensus including an avoidance of overt conflict in

> social relations, an emphasis on law and order and a desire not to have individual liberty undermine personal security concerns, an emphasis on stability to promote economic and social development, a reverence for traditional values and culture, an emphasis on education and self-discipline, and acceptance of diversity of spiritual and philosophical authority in theory, but enforced social consensus among such diversity in practice (Mendes 1994).

Thus, given the plurality of cultural values, so-called human rights have no legitimate normative basis and when Eastern leaders run up against people who assert these rights against them, they are justified in denying their demands. As a white paper written by the Chinese government in 1991 asserted:

> No country has the in its effort to realize and protect human rights can take a route that is divorced from its history and its economic, and political realities … It is neither proper nor feasible for any country to judge other countries by the yardstick of its own mode or to impose its own mode on others (Information Office of the State Council of PRC 1991).

Given the fact that human rights are relative to cultures, Western leaders should refrain from criticizing these countries. When these leaders "oppress" their people, they are only governing them in the manner appropriate to their own values and traditions.

Additionally, proponents of Eastern values have asserted that liberal democratic institutions, inextricable from the modern ideology of human rights (as enshrined in a number of human rights treaties), are unnecessary for Eastern economic and social development and ultimately undermined the progress of Asian societies. This right to cultural development is more important than the liberal, democratic freedoms cherished by the West. "China pays close attention to the issue of the right to development … To the people in the developing countries, the most urgent human rights are still the right to subsistence and the right to economic, social and cultural development (1991)." And the former Prime Minster of Singapore:

> For success to continue, correct economic policies alone are not enough. Equally important are the noneconomic factors – a sense of community and nationhood, a disciplined and hardworking people, strong moral values and family ties. The type of society determines how we perform. It is not simply materialism and individual rewards which drive Singapore forward. More important, it is the sense of idealism and service born out of a feeling of social solidarity and national identification. Without these crucial factors, we cannot be a happy or dynamic society (Goh Chok Tong 1994).

Liberal political rights are foreign to Asia and are only Western ideology foisted upon traditional societies that undermines the right of development, which has priority. Thus, while Eastern countries may legitimately accept certain aspects of the international law of human rights, those aspects of human rights that do not cohere with the Eastern way of life ought to be ignored by those countries.

Of course, these criticisms of international law do not cut very deeply, especially as I set out the various forms of relativism earlier. Soft relativists are not critics of international law as such, but merely target particular domains within the law.

China, for example has not rejected human rights in their entirety, but has sought to promote what they see as an Asian consensus on the matter. Further, many of the rejections of the soft relativists have been incorporated into legal doctrine in the present day. The Third World has come a long way since released from submission to colonial rule and as an organized faction they have changed many international legal rules so that they are in the perceived interests of these nations. The doctrine of state succession, for example, has sought to accommodate the concerns of the Third World in providing new states with a certain amount of leeway in determining the legal and economic obligations that remain through a transition from colonial power (Henkin1979, 126).

Further, the previously discussed doctrine of the *margin of appreciation* sensitizes the demands of the human rights regime to the differences of particular cultures. This principle (again, conceived as a general principle of international law)[19] allows us to temper the universalist claims of law to fit unique political and cultural backgrounds. The European Court of Human Rights has argued that local regimes were best suited to understand the values of their own particular communities and the most appropriate way to deal with human rights issues there (Shany 2005, 712):

> [I]t is not possible to find in the domestic law of the various Contracting States a uniform European conception of morals. The view taken by their respective laws of the requirements of morals varies from time to time and from place to place, especially in our era which is characterised by a rapid and far-reaching evolution of opinions on the subject. By reason of their direct and continuous contact with the vital forces of their countries, State authorities are in principle in a better position than the international judge to give an opinion on the exact content of these requirements as well as on the "necessity" of a "restriction" or "penalty" intended to meet them.[20]

This practice, which many argue can be translated beyond Europe into other regional human rights systems, allows for human rights norms to have a certain degree of flexibility when dealing with different contexts. While most international human rights bodies are not judicial in form (usually they work through international committees and commissions), nonetheless the appeal to domestic norms and cultural values provides states with enough leeway to accommodate the concerns of the soft relativists.[21] Further, the give and take that is essential to the vitality and growth of any legal system has absorbed and transformed non-Western perspectives,

---

19 As Benvenisti points out, the ECHR jurisprudence in this field, "Has become an indelible source of inspiration for judges in national courts around the globe" (1999, 843).

20 *Handyside v. United Kingdom*, Judgment of 7 December 1976, A. 24, para. 48. For a particularly useful analysis of the doctrine of the margin of appreciation in relation to cultural difference see van Dijk and van Hoof (1998, 82–95).

21 As Eve Brems argues:

> The non-Western critical human rights discourse does not threaten the universality of human rights because it can be read as a demand for more universality through the increased inclusion of non-Western concerns and values in international human rights, a demand which can be met to a significant extent without upsetting the human rights system (Brems 2001, 513).

interests, and concerns in developing new legal doctrine.[22] Thus, soft relativism is no real threat to the international legal regime but rather serves as a call for more inclusiveness in the development of legal doctrine, a call that all fair-minded jurists ought to heed. More extreme forms of relativism take a good deal more work to adequately confront.

Hard relativism

Hard relativists make a substantially different and significantly deeper claim than their softer counterparts. The hard relativists do not say that this or that particular aspect of the international legal order is somehow biased against states who are marginalized in the international community, but rather they maintain that there is something incoherent about the notion of an international law as such. Notions of "legality," "due process," and even "justice" vary dramatically from culture to culture, as does the understanding of correct legal practice (including correct forms of legal reasoning, conclusions that might be derived from evidence, and so on). As MacIntyre puts it: "[Socially established] sets of rules only come into existence at a particular social circumstance. They are in no way universal features of the human condition" (1984, 65). Given this reality, there is no reason to think that an international law could have normative legitimacy, which is to say that there is no reason why international laws *should* be followed. While regional legal systems may have some possible shared cultural understandings in relation to law, international law writ large cannot. This being the case, there is no international law, regardless of whether these rules play some determinate role in international politics.

Unlike soft relativism, I cannot simply cite particular rules of international law, showing portions that display some form of sensitivity to cultural or economic difference in response, because this would simply beg the question for the hard relativist. The hard relativist is not saying that some of the rules are congenial to some cultural values, but that the very notion of international law is based upon a false legal universalism. The objection of the hard relativists is not with this or that international rule, but with the very concept of international law as such. As D.P. Chattopadhyaya puts the matter in relation to human rights, "(Natural) human rights and justice have to be understood in their proper social context and ... any attempt to decontextualize and thus *universalize* them is bound to prove more or less meaningless" (1980, 169).[23] This brand of law cannot be reformed because at its philosophical core it is irredeemable. If this brand of relativism is correct,

22 For a brief and interesting summary of some attempts to find common ground between Asian values and Western conceptions of human rights, see Choi (2001).

23 It is worth noting that Chattopadyaya's account of human rights is much more nuanced than this quote may make it seem. Nonetheless it is indicative of the hard relativist approach. He does think that, under the proper economic conditions, these rights can be *generalized*, but that "The structural conditions necessary for the realization of human rights are, in most nations of the world, minimal and in some cases almost absent." This, of course means that there are logistical, not philosophical impediments to human rights and international law and not, that these rights are "meaningless" in any strict sense of the word.

then it makes sense to ditch international law and accept the impossibility of legal obligations that stretch beyond the borders of a particular state.

One traditional response to relativism has been to point out that no modern state, regardless of its geographical situation, cultural heritage, or political ideology has rejected international law *en totum*. Even the Marxist states that assumed power in the last century did not reject having international legal relations with the capitalist states that they saw as illegitimate. As Upendra Baxi eloquently reminds us:

> All emancipated nations are groomed in, and have an interest in the corpus of international law as developed in the preceding three centuries. No doubt they have protested against, and in some cases flouted, some of its norms and have also, with some vehemence, sought reconstruction of some aspects of the law so as to take their particular needs and expectations into account. But all their impatience and anxieties have a meaning because they acquiesce in most of the fundamentals of international law. In other words, no "new" nation has, or probably will, seek with anything even faintly approaching serious commitment, a total renovation either of salient norms of international law or a fixed pattern of international behavior and relations in the light of its pre-colonial and indigenous traditions of statecraft. Making use of the letter for political or other purposes is something entirely different from crusading to establish the relevance of such traditions in international order (1972, 6–7).

Certainly, each state has had problems with this or that part of the law (again, soft relativism), but the belief that the new state has no international legal obligations or any standing in international law has been a non-starter. The fact that all states are willing, in principle, to accept the international legal order shows that international law has a certain universal authority, if only as a form of *modus vivendi*.

Of course, the political calculations behind the acceptance of the bulk of international law on the part of new states are obvious. New states are frequently in an insecure position both domestically and internationally, and any external recognition they might achieve would only benefit them, regardless of the cost of this in the long run. Beyond this point, when these new states quarrel with this or that particular rule *within* the international legal system after accepting the system in general, they are taking the point of view of soft relativists, whom I have already addressed in this chapter. It is perhaps best to describe the logic of new states in relation to international law as dialectical in nature: new states gain an international status by accepting the international legal system – which simultaneously structures any further ambitions they have in world politics.

Extreme relativism

This response may initially seem persuasive, but would only force the relativist to retreat to higher ground in order to mount a stronger defense. She can respond to this fact by asserting that the legitimacy or illegitimacy of international rules does not depend upon the acquiescence of a set of arbitrary political leaders. As previously mentioned, the present states system as it exists in the Third World is an arbitrary imposition on traditional ways of life. A relativist writing in the Third World does not need to accept the legitimacy of her domestic political leadership any more than she must accept the legitimacy of the international legal norms that this government has accepted. She need not concern herself with what these leaders do, nor with what she would do were she suddenly given control of the reins of the state. To submit to the pragmatic necessities of a state's survival in international society would be to accept the rules of a game which she has refused to play. Through her eyes her own government is as much a foreign imposition as international law itself.

Already, in detailing the position of the hard relativist, we can see the beginnings of a response to their concerns. Throughout this work I have eschewed the concept of a deep philosophical foundation for international law. For example, I dismissed the notion of "national interest" as foundational in Chapter 3, because, I argued, such approaches unrealistically seek a theoretical skeleton key that will somehow unlock the complexities and contradictions of international political and legal practice. Such a non-foundationalist approach does not require a basis in some deeply felt cultural imperative or some other metaphysical basis for the normative status of international legal rules. This means that the terms and values embodied in international law are culturally agnostic – they require appeal to no particular set of beliefs about the world, or any set of values to exist and properly function. International law is valid because it is recognized to be so by those in the know, and there is no need to turn to some deeper bedrock justification for its validity, be this justification spiritual, cultural, or something more base.

How does this approach respond to the concerns of the extreme relativist? Simply put, the fact that international law functions and continues to function in the international system is enough to show that international law does not violate some sacred norms of a particular culture. Were the "values" embodied in international law so different from those found in certain cultures, there would have to be a complete breakdown of international law. Not only would states be unwilling to recognize the legitimacy of international legal norms, but most likely, they would be oblivious to the meaning of its central concepts. International law, to such alien states, would be akin to a language that nobody in their community speaks – there wouldn't be a rejection as much as there would be a complete failure in comprehension.[24] As this is clearly not the case, we need not concern ourselves with some normative foundation for international law and whether such a foundation can be made to cohere with different cultures or traditions.

The final move presented to the relativist is that she could either reject the possibility of cross cultural understanding in general (and thus to reject any cross-cultural legal system), or resort to a dogmatic assertion that her own way of life is the superior one. The former view, associated with postmodernists such as Lyotard (1988) asserts that there is no cross-cultural "metanarrative" which could legitimize a universal discourse of any kind. Cultural languages of law and justice (not to mention discourses on more banal subjects) are ultimately untranslatable into each

---

24 Of course, it is a mistake to think that there is anything more to cross-cultural understanding than the fact that we are capable of coordinating a shared world. There is no unattainable secret to understanding other cultures or other languages (see Davidson 1984). For a direct application of Davidson's ideas to Lyotard, see Rorty (1991).

other, as they represent fundamentally incompatible ways of thinking, speaking, and living.[25] The latter view, a kind of cultural chauvinism, would require an argument for the superiority of a particular way of life. If it devolves into *mere* chauvinism *sans* argument, then it is ultimately an untenable dogmatism which need not be taken seriously. Further, chauvinism (the dogmatic assertion that one way of life is the superior one) is no longer relativism and thus the debate shifts away from the possibility of a transcultural legal system to the type of transcultural legal system that we wish to envision and this would be a very different kind of debate.

However, just as with its softer counterpart, beneath the flawed objection of the extreme relativists stands an important insight about international law and international relations. International legal rules and the organizations that create, promote, and enforce compliance with these rules must negotiate between different cultures and groups each with very different interpretations of the aims of political life and the facts of history along with deep disagreements about right and wrong. Certainly, there is a common assumption among practicing international lawyers and other legal practitioners that some of the basic notions of law are somehow by their very nature universal in scope. We assume that we have relatively clear and established conceptions of "justice," "treaty," and "compliance," and similar concepts, and that these understandings may be applied across cultures and across diverse political systems. This belief may be true but ought not be assumed or asserted as an *a priori* truth. Patient, empirical research must take place to understand how these concepts fit into different cultural contexts and where international laws might find a home in indigenous legal systems. There may be some basis for values extending across humanity (and perhaps beyond), but even if there are such values, it could not be proven deductively but should also be validated empirically.

This need for cross-cultural understanding is, however, quite different from the claim that all cultures at all times must be equally satisfied with particular international laws and international decisions. There will be conflicts between communal values and communal understandings of the law and the rules and understandings of international law. These gaps may produce confusion and at times immense hostility, however, this does not create a real problem for international law. To use an extreme example, a culture might value genocide and consider an ethnic group under its dominion to be a purveyor of dark powers. Their efforts to eliminate this group would be in contradiction to international law, regardless of how esteemed this value is within the culture. International law is malleable and margins of appreciation exist, but these margins are not so wide as to render the values found in the law meaningless. Minimally, laws delineate certain behavior as acceptable and other behavior as unacceptable, and thus there will be some cut off point beyond which cultures, communities, or state may not stretch their understandings of the law. Just as with the prudential diplomat's concerns about flexibility in law, there are limits to the demand for cultural sensitivity.

---

25 As Lyotard puts it, "A differend [*différend*] would be a case of conflict, between (at least) two parties, that cannot be equitably resolved for lack of a rule of judgment applicable to both arguments. One side's legitimacy does not imply the other's lack of legitimacy … [A] universal rule of judgment between heterogeneous genres is lacking in general" (1988, xi).

Republicanism

The belief that the primary task of legitimate political authority is to improve the welfare of its people and to represent their interests (as opposed to, say, owning them as mere property) is the bedrock of modern political thought, both academically as well as in the popular mind. Governments, whether democratic or autocratic, are responsible, albeit each in their own way, for the well being of all of their citizens. What this political ideal entails may differ among states and across cultures (a fundamentalist theocracy will differ dramatically from a liberal democracy in the policies it promotes) and the range of acceptable means by which they may achieve this goal will likewise differ, it nonetheless stands at the center of modern political life. Even many of the most arbitrary and brutal dictatorships pay lip service to this ideal, and few if any question its status as an axiom of modern political philosophy. Even though it rarely matches up with the real practices of many governments, the republican belief that governments exist in some sense by and for the people remains a central assumption of modern political philosophy and practiced ideologies throughout the world.

By using the term "republicanism" to denote this view, I do not refer simply to the political philosophy of republicanism, much less the views of a particular political party, but rather the overarching idea of which republicanism is the clearest philosophical variant. Republicanism, as a political philosophy, argues that the state is to represent the moral life of a people and that a legitimate government represents the interests of its people. "[A] republic is a human association, but not just any association created for narrowly instrumental purposes. A republic exists for the common good" (Onuf 1998, 6). What makes political authority legitimate in a republican state is that leaders are concerned with what is good for everyone under its dominion and puts this ahead of all else, including personal gain or glory. This common thread runs through republican political thought from Aristotle and Cicero to the contemporary scene and shapes the discourse of modern political thought. Sometimes this ideal is represented as *raison d'état* – that the people of the state ought to take priority in the deliberations of its leadership. A republican government in the modern mind is entrusted with the well being of its people, but, as I just argued, so are all governments that are considered legitimate in the modern world.

When this maxim of domestic political legitimacy is transferred to the international arena, it is taken as the view that the primary aim of the state in its foreign policy is to represent the interests of its own people abroad. This means that a ruler must contend with other leaders who are equally obliged to pursue the ends of their own people in the international sphere. When a republican leader engages in foreign affairs for the sake of her own wealth, power, or glory, she has stepped beyond the bounds of her legitimate political authority. A just leader should avoid any foreign entanglements, however fair or just, that do not ultimately advance the interests of her people. Even those moral obligations that a political leader has personally assumed to foreign powers do not merit abandoning her people's interests. The public trust does not permit the just leader to betray her people for *any* other reason be it personal, moral, or otherwise. She has no obligations superior to the interests of her people.

It should be clear how such a political philosophy turns into a critique of the normative basis for international law. The basis of authority for international law is not the consent of the people that a legitimate domestic government is obliged to represent, but rather comes from other international bodies with which the government relates. This is to say that the leadership of State A has an international legal obligation to do or refrain from doing X to State B, and does not have an obligation to do or refrain from doing X to its own citizens. These other states will invariably have interests that may differ dramatically from the interests of the people whom the leader represents. When X is not in the interests of the people of A, there is no good reason why the leaders of the state in question should consider themselves bound to perform X. Political authority and legal obligation are horizontal relationships between the ruler and the ruled, international legal obligations are horizontal obligations between rulers (or governments). Given that it is the leaders' moral obligation to protect the interests of its own people (and not the interests of others), when necessary, a political leader must break an international obligation for normative reasons alone. When all repercussions have been properly considered, the leader should do whatever she can to promote her peoples' well being regardless of any international legal obligation to the contrary.

No leader should enter into quarrels with other states lightly, nor should she be completely unwilling to make legal commitments with other states and to keep them when possible (sometimes paying a price in the short term). But, the republican would assert that one must be completely clear about where the ruler's true loyalties and obligations lie. She is only obliged to follow international agreements because it is in the best interests of her people as she perceives them, and not because of some sort of obligation to the law as such. External laws are only followed when and to the extent that they represent the interests of her people. When a state violates its international legal obligations in order to serve the interests of its citizens, it not only can, but *ought* to do so. In democratic societies, this point is underscored by the fact that it is the people within her own state who have put her in a position of leadership and it is their interests that she is duty-bound to follow (but as I have previously asserted, this principle is common to all modern political ideologies in some form or other). She has no *real* legal obligations to other states and thus has no legitimate reason to consider putative obligations to these other states in her deliberations.

Of course, this view has a long history in political philosophy. However, a particularly famous and influential version comes from no less than the German philosopher G.W.F. Hegel.[26] For Hegel, the modern state stands in a particular relation to its own development and the people who comprise it. In his eyes, the state

26 I should note that this reading of Hegel will differ in some significant ways from another influential reading in international legal theory: that of Fernando Téson, who reads Hegel as a kind of relativist (1997). While I am disagreeing with Téson's interpretation, I do not believe it is wholly wrong. Rather, I wish to emphasize a different side of Hegel's political philosophy, more to make a broader philosophical point than to engage in any scholarly debate. Further, I disagree with scholars such as Verene and Harris who seek to downplay the normative aspect of Hegel's account of the state in international relations. See Verene (1971, 171), and Harris (1993).

represents the highest level of the development of the spirit of a people (a *Volk*, to be precise). The state crystallizes and fulfills the collective wills of its citizens, unifying them under one political (and spiritual) body:

> The state is the actuality of the substantial will, an actuality which it possesses in the particular self consciousnesses when this has been raised to its universality; as such, it is the *rational* in and for itself. *This substantial unity is an absolute and unmoved end in itself*, and in it, freedom enters into its highest right, just as this ultimate end possesses the highest right in relation to individuals, whose highest duty is to be members of the state (Hegel 1991, 275).

The state is the supreme embodiment of right (*recht*), and thus can be the only source of political or legal authority. It has developed in a more or less organic relationship with the cultural life and unique experiences of its people and represents their self-understanding as a people. Right does not exist without such organic conditions.

It is not simply that the state is the sole source of the enforcement power required of law (as was Austin's view), but rather it is the source of justice and legitimacy in its entirety. Justice and law, for Hegel, are not simply rules enforced by a sovereign but are inextricably bound up with a process of political and cultural development and the general will that is particular to a group. The state is the embodiment of the people, realizing it as an organic whole.

> The nation state [*das Volk als Staat*] is the spirit in its substantial rationality and immediate actuality, and is therefore the absolute power on earth; each state is consequently a sovereign and independent entity in relation to others. The state has a primary and absolute entitlement to be sovereign... (Hegel 1991, 367).

Thus, there cannot be law beyond the state, because there is no true right (or wrong) beyond the bounds of the state, which is the same as saying that there is no justice beyond a group of people.

> The relationship of states to one another is a relationship between independent entities and hence between *particular* wills, and it is on this that the very validity of treaties depends. But the *particular will* of the whole, *as far as its content is concerned*, is its own *welfare* in general. Consequently, this welfare is the supreme law for a state in its relations with others... (Hegel 1991, 369).

Any attempt to impose principles of justice from without can only end in disaster, a false abstraction that sees right as having an existence independent of the political life and experiences of a people:

> The universal determination of international law remains only an *obligation*, and the [normal] condition will be for relations by treaties to alternate with the suspension [*Aufhebung*] of such relations (Hegel 1991, 368).

Therefore international law is invalid, precisely because there is no legality beyond a particular people, a particular *Volk*, who have expressed their freedom through the formation of a particular *Staat*.[27]

To put the finest point possible to the republican criticism expressed by thinkers such as Hegel, we can say that their argument is first and foremost one about the basis of political obligation and how this relates to international law. Political leaders are obliged to follow international law only because it is in the interests of their people to do so, and when it isn't, they are not. Cases where it is in the interests of their people to violate international law may be rare, but they make (so the republican would argue) a rather profound point about the law: that normatively it is irrelevant. In effect there is no merit in following international law for its own sake. This means that the law does not have any independent, normative force that would provide it with an autonomous life in international relations. Just as the descriptive realist asserted that the law is "epiphenomenal" in global politics, that it plays no independent roles in the causal chain of international relations, international law is "normatively epiphenomenal" for the republican in that it plays no role in the chain of political norms. Where the dictates of international law conflict with the obligations of political leadership (advancing the interests of the people of the state in question), these laws should be followed. However, where the law does not advance the interests of the people to whom the ruler owes his allegiance, international law is only words on paper akin to the Ten Commandments to an atheist.

Such appeals to *raison d'état* have a mixed character in international politics. It is undeniable that at times states violate their international legal obligations in deference to domestic politics or perceived domestic interests. Sometimes, of course, this is done because the political leadership of the state in question has genuine concerns about the onerous consequences of fulfilling its legal obligations – concerns that invoke a genuine conflict of obligations. Other times, of course, international obligations are shirked for less noble reasons: a treaty creates obligations which would hurt the domestic economy of a state and which could influence future elections, or nationalistic sentiment plays well on domestic television screens. The well being of a citizenry can often be a less than subtle rationalization for crass political calculation, crude political opportunism, or pandering to a domestic constituency. It is only the cases where the leaders genuinely believe that their national interests are at stake and these interests are not trivial that this critique gains plausibility. Not every perceived conflict is one by which a republican can justifiably ignore its international legal obligations. There are times, however, when genuine national interest and craven political calculation are unfortunately confused.

We have already developed our response to the republican in part when we dealt with the relativist. By saying that international legal norms are nominalist, that is, that there is no deep normative structure to international law, no particular set of values that this legal regime is beholden to, we can grant much of what the republican asserts regarding the basis of legal and political obligation in international law but deny that

27 One attempt to reconcile the Hegellian worldview with the existence of international law is Georg Jellinek. But as Hall (2001, 282) observes, "Jellinek strengthened the jurisprudential character of international law only by weakening the juridical character of law itself."

this entails that the rulers ought to ignore international law. Arguments about the source or basis of obligation for international law are misguided, overlooking the nuances of international political life and the role that law plays within this life. If the republican wishes to assert that domestic interest is why the state ought to follow international law, than so be it. This reason is as good as a host of others and just as irrelevant to understanding the actual functioning of international law in international relations.

Second and more significantly, the divide between domestic law and international law is not as stark as the republican makes it out to be, an insight that has important normative implications for the republican. Not all constitutions or courts recognize a dramatic split between international legal obligations and domestic ones. For "monists" the ratification of treaties by these states *immediately* creates binding legal obligations not only in relations between the state and its peers, but also within the domestic sphere.[28] In a "dualist" regime most international obligations have no direct domestic legal status without additional legislation passed by a legislature.[29] While the distinction between monism and dualism is not a hard and fast one,[30] the interconnections between municipal and international legal systems undermine the claim that a leader has obligations in regards to some legal norms that she doesn't have towards others. The fuzzier the conceptual distinction between municipal and international laws, the fuzzier a distinction between the normative basis of each set of laws becomes.

Clearly for monists, the republican objection does not gain any traction: a leader is just as bound (as a matter of political authority) to uphold her international obligations as she is her domestic ones. "For monists... the legal system of every state is a single system... The national executive is constitutionally required to take care that international law be faithfully executed" (Henkin 1995, 64). From a normative standpoint, this means that a leader's obligation to uphold the laws of the state and a judge's obligations to apply said laws includes any international laws that the state has recognized (either formally or informally). A leader is bound to accept an existing treaty obligation that imposes duties upon her and her people when she assumes power or she assents to be bound by the treaty. In monistic systems, there is no strict divide between internal and external legal obligations and therefore there is

28 As Bederman puts it: "Reduced to its essentials, *monism* is the idea that international law and domestic law are parts of the same legal system, but that international law is higher in prescriptive value than municipal law. *Dualism* is the position that international law and municipal law are separate and distinct legal systems which operate on different levels, and that international law can only be enforced in national law if it is incorporated or transformed" (2001b, 151–152).

29 The "monism-dualism" debate is often conducted on two levels. Many legal theorists argue from a conceptual standpoint that one or the other must capture the "essence" of international law. However, in most modern versions of the debate, monism and dualism are seen through the lens of specific states. "The relation of domestic law to international law, then, is principally an issue for each state rather than for the international political system" (Henkin 1995, 66).

30 For a more sophisticated analysis of the connections between domestic and international legal systems see; International Law Association (1996, 570, 572–7, 587–90).

no separation between the authority of each sort of law. The leader may not pick and choose which of her domestic laws she must obey. They all bind her. This includes those laws that originate in treaty obligations with other states or from general principles of international law.

Even from a dualist perspective, from states that accept a sharp distinction between domestic and international law, the border between international legal obligations and domestic ones is a porous one. All states have some means to incorporate international legal norms into their own domestic legal systems. In many states, legislatures play a role in ratifying international agreements, making it a quasi-legislative act (Malanczuk 1997, 66). Other states must incorporate international obligations into their own domestic legal systems by separate legislative acts. Finally, customary norms are often taken to be law of the land in most legal systems, a part of domestic and international law (in the US, for example, the Supreme Court ruled in *Sosa v. Alvarez Machain* (542 US 692 (2004)) that, to a certain extent, customary international law may be used by federal courts in interpreting the Alien Tort Statute (2004, §789; Lynch 2006, 768)).

However brief this short survey of the interconnections between international law and domestic law may be,[31] there are some clear consequences: lacking a strict border between domestic law and international law, whether the legal culture of the state is a monistic or dualistic one, the borders of normative legitimacy of domestic and international law are similarly vague. The responsibility of leaders is to promote the best interests of their own citizens within the constitutional framework in which they function, and requires that they pay heed to the rule of law as understood by their legal culture. This means that if a domestic legal culture accepts the legitimacy of international legal rules, then the republican is obliged to follow these laws regardless of how they may feel about said laws or if they are in the national interest as she perceives them. A republican political leader may not be pleased with certain international laws (presumably, because they do not sufficiently promote the well-being of her people), but these are grounds for changing the present law and for greater care in creating new laws. Insofar as the framework of her constitution and its rule of law bind her, she is bound by her international legal obligations. The conceptual relations between international law and domestic law in a given state entails that the former be given the same normative value as the latter (at least insofar as the constitution allows).

My defense of international law against the republican model assumes that political legitimacy is fundamentally legal and constitutional in character. This means that legitimate political leaders operate within the framework of their laws and their respective constitutions. It is not incoherent (nor unheard of) that leaders violate domestic and international laws because such leaders believe that the laws do not serve the public interest. Were such actions normatively justified, were a leader justified in violating a law whatever its origins, when such laws are not in the best interest of the people under her charge, then it follows that international law has no legitimacy. However, it would also be true that domestic laws would also lack

31 For a much more in-depth analysis of the relationship between United States' law and international law see Paust (1996).

justification and any substantive and procedural legal constraints on political power would disappear from the landscape of normative political philosophy. While I admit that I would not have a good response to such a radical conception of political legitimacy (as I have simply claimed that in a good number of cases international law has about the same legitimacy as municipal law), I suspect that such radicalism would find few adherents, especially among the legal community.

Conclusion

If my argument here is correct, none of the prescriptive realists are justified in their skepticism and there is no valid reason why political leaders, diplomats, or lawyers of any stripe *ought* to ignore or reject international law. Either these critics have misunderstood the nature and mechanisms of the international legal system, attacking a straw man, or they have misunderstood the values underlying international law (there are none). One may remain committed to the ideals of prudence, difference, and representative government and accept that international law is *real* in the normative sense that it should be followed. Of course, there is no one reason why international law should be followed; there is no single decisive normative argument *for* international law, just as there is no single decisive normative argument *against* international law. The complexities and subtleties of international politics (including its moral and political complexities) are mirrored in international law and just as international relations as such are normatively unjustified, so is international law.

The nominalist approach toward international law that I have advocated throughout this work avoids a great number of the concerns of the prescriptive realists by refusing to enter into a debate at the level of values. Both the relativist and the republican mistakenly assume that there must be some deep normative structure to international law, some "source" to which we can refer to somehow show why the law ought to be followed. As I argued in Chapter 6, this simply is not the case: we may be deemed "law abiding," and our behavior may be determined to be "following the law" for a vast number of reasons. Legal behavior does not require some deep moral proof to justify its existence any more than any other social practice requires such a justification. Its existence is real simply because it plays a real role in international affairs, a fact which can (and must) be proven empirically, in the course of actual research, any further argument is superfluous.

Of course, like the descriptive realists, the prescriptive realists have a point and their skepticism is not completely without merit. They expose a number of weaknesses of the modern international legal system, weaknesses that anyone concerned with its future (as well as the common good of mankind) must address. The fact is that much of this legal regime is tilted towards Western values (as the relativists charge). It can be an undue threat to popular sovereignty (as the republicans charge), and it can, if misconstrued, force a constraining rigidity on international politics that could ultimately prove destructive. The fits and starts of international law throughout the previous century, and the many stumbling blocks that it presently faces are to a large degree a result of international law's inability to address the concerns of the prescriptive realists. The critical perspectives they offer are valuable ones, despite their common mischaracterization of the international law.

By avoiding the postmodern metaphysics of the New Stream, the rationalist metaphysics of the descriptive realists, and the normative skepticism of the prescriptive realists, we have stepped around their objections whenever possible. When this is not possible, when the skeptics have a genuine complaint against the system, we have absorbed their concerns into a broader theory of law. By understanding the depth of these objections, and presenting them in their clearest and most defensible forms, we can transform their criticisms into warnings and strategies for the further development of international law. International law is a work in progress, and will always be in development, changing its dictates and broad principles as new dilemmas and crises arise. This is the work of the coherence approach outlined in Chapter 2: we modify our theory of law both in terms of the empirical data *and* the broader theories to which we are committed. The skeptics, when properly understood, are not rejecting international law, but offering constructive criticisms and a few well-placed warnings. These criticisms point out places where legal theorists and concerned international lawyers ought to develop and refine the law to better serve the needs and values of humankind.

Conclusion

As mentioned in the Introduction, one of the central themes of this work is that international law does not need to look beyond itself and rely on normative or political theories to justify itself or prove its relevance to the contemporary world. While it is undoubtedly true that international legal theory and theories of international politics are useful and important fields and contribute much to our thinking about international law, they ultimately conceal as much as they reveal about the nature and function of international law. Their questions can be reductive or misleading and may depend on a number of discipline-specific assumptions which are unfamiliar or unnecessary for those engaged in legal practice – where the "action" is. Their answers likewise are limited and often ignore some of the most compelling points where international law connects with the modern world. They can illuminate useful features of the international legal system, suggesting corrections or places where the law could be improved, however, they need not play a foundational role in international law.

The search for "foundations" for international law denotes a sort of anxiety about the field, a concern that if such foundations are not provided, international law would somehow collapse upon itself. However, in reality, theories, even compelling foundationalist theories of social practices like law do not play such an essential role in human life. They can help make sense out of law, help make our legal practices more coherent, but they do not legitimize the law or somehow make it relevant to those who would otherwise reject it. A theory, no matter how logically sound or intuitively compelling, will not convince a committed skeptic of the value of international law. The prevailing prejudices against international law are widespread and mainstream enough that it is doubtful that foundationalist theories would do much to sway the devout skeptic towards international law.

Rather, international law is legitimate because the professional communities that use it acknowledge that it is legitimate in both their actions and their words. It is increasingly taught in law schools, more and more as a required course, and increasingly operates as a part of the professional attorney's toolkit. Foreign ministries and state departments rely on the advice of lawyers and militaries, and companies that deal with global trade similarly turn to attorneys when there are legal matters that need to be addressed. They do this because they believe the law is an important part of the world that they must navigate. Regardless of whether or not this legal regime has foundations that philosophers, legal scholars, or political theorists would recognize, international law proves its relevance in practice, not theory. International law matters because lawyers and other important actors use it. It is this reality that I have sought to capture in this work.

Furthermore international law is relevant because it impacts upon the outcomes of actual events in innumerable small and large ways. One hands one's passport to customs officials because of international law. Combatants captured on the battlefield are (sometimes) not immediately shot in the head because of law. Traffic tickets are not paid by diplomatic officials because of the international laws governing diplomatic and consular immunities. Emphasis on enforcement or obedience to law overlooks the innumerable mundane ways that law, even international law structures our daily existence. Similarly, emphasis on deliberation in the UN Security Council or in the offices of heads of state in understanding international law ignores the fact that law is significant to microanalyses as well as macroanalyses.

Of course, skepticism towards international law remains endemic both inside and outside the academy (particularly in the United States) and it will most likely not dissipate any time soon. However, emphasis on the law's "failures" is in many ways a misleading proposition. The continued prominence of "failures" of law (wars waged without Security Council resolutions, prisoners tortured in violation of the Geneva Conventions, to name only a couple) lead one to overlook cases, both innumerable and important, where the law *does* matter, places where law plays an important, even crucial role in the outcome of many complex events in international affairs. These cases do not necessarily grab the attention of newspapers and are often unglamorous, but they are extremely important and we overlook them at our peril.

Bibliography

Abbott, K. (1989), 'Modern International Relations Theory: A Prospectus for International Lawyers,' *Yale Journal of International Law* 14:2, 335–411.

Abiew, F. (1999), *The Evolution of the Doctrine and Practice of Humanitarian Intervention* (The Hague: Kluwer Law International).

Acheson, D. (1967), 'Cuban Quarantine: Implications for the Future,' *American Society of International Law: Proceedings of the 57th Annual Meeting*, 13–15.

—— (1963), 'Remarks,' in Beck et al. (1996).

Adler, E. and Haas, P. (1992), 'Conclusion: Epistemic Communities, World Order, and the Creation of a Reflective Research Program,' *International Organization* 46:1, 367–90.

Allan, T.R.S. (1998), 'Rule of Law (Rechtstaat),' in Craig (1998).

Altman, A. (1995), 'Legal Realism, Critical Legal Studies, and Dworkin,' in Feinberg and Gross (1995).

Amerasinghe, C.F. (2005), *Principles of the Institutional Law of International Organizations*, 2nd edn (New York: Cambridge University Press).

Anand, R.P. (ed.) (1972), *Asian States and the Development of International Law* (Delhi: Vikes Publications).

An-Na'im, A. (1990), *Toward an Islamic Reformation: Civil Liberties, Human Rights, and International Law* (Syracuse, NY: Syracuse University Press).

Aquinas, T. (1996), *Treatise on Law* (Washington, DC: Regnery Publishing, Inc.).

Arangio-Ruiz, G. (1997), 'The "Federal Analogy" and UN Charter Interpretation: A Crucial Issue,' *European Journal of International Law* 8:1, 1–28.

Arend, A. and Beck, R. (1993), *International Law and the Use of Force: Beyond the UN Charter Paradigm* (New York: Routledge).

Arend, A. (1999), *Legal Rules and International Society* (Oxford: Oxford University Press).

Asrat, B. (1991), *Prohibition of the Use of Force Under the UN Charter: A Study of Art. 2(4)* (Uppsala: Iustus Förlog).

Audi, R. (1995), *The Cambridge Dictionary of Philosophy* (Cambridge: Cambridge University Press).

Aufricht, H. (1943), 'Personality in International Law,' *The American Political Science Review* 37:2, 217–43.

Austin, J.L. (1962), *How to Do Things with Words* (Cambridge, MA: Harvard University Press).

Austin, J. (1995), *The Province of Jurisprudence Determined* (Cambridge: Cambridge University Press).

Bailey, S. (1994), *The UN Security Council and Human Rights* (New York: St. Martin's Press).

Bass, G. (2000), *Stay the Hand of Vengeance: The Politics of War Crimes Tribunals* (Princeton, NJ: Princeton University Press).

Baxi, U. (1972), 'Some Remarks on Eurocentrism and the Law of Nations,' in Ram Prakash Anand (1972).

Beck, R., et al. (eds) (1996), *International Rules: Approaches from International Law and International Relations* (Oxford: Oxford University Press).

Beckett, A. (2003), *Pinochet in Piccadilly* (London: Faber and Faber).

Bederman, D. (1996), 'The Souls of International Organizations: Legal Personality and the Lighthouse at Cape Spartel,' *Virginia Journal of International Law* 36, 275.

—— (2001a), *International Law in Antiquity* (Cambridge: Cambridge University Press).

—— (2001b), *International Law Frameworks* (New York: Foundation Press).

—— (2002), *The Spirit of International Law* (Athens, GA: The University of Georgia Press).

Bedi, S.D. (2001), *Extradition: A Treatise on the Laws Relevant to the Fugitive Offenders Within and with the Commonwealth Countries* (Buffalo, NY: Wm. S. Hein Publishing).

Beitz, C. (1999), *Political Theory and International Relations* (Princeton, NJ: Princeton University Press).

Bentham, J. (1970), *An Introduction to the Principles of Morals and Legislation* (Darien, CT: Hafner Publishing Company).

Benvenisti, E. (1999), 'Margin of Appreciation, Consensus, and Universal Standards,' *New York University Journal of International Law and Policy* 31, 843–55.

Benevisti, E. and Hirsch, M. (eds) (2004), *The Impact of International Law on International Cooperation* (New York: Cambridge University Press).

Bhiku, P. (ed.) (1993), *Jeremy Bentham: Critical Assessments* (New York: Routledge).

Bianchi, A. (1999), 'Immunity versus Human Rights: The Pinochet Case,' *European Journal of International Law*, 10:2, 237–77.

Blackstone, W. (2003), *Commentaries on the Laws of England* (Clark, NJ: Lawbook Exchange).

Blakesley C. (2000), 'Autumn of the Patriarch: The Pinochet Extradition Debacle and beyond: Human Rights Clauses Compared to Traditional Derivative Protections Such as Double Criminality,' *The Journal of Criminal Law and Criminology* 91:1, 1–98.

Bodin, J. (1992), *On Sovereignty* (Cambridge: Cambridge University Press).

Bowett, D.W. (1963), *The Law of International Institutions* (New York: Praeger Publishers).

Bowie, R. (1974), *Suez 1956* (Oxford: Oxford University Press).

Boyd, G. (1986), 'Reagan says the Choice is Between Backing Him or Communists,' *New York Times*, 7 March.

Boyle, J. (1990), 'Ideals and Things: International Legal Scholarship and the Prison-house of Language,' in Koskenniemi (1990).

Bradley, C. and Goldsmith, J. (1999), 'Pinochet and International Human Rights Litigation,' *Michigan Law Review* 97:7, 2129–84.

Brems, E. (2001), *Human Rights: Universality and Diversity* (The Hague: Martinus Nijhoff Publishers).
Brierly, J.L. (1963), *The Law of Nations: An Introduction to the International Law of Peace*, 6th edn (New York: Oxford University Press).
Briggs, H. (1959), 'The United States and the International Court of Justice: A Reexamination,' *The American Journal of International Law* 53:2, 301–18.
Brody, R. and Ratner, M. (2000), *The Pinochet Papers* (The Hague: Kluwer Law International).
Bronson, R. (1999), 'Think It Over: Indicting Today's Dictators Is Not a Good Idea,' *Los Angeles Times*, 3 December.
Brownlie, I. (1963), *International Law and the Use of Force by States* (Oxford: Oxford University Press).
— (1973), 'Thoughts on Kind-Hearted Gunmen,' in Lillich (1973).
— (2003), *Principles of Public International Law*, 6th edn (New York: Oxford University Press).
Bull, H. (1977), *The Anarchical Society: A Study of Order in World Politics* (New York: Columbia University Press).
Burbach, R. (2003), *The Pinochet Affair: State Terrorism and Global Justice* (New York: Zed Books).
Byers, M. (2000), 'The Law and Politics of the Pinochet Case,' *Duke Journal of Comparative and International Law* 10:2, 415–442.
Campbell, K. and Smith, N. (1998), 'Epiphenomenalism,' in Craig (1998).
Carty, A. (1991), 'Critical International Law: Recent Trends in the Theory of International Law,' *European Journal of International Law* 2:1, 66–96.
— (1993), 'Intervention and the Limits of International Law,' in Forbes and Hoffman (1993).
Cassese, A. (1986), *International Law in a Divided World* (Oxford: Oxford University Press).
— (2001), *International Law* (Oxford: Oxford University Press).
Chattopadhyaya, D.P. (1980), 'Human Rights, Justice, and Social Context,' in Rosenbaum (1980).
Checkel, J. (1998), 'The Constructivist Turn in International Relations Theory,' *World Politics* 50:2, 324–48.
Chen, L. (1989), *An Introduction to Contemporary International Law: A Policy-Oriented Perspective* (New Haven, CT: Yale University Press).
Chesterman, S. (2001), *Just War or Just Peace? Humanitarian Intervention and International Law* (New York: Oxford University Press).
Chimni, B. (1986), 'The International Court and the Maintenance of Peace and Security: The Nicaragua Decision and the United States Response,' *The International and Comparative Law Quarterly* 35:4, 960–70.
Chomsky, N. (1989), *Necessary Illusions: Thought Control in Democratic Societies* (Toronto: Anansi Press).
Choi, C. (2001), 'Human Rights and Human Responsibilities: An East Asian Perspective,' in Leiser and Campbell (2001).
Claude R., and Weston, B. (eds) (1989), *Human Rights and the World Community* (Philadelphia, PA: University of Pennsylvania Press).

Collier, J. and Lowe, V. (2000), *The Settlement of Disputes in International Law: Institutions and Procedures* (New York: Oxford University Press).

Craig, Edward (ed.) (1998), *Routledge Encyclopedia of Philosophy*, Vol. 3 (New York: Routledge).

—— (1998b) *Routledge Encyclopedia of Philosophy* Vol. 8 (New York: Routledge).

Cullet, P. (1999), 'International Environmental Law in Domestic Courts: Switzerland,' *IELC Working Paper 1999–1.* [website] < http://www.ielrc.org/content/w9901.pdf >.

Cutler, A. (2001), 'Critical Reflections on the Westphalian Assumptions of International Law and Organization: A Crisis of Legitimacy,' *Review of International Studies* 27, 133–150.

D'Amato, A. (1985), '*Nicaragua* and International Law: The "Academic" and the "Real",' *The American Journal of International Law* 79:3, 657–64.

—— (1987), 'Trashing Customary International Law,' *The American Journal of International Law* 81:1, 101–105.

Daniels, N. (1980), 'On Some Methods in Ethics and Linguistics,' *Philosophical Studies* 37:1, 21–36.

Darwall, S. et al. (eds) (1996), *Moral Discourse and Practice* (Oxford: Oxford University Press).

Darwall, S. (1996), 'Reasons, Motives, and the Demands of Morality: An Introduction,' in S. Darwall et al. (1996).

Davidson, D. (1984), 'On the Very Idea of a Conceptual Scheme,' in *Inquiries into Truth & Interpretation* (Oxford: Oxford University Press).

Davis, K. (1980), *Discretionary Justice* (Westport, CT: Greenwood Press).

Davis, M. (2003), 'The Politics of the Pinochet Case in the United Kingdom,' in M. Davis (2003).

Davis, M. ed. (2003), *The Pinochet Case Origins, Progress, and Implications* (London: Institute of Latin American Studies), 125–44.

De Wet, E. (2004), 'The Prohibition of Torture as an International Norm of *jus cogens* and Its Implications for National and Customary Law,' *European Journal of International Law* 15:1, 97–121.

D'Entrèves, A.P. (1970), *Natural Law*, 2nd edn (London: Hutchison & Co.).

Dupuy, R-J. (ed.) (1993), *Le Développement du Rôle du Counseil De Sécurite* (Dordrecht: Martinus Nijhoff Publishers).

Durkheim, E. (1997), *The Division of Labor in Society* (trans. W.D. Halls), (New York: The Free Press).

Dworkin, R. (2001), *The Sovereign Virtue* (Cambridge, MA: Harvard University Press).

Fain, H. (1987), *Normative Politics and the Community of Nations* (Philadelphia, PA: Temple University Press).

Feinberg, J. and Gross H. (eds) (1995), *Philosophy of Law* (Belmont, CA: Wadsworth Publishing Company).

Ferdinandusse, W. (2004), 'The Interaction of National and International Approaches in the Repression of International Crimes,' *European Journal of International Law* 15:5, 1041–53.

Fichtelberg, A. (2007), *Crime Without Borders: An Introduction to International Criminal Justice* (New York: Prentice Hall).
Finnis, J. (1980), *Natural Law and Natural Rights* (Oxford: Clarendon Press).
Fitzmaurice, G. (1956), 'Draft Convention on the Law of Treaties,' *United Nations Yearbook of International Law*, II, 118.
Forbes, I. and Hoffman, M. (eds) (1993), *Political Theory, International Relations, and the Ethics of Intervention* (New York: St. Martin's Press).
Forsythe, D. (2001), *Human Rights in International Relations* (Cambridge: Cambridge University Press).
Fotion, N. (1968), *Moral Situations* (Kent, OH: Kent State University Press).
Fox, H. et al. (1999), 'The First Pinochet Case: Immunity of a Former Head of State,' *The International and Comparative Law Quarterly* 48:1, 207–16.
Franck, T. and Rodley, N. (1973), 'After Bangladesh: The Law of Humanitarian Intervention by Military Force,' *The American Journal of International Law* 67:2, 275–305.
Franck, T. (1985), 'Icy Day at the ICJ,' *The American Journal of International Law* 79:2, 379–84.
—— (1995), *Fairness in International Law and Institutions* (Oxford: Oxford University Press).
Friedman, R. (1998), 'Some Thoughts on Natural Law and International Order,' in Nardin and Mapel (1998).
Friedman, T. (1991), 'US Suspends Assistance to Haiti and Refuses to Recognize Junta,' *New York Times*, 2 October.
Fuller, L. (1995), 'Positivism and Fidelity to Law – A Reply to Professor Hart,' in Feinberg and Gross (1995).
Gabbay, D. and Guenthner, F. (eds) (1984), *Handbook of Philosophical Logic, Vol. II* (New York: Springer).
Gardner, R. (1986), 'A Reagan Fiasco in the World Court,' *New York Times*, 2 July.
Gilbert, G. (1991), *Aspects of Extradition Law* (New York: Springer).
Gill, T. (2003), *Rosenne's The World Court: What It Is And How We Use It*, 6th edn, (Herndon: Brill Academic Publishers).
Goh Chok Tong. (December 1994), 'Social Values, Singapore Style.' *Current History* 417–22, and reprinted in E. Mendes (1994).
Goodman, N. (1965), *Fact, Fiction, and Forecast* (Cambridge, MA: Harvard University Press).
Grant, E. (2000), 'Pinochet 2: The Questions of Jurisdiction and Bias,' in Woodhouse (2000).
Green, D. and Shapiro, I. (1996), *Pathologies of Rational Choice Theory* (New Haven, CT: Yale University Press).
Greenhouse, L. (1986), 'House Votes, 221–209, to Aid Rebel Forces in Nicaragua; Major Victory for Reagan,' *New York Times*, 26 June.
Greig, D.W. (1991), 'Nicaragua and the United States: Confrontation Over the Jurisdiction of the International Court,' *British Yearbook of International Law* 62, 119–281.
Grotius, H. (Louise Ropes Loomis, trans.) (1949), *The Law of War and Peace* (De jure belli ac pacis) (New York: Pub. for the Classics Club by W.J. Black).

Grotius, H. (Willey F. trans.) (1962), *The Law of War and Peace: De Jure Belli Ac Pacis Libri Tres* Kelsey Published (Indianapolis, IN: Bobbs-Merrill).
Hall, S. (2001), 'The Persistent Spectre: Natural Law, International Order and the Limits of Legal Positivism,' *European Journal of International Law* 12:2, 269–307.
Hall, W.E. (1904), *A Treatise on International Law* (New York: Oxford University Press).
Harrah, D. (1984), 'The Logic of Questions' in Gabbay and Guenthner (2004), 715–64.
Harris, D.J. (1998), *Cases and Materials in International Law*, 5th edn (London: Sweet & Maxwell).
Harris, E. (1993), 'Hegel's Theory of Sovereignty, International Relations, and War,' in Stepelevich (1993).
Hart, H.L.A. (1958), 'Positivism and the Separation of Law and Morals,' *Harvard Law Review*, 71, 593–629.
— (1994), *The Concept of Law* (Oxford: Oxford University Press).
Hayner, P. (1994), 'Fifteen Truth Commissions-1974–1994: A Comparative Study,' *Human Rights Quarterly* 16:4, 597–655.
Hegel, G.W.F. (1991), *Elements of the Philosophy of Right*, translated by H.B. Nisbet (Cambridge: Cambridge University Press).
Helfer, L. (2004), 'Constitutional Analogies in the International Legal System,' *Loyola of Los Angeles Law Review* 37:2, 193–237.
Hempel, C. (1994), 'The Logic of Functional Analysis,' in Martin and McIntyre (1994).
Hempel, C. and Oppenheim, P. (1948), 'Studies in the Logic of Explanation,' *Philosophy of Science* 15:2, 135–75.
Henkin, L. (1979), *How Nations Behave*, 2nd edn (New York: Columbia University Press).
— (1995), *International Law: Politics and Values* (Dordrecht: Springer).
— (1999), 'That "S" Word: Sovereignty, and Globalization, and Human Rights, et cetera,' *Fordham Law Review* 68:1, 1–14.
Henkin, L., et al. (eds) (1993), *International Law: Cases and Materials*, 3rd edn (St. Paul. MN: West Group).
Hertogh, M. (2004), 'A "European" Conception of Legal Consciousness: Rediscovering Eugen Ehrlich,' *Journal of Law and Society* 31:4, 457–81.
Higgins, R. (1994), *Problems and Process: International Law and How We Use It* (Oxford: Oxford University Press).
Hitchins, C. (2001), *The Trial of Henry Kissinger* (New York: Verso Publishers).
Hobbes, T. (1991), *Leviathan* (Cambridge: Cambridge University Press).
Hoffmann, S. (1960), *Contemporary Theory of International Relations* (Englewood Cliffs, NJ: Prentice-Hall).
Hoge, W. (2000), 'After 16 Months of House Arrest, Pinochet Quits England,' *New York Times*, 3 March.
Hopkins, J. (1982), 'Introduction,' in Hopkins and Wollheim (1982).
Hopkins, J. and Wollheim, R. (eds) (1982), *Philosophical Essays on Freud* (New York: Cambridge University Press).

Hudson, W.D. (ed.) (1975), *The Is-Ought Question* (New York: St. Martin's Press).
Human Rights Watch (2002), 'The Pinochet Precedent: The End of Impunity?' *Human Rights Watch* [website] (updated 1 July 2002) <http://www.hrw.org/campaigns/chile98/index.htm>.
Hume, D. (1978), *A Treatise on Human Nature*, 2nd edn (New York: Oxford University Press).
Ignatieff, M. (2001), *Human Rights as Politics and Idolatry* (Princeton, NJ: Princeton University Press).
Information Office of the State Council Of the People's Republic of China, 'Human Rights in China' [website], (published online Nov. 1991) <http://english.people.com.cn/whitepaper/4(10).html>.
International Law Association (1996), 'Report of the Committee on International Law in National Courts,' Sixty-Seventh Conference, Helsinki. Reprinted in Paust et al. (2000).
Jacobs, Francis G. and White, Robin C.A. (1996), *The European Convention on Human Rights*, 2nd edn (NewYork: Oxford Press).
Janis, M. (1984), 'Individuals as Subjects of International Law,' *Cornell International Law Journal* 17:1, 61–78.
—— (1987), 'Somber Reflections on the Compulsory Jurisdiction of the International Court,' *The American Journal of International Law* 81:1, 144–46.
—— (1993a), 'Jeremy Bentham and the Fashioning of International Law,' in Bhiku, Parekh (ed.), *Jeremy Bentham: Critical Assessments* (New York: Routledge).
—— (1993b), *An Introduction to Contemporary International Law* (Aspen, CO: Aspen Law & Business).
—— (1997), *International Law: Cases and Materials* (St. Paul, MN: West Group).
Janis, M., and Noyes, J. (eds) (1997), *International Law: Cases and Commentary* (St. Paul, MN: West Group).
Jenks, W. (1962), *The Proper Law of International Organizations* (Dobbs Ferry, NY: Oceana Publications).
Johnston, D. (1988), 'Functionalism in the Theory of International Law,' *The Canadian Yearbook of International Law* 26, 3–60.
Kagan, R. (1996), *A Twilight Struggle: American Power and Nicaragua, 1977–1990* (New York: Free Press).
Kant, I. (1996), *The Metaphysics of Morals*, trans. Mary Gregor (Cambridge: Cambridge University Press).
—— (1993), *Grounding for the Metaphysics of Morals*, 3rd edn. trans. James W. Ellington (Indianapolis. IN: Hackett Publishers).
—— (1983) *Perpetual Peace and Other Essays*, trans. Ted Humphrey (Indianapolis, IN: Hackett Publishers).
—— (1983b), 'To Perpetual Peace: A Philosophical Sketch,' in Kant (1983).
Kaufmann, W. (ed.) (1989), *Existentialism from Dostoevsky to Sartre* (New York: Meridian Press).
Kelsen, H. (1952), *Principles of International Law* (New York: Reinhardt and Co.)
—— (1945) *General Theory of Law and the State* (Cambridge, MA: Harvard University Press).

Kennan, G. (1985), *American Diplomacy*, expanded edn (Chicago, IL: University of Chicago Press).
— (1996), 'Diplomacy in the Modern World,' in R. Beck (1996).
Kennedy, D. (1987), *International Legal Structures* (Baden-Baden: Nomos).
— (1988), 'A New Stream of International Law Scholarship,' *Wisconsin International Law Journal* 7, 1–49.
— (1996), 'A New Stream of International Legal Scholarship,' in Beck, et al. (1996).
— (1997), *A Critique of Adjudication (fin de siècle)* (Cambridge, MA: Harvard University Press).
Kessler, G. (ed.) (2000), *Voices of Wisdom*, 4th edn (Belmont, CA: Wadsworth Publishing Company).
Khalifa, K. (2004), 'Erotetic Contextualism, Data-Generating Procedures, and Sociological Explanations of Social Mobility,' *Philosophy of the Social Sciences* 34:1, 38–54.
Kierkegaard, S. (1989), 'Authority,' in W. Kaufmann (1989).
King, G. et al. (1994), *Designing Social Inquiry* (Princeton, NJ: Princeton University Press).
King Jr., M.L. (2000), 'Letter from Birmingham Jail,' in Kessler (2000).
Kissinger, H. (1957), *A World Restored* (Boston, MA: Houghton Mifflin).
— (2001), *Does America Need a Foreign Policy?* (New York: Simon & Schuster).
Klintworth, G. (1989), *Vietnam's Intervention in Cambodia in International Law* (Canberra: Australian Government Publishing Service).
Kooijmans, P. (1993), 'The Enlargement of the Concept "Threat to the Peace",' in Dupuy (1993).
Koremenos, B. (2001), 'Loosening the Ties That Bind: A Learning Model of Agreement Flexibility,' *International Organization* 55:2, 289–325.
Koskenniemi, M., (1990), 'Introduction,' in M. Koskenniemi (ed.), *International Law* (New York: New York University Press).
— (2001), 'Introduction,' in Koskenniemi, M. (ed.), *Sources of International Law* (The Library of Essays in International Law), (Aldershot: Ashgate).
— (2005), *From Apology to Utopia*, 2nd edn (New York: Cambridge University Press).
Kothari, R. (1989), 'Human Rights as a North-South Issue,' in Claude and Weston (1989).
Krasner, S. (1999), *Sovereignty: Organized Hypocrisy* (Princeton, NJ: Princeton University Press).
Krauss, C. (2000), 'Ruling on Immunity Puts Chile Closer to Trial of Pinochet,' *New York Times*, 25 May.
Kripke, S. (1980), *Naming and Necessity* (Cambridge, MA: Harvard University Press).
Kuhn, T.S. (1962), *The Structure of Scientific Revolutions* (Chicago, IL: University of Chicago Press).
Lamont, N. (1999), 'Double Standards, Treachery and Easy Hypocrisy. How this Country has Betrayed Pinochet,' *Daily Mail*, 18 January (London).

Lauterpacht, H. (1970), *International Law: Being the Collected Papers of Hersch Lauterpacht* (Cambridge: Cambridge University Press).

Leigh, M. (1985), 'Military and Paramilitary Activities in and Against Nicaragua (Nicaragua v. United States of America),' *The American Journal of International Law* 79:2, 442–6.

Leiser, B, and Campbell, T. (eds) (2001), *Human Rights in Philosophy and Practice* (Burlington, VT: Dartmouth Publishing Company).

Lejbowicz, A. (1999), *Philosophie du droit international* (Paris: Presse Universitaires de France).

Lennon, K. (1994), 'Reasons,' in *Blackwell Companion to the Philosophy of Mind*, ed. Samuel Gutenplan (Boston, MA: Blackwell), 531–4.

Lewis, I. and Mayall, J. (1996), 'Somalia,' in Mayall (1996).

Lewis, P. (1986), 'World Court Supports Nicaragua after U.S. Rejected Judges' Role,' *New York Times*, 28 June.

Lillich R. (ed.) (1973), *Humanitarian Intervention in the United Nations* (Charlottesville, VA: University Press of Virginia).

Lissitzyn, O. (1966), 'Foreword,' in Sinha (1966).

Locke, J. (1959), *An Essay Concerning Human Understanding* (New York: Dover Publications).

Lowe, V. (1992), 'The Role of Equity in International Law,' *Australian Yearbook of International Law* 12, 54–81.

Lynch, H. (2006), 'Liability for Torts in Violation of International Law: No Hook under *Sosa* for Secondary Complicit Actors,' *New York Law School Law Review* 50:3.

Lyotard, J-F. (1988), *The Differend: Phrases in Dispute* (Minneapolis, MN: University of Minnesota Press).

McDougal, M. et al. (1981), 'Theories about International Law: Prologue to a Configurative Jurisprudence,' in McDougal et al. (eds).

McDougal, M. and Reisman, W. (eds) (1988), *International Law Essays: A Supplement to International Law in Contemporary Perspective* (New York: Foundation Press).

MacDonald, R. St. J. and Johnston, D (eds) (1983), *The Structure and Process of International Law* (The Hague: Martinus Nijhoff Publishers).

MacIntyre, A. (1984), *After Virtue*, 2nd edn (Notre Dame, IN: University of Notre Dame Press).

Maher, G. (1978), 'Analytical Philosophy and Austin's Philosophy of Law,' *Archiv für Rechts- und Sozialphilosophie* 64:3, 401–16.

Malanczuk, P. (1997), *Akehurst's Modern Introduction to International Law*, 7th edn, (New York: Routledge).

Malone, D. (1998), *Decision-Making in the UN Security Council: The Case of Haiti* (Oxford: Clarendon Press).

Mani, V.S. (1972), 'The 1971 War on the Indian Sub-Continent and International Law,' *The Indian Journal of International Law* 12:1, 83–99.

Martin, M. and McIntyre, L. (eds) (1994), *Readings in the Philosophy of Social Science* (Cambridge, MA: MIT Press).

Mason, J. (1998), 'Red Faces in UK After Reversal of Pinochet Ruling,' *Financial Times*, 11 December.

Mayall, J. (ed.) (1996), *The New Interventionism 1991–1994: United Nations experience in Cambodia, for Yugoslavia, and Somalia* (Cambridge: Cambridge University Press).

Mazrui, A. (1998), *The Power of Babel: Language and Governance in the African* Experience (Chicago, IL: University of Chicago Press).

Mendes, E. (1994), 'Asian Values and Human Rights: Setting the Tigers Free,' *Human Rights Research and Education Center* [website] (updated 31 December 1994) <http://www.uottawa.ca/hrrec/publicat/asian_values.html>.

Meron, T. (1986), 'On a Hierarchy of International Human Rights,' *The American Journal of International Law* 80:1, 1–23.

Meyer, H. (2002), *The World Court in Action* (Lanham: Rowman & Littlefield).

Moore, J. (1987), 'The Nicaragua Case and the Deterioration of World Order,' *American Journal of International Law* 81:1, 151–9.

Morgenthau, H. (1967), *Politics Among Nations: The Struggle for Power and Peace* (New York: Knopf).

Morrison, Fred L. (1987), 'Legal Issues in the Nicaragua Opinion,' *American Journal of International Law*, 81:1, 160–66.

Mugerwa, Nkambo (1968), 'Subjects of International Law', in Max Sørensen (ed.) (1968), *Manual of Public International Law* (New York: St Martin's Press).

Murphy, S. (1996), *Humanitarian Intervention: The United Nations in an Evolving World Order* (Philadelphia, PA: University of Pennsylvania Press).

Napley, K. (2000), Letter to Home Secretary Jack Straw, 21 October 1998 reprinted in Brody and Ratner (2000).

Nardin T. and Mapel D. (eds) (1992), *Traditions in International Ethics* (Cambridge: Cambridge University Press).

—— (1998), *International Society: Diverse Ethical Perspectives* (Princeton: Princeton University Press).

Nardin, T. (1983), *Law, Morality, and the Relations of States* (Princeton, NJ: Princeton University Press).

—— (1998), 'Legal Positivism as a Theory of International Society,' in Nardin, and Mapel (1998).

Nussbaum, A. (1954), *A Concise History of the Law of Nations* (New York: Macmillan).

Nussbaum, M. (1996), *For Love of Country: Debating the Limits of Patriotism* (Boston, MA: Beacon Press).

Obdrzalek, M. (1992), 'Tropical Deforestation and International Environmental Negotiation: An Illustration of the North-South Confrontation,' in Susskind et al. (1992).

O'Connell, M. (1990), 'The Prospect of Enforcing Monetary Judgments of the International Court of Justice: A Study of Nicaragua's Judgment against the United States,' *Virginia Journal of International Law* 30, 891.

O'Connell, D.P. (ed.) (1982), *International Law*, 2nd edn (London: Stevens).

Okeke, C. (1974), *Controversial Subjects of Contemporary International Law* (Rotterdam: Rotterdam University Press).

Onuf, N. (1994), 'The Constitution of International Society,' *European Journal of International Law* 5:1, 1–19.

—— (1998), *The Republican Legacy in International Thought* (New York: Cambridge University Press).

Oppenheim, L. (1912), *International Law: A Treatise*, 2nd edn (London: Longmans Green, & Co.).

—— (1947), *International Law Vol. 1: Peace*, 6th edn (New York: Longman's Green & Co).

Paust, J. et al. (eds) (2000), *International Criminal Law: Cases and Materials* (Durham, NC: Carolina Academic Press).

Paust, J. (1996), *International Law as Law of the United States* (Durham, NC: Carolina Academic Press).

—— (2000), *International Law and Litigation in the US* (St. Paul, MN: West Group).

Pelczynski, Z.A. (1971), *Hegel's Political Philosophy: Problems and Perspectives* (Cambridge: Cambridge University Press).

Popper, K. (1992), *Conjectures and Refutations: The Growth of Scientific Knowledge* (New York: Harper Torchbooks).

Posner, E. and Goldsmith, J. (2005), *The Limits of International Law* (New York: Oxford University Press).

Quine, W.V.O. (1961), 'Two Dogmas of Empiricism,' in Quine, W.V.O. (ed.).

—— (ed.) (1980), *From a Logical Point of View* (Cambridge, MA: Harvard University Press).

Rama-Montaldo, M. (1970), 'International Legal Personality and Implied Powers of International Organizations,' *British Yearbook of International Law* 44, 111–56.

Ratner, S. and Abrams, J. (2001), *Accountability for Human Rights Atrocities in International Law*, 2nd edn (New York: Oxford University Press).

Rawls, J. (1971), *A Theory of Justice* (Cambridge, MA: Harvard University Press).

—— (1999), *The Law of Peoples* (Cambridge, MA: Harvard University Press).

Reichler, P. (2001), 'Holding America to its Own Best Standards: Abe Chayes and Nicaragua in the World Court,' *Harvard International Law Journal*, 15–46.

Reisman, W.M. (1986), 'Has the International Court Exceeded its Jurisdiction?,' *The American Journal of International Law*, 80:1, 128–34.

Reus-Smit, C. (2004), 'The Politics of International Law,' in Reus-Smit, *The Politics of International Law* (Cambridge: Cambridge University Press).

Riding, A. (1998), 'A Mother Country's Advice: Do as I Say, Not as I Did,' *New York Times*, 13 December.

Risjord, M. (1998), 'Norms and Explanation in the Social Science,' *Studies in the History and Philosophy of Science* 29:2, 223–37.

—— (2000), *Woodcutters and Witchcraft: Rationality and Interpretive Change in the Social Sciences* (New York: SUNY Press).

Roberts, A. (2001), 'Traditional and Modern Approaches to Customary International Law: A Reconciliation,' *The American Journal of International Law*, 95:4, 757–91.

Robertson, D. (2000), 'The House of Lords as a Political and Constitutional Court' in Woodhouse (2000).

Roht-Arrazia, N. (2003), 'Of Catalysts and Cases: Transnational Prosecutions and Impunity in Latin America,' in Davis (2003).

Ronzitti, N. (1985), *Rescuing Nationals Abroad through Military Coercion and Intervention on Grounds of Humanity* (Dordrecht: Martinus Nijhoff Publishers).

Rorty, R. (1991), *Objectivity, Relativism, and Truth: Philosophical Papers, Volume I* (Cambridge: Cambridge University Press).

Rosenbaum, A. (ed.) (1980), *The Philosophy of Human Rights: International Perspectives* (Westport, CT: Greenwood Press).

Rossi, C. (1993), *Equity and International Law* (Irvington, NY: Transnational Publishers).

Roth, B. (1999), *Governmental Illegitimacy in International Law* (New York: Oxford University Press).

Rozakis, C. (1976), *The Concept of Jus Cogens in the Law of Treaties* (Amsterdam: North Holland Publishing Company).

Rubin, A. (1997), *Ethics and Authority in International Law* (Cambridge: Cambridge University Press).

Sadat, L. (2002), *The International Criminal Court and the Transformation of International Law: Justice for the New Millennium* (Ardsley: Transnational Publishers).

Sand, P. (1993), 'International Environmental Law After Rio,' *European Journal of International Law* 4:1 377–89.

Sands, P. (2003), 'International Law Transformed? From Pinochet to Congo..?,' *Leiden Journal of International Law* 16:1, 37–53.

Schabas, W. (2000), *Genocide in International Law: The Crimes of Crimes* (New York: Cambridge University Press).

Scharf, M. (1999), 'The Amnesty Exception to the Jurisdiction of the International Criminal Court,' *Cornell International Law Journal* 32:3, 507–27.

Scheffer, D. (1986), 'U.S. Must Not Be the Outlaw on Nicaragua,' *Los Angeles Times*, 11 July, Metro 5.

Schemo, D. (2001), 'New Files Tie U.S. to Deaths Of Latin Leftists in 1970s,' *New York Times*, 6 March.

Schneewind, J.B. (1998), *The Invention of Autonomy* (Cambridge: Cambridge University Press).

Schneider, J. (1963), *Treaty-making Power of International Organizations* (Ann Arbor, MI: University of Michigan Press).

Sciolino, E. (2006), 'Spanish Judge Calls for Closing U.S. Prison at Guantánamo,' *New York Times*, 4 June.

Searle, J. (1975), 'How to Derive "Ought" from "Is",' in Hudson (1975).

Sen, A. (1999), *Development as Freedom* (New York: Knopf).

Sen, S. (1971), 'Statement of Mr. S. Sen, The Permanent Representative of India to the UN, in the General Assembly on the Situation in Bangladesh, 7 December. 1971,' *Indian Journal of International Law* 11, 690–99.

Shany, Y. (2005), 'Toward a General Margin of Appreciation Doctrine in International Law?,' *The European Journal of International Law* 16:5, 907–40.

Shaw, M. (ed.), (1991), *International Law*, 3rd edn (Cambridge: Cambridge University Press).

Shen, J. (2001), 'The Non-Interventional Principle and Humanitarian Interventions,' *International Legal Theory* 7, 77–36.

Shipler, D. (1986), 'U.S. Assails Court Ruling and Closing of La Prensa,' *New York Times*, 28 June.

Sisson, R. and Rose, L. (1990), *War and Secession: Pakistan, India, and the Creation of Bangladesh* (Berkeley, CA: University of California Press).

Simons, M. (2001), 'Human Rights Cases Begin to Flood Into Belgian Courts,' *New York Times*, 27 December.

Singer, P. (2002), *One World* (New Haven, CT: Yale University Press).

Sinha, Bhek Pati (1966), *The Unilateral Denunciation of Treaty Because of Prior Violations of Obligations by Other Party* (The Hague: Matinus Nijhoff).

Slaughter, A-M. (1998), 'International Law and International Relations Theory: A New Generation of Interdisciplinary Scholarship,' *American Journal of International Law* 92:3, 367–397.

—— (2004), 'International Law and International Relations Theory: A Prospectus,' in Benvenisti and Hirsh (2004).

Slomanson, W. (1995), *Fundamental Perspectives on International Law*, 2nd edn (St. Paul, MN: West Group).

Spooner, M. (1994), *Soldiers in a Narrow Land: The Pinochet Regime in Chile*, (Berkeley, CA: University of California Press).

Steiner, H. and Alston P. (eds) (1996), *International Human Rights in Context: Law, Politics, Morals* (Oxford: Oxford University Press).

Stepelevich, L. (ed.) (1993), *Selected Essays on G.W.F. Hegel* (Atlantic Highlands, NJ: Humanities Press).

Stich, S.P. (1988), 'Reflective Equilibrium, Analytic Epistemology and the Problem of Cognitive Diversity,' *Synthese* 74:3, 391–413.

Stiles, K. (2000), 'U.S. Responses to Defeat in International Courts: A Contingent Model of Rule Compliance,' *Political Research Quarterly* 53:2, 401–25.

Susskind, L.E. et al. (eds) (1992), *International Environmental Treaty Making* (Cambridge, MA: Program on Negotiation).

Tesón, F. (1997), *Humanitarian Intervention: An Inquiry into Law and Morality* (New York: Transnational Publishers).

—— (1998), *A Philosophy of International Law* (Boulder, CO: Westview Press).

Lawyers Committee on American Policy Towards Vietnam (1967), *Vietnam and International Law* (Flanders: O'Hare Books).

Taylor, S. (1985), 'U.S. Plans to Quit World Court Case on Nicaragua Suit,' *New York Times*, 19 January.

Tuck, R. (1999), *The Rights of War and Peace* (Oxford: Oxford University Press).

Tweedie, N. (2006), 'Pinochet, the Friend of Britain Who Ruled His Country By Fear,' *Daily Telegraph*, 11 December.

Twinning, W. (2000), *Globalization and Legal Theory* (London: Butterworths).

Tyler, T. (1990), *Why People Obey the Law* (New Haven, CT: Yale University Press).

Uhlig, M. (1990), 'U.S. Urges Nicaragua to Forgive Legal Claim,' *New York Times*, 30 September.

US State Department (1981), *State Department Report on Communist Support of Salvadoran Rebels*.
Valenzuela, A. (1991), *A Nation of Enemies: Chile Under Pinochet* (New York: WW Norton).
van Dijk, P., and van Hoof, G.J.H. (1998), *Theory and Practice of the European Convention on Human Rights* (The Hague: Kluwer Law International).
Verdross, A.V. (1949), 'On the Concept of International Law,' *The American Journal of International Law* 43:3, 435–40.
Verdross, A., and Koeck, H. (1983), 'Natural Law: The Tradition of Universal Reason and Authority,' in MacDonald and Johnston (1983).
Verene, D.P. (1971) 'Hegel's Account of War,' in Pelczynski (1971).
Verwey, W. (1992), 'The Idea of Rights in International Ethics,' in Nardin and Mapel (1992).
Verzijl, J.H.W. (1955), 'Western European Influence on the Foundation of International Law,' *International Relations* 1:4, 137–46.
Vincent, R.J. (1986) *Human Rights and International Relations* (New York: Cambridge University Press).
Wallace, R. (1990), 'How to Argue about Practical Reason,' *Mind* 99, 355–85.
Waltz, K. (1959), *Man, The State, and War: A Theoretical Analysis* (New York: Columbia University Press).
Watson, J.S. (1979), 'Legal Theory, Efficacy and Validity in the Development of Human Rights Norms in International Law,' *The University of Illinois Law Forum* 3, 609–641.
Weil, P. (1983), 'Towards Relative Normativity in International Law,' *American Journal of International Law* 77:3, 413–442.
Weinraub, B. (1985), 'U.S. Limits its Role at Court in Hague,' *New York Times*, 8 October.
Weisburd, A. (1997), *Use of Force: The Practice of States since World War II* (University Park, PA: Pennsylvania State University Press).
Weller, M. (1999), 'On the Hazards of Foreign Travel for Dictators and Other International Criminals,' *International Affairs* 75:3, 599–617.
Wendt, A. (1999), *Social Theory of International Politics* (New York: Cambridge University Press).
Williams, G. (1945), 'International Law and the Controversy Concerning the Word "Law",' *British Yearbook of International Law* 22, 146–63.
Wirth, S. (2002), 'Immunity for Core Crimes? The ICJ's Judgment in the Congo v. Belgium Case,' *European Journal of International Law* 13:4, 877–93.
Wittgenstein, L. (1963), *Philosophical Investigations* (Oxford: Basil Blackwell Publishers).
Woodhouse, D. (ed.) (2000), *The Pinochet Case: A Legal and Constitutional Analysis* (Portland, OR: Hart Publishing).
—— (2003), 'The Progress of Pinochet Through the UK Extradition Procedure: An Analysis of the Legal Challenges and Judicial Decisions,' in Davis (2003).
Yagisawa, T. (1995), 'Definition,' in Audi (1995).
'A Strange Procedure – But Justice Was Done,' *The Independent* (London), 16 April 1999.

'Europeans say U.S. should pay Nicaragua,' *The Guardian*, 16 March 1990, 18A.
'Security Council does not adopt text calling for full compliance with International Court ruling in case of military and paramilitary activities in and against Nicaragua' (1986), *UN Chronicle*.
'Profile: Judge Baltasar Garzón,' BBC News, [website], (updated 26 September 2005) <http://news.bbc.co.uk/2/hi/europe/3085482.stm>.

Cases

'Arrest warrant of 11 April 2000,' (*Democratic Republic of the Congo v. Belgium*) Judgment of 14 February 2002.
Military and Paramilitary Activities in and against Nicaragua (*Nicaragua v. US*), Merits, 1986, ICJ Rep. 14 (Judgment of 7 June) at 146.
Decision of the High Court of Justice for England and Wales, 28 October 1998, paragraph 33. Reprinted in Brody and Ratner (2000), pp. 71–93.
Decision by the Appellate Committee of the House of Lords, 25 November 1998. Reprinted in Brody and Ratner (2000), 121–87.
Decision by the Appellate Committee of the House of Lords, 15 January 1999 (lead opinion of Lord Browne-Wilkinson).

Index

www.ingramcontent.com/pod-product-compliance
Ingram Content Group UK Ltd.
Pitfield, Milton Keynes, MK11 3LW, UK
UKHW020158200926
475702UK00004B/520

9780754672517